DOROTHEA LANGE, DOCUMENTARY PHOTOGRAPHY, AND TWENTIETH-CENTURY AMERICA

Dorothea Lange, Documentary Photography, and Twentieth-Century America charts the life of Dorothea Lange (1895–1965), whose life was radically altered by the Depression, and whose photography helped transform the nation. The book begins with her childhood in immigrant, metropolitan New York, shifting to her young adulthood as a New Woman who apprenticed herself to Manhattan's top photographers, then established a career as portraitist to San Francisco's elite. When the Great Depression shook America's economy, Lange was profoundly affected. Leaving her studio, Lange confronted citizens' anguish with her camera, documenting their economic and social plight. This move propelled her to international renown.

This biography synthesizes recent New Deal scholarship and photographic history and probes the unique regional histories of the Pacific West, the Plains, and the South. Lange's life illuminates critical transformations in the U.S., specifically women's evolving social roles and the state's growing capacity to support vulnerable citizens. The author utilizes the concept of "care work," the devalued nurturing of others, often considered women's work, to analyze Lange's photography and reassert its power to provoke social change. Lange's portrayal of the Depression's ravages is enmeshed in a deeply political project still debated today, of the nature of governmental responsibility toward citizens' basic needs.

Students and the general reader will find this a powerful and insightful introduction to Dorothea Lange, her work, and legacy. *Dorothea Lange, Documentary Photography, and Twentieth-Century America* makes a compelling case for the continuing political and social significance of Lange's work, as she recorded persistent injustices such as poverty, labor exploitation, racism, and environmental degradation.

Carol Quirke is a professor of American Studies at the State University of New York, Old Westbury, USA. She teaches women's history, U.S. history, and visual culture. Her previous book *Eyes on Labor: News Photography and America's Working Class* (2012) examines the political stakes of news photography for organized labor in America's midcentury. Her essays appear in *American Quarterly, Radical History Review, History Today*, and *Reviews in American History*.

LIVES OF AMERICAN WOMEN

Series editor: Carol Berkin

Selected and edited by renowned women's historian Carol Berkin, these brief, affordably priced biographies are designed for use in undergraduate courses. Rather than taking a comprehensive approach, each biography focuses instead on a particular aspect of a women's life that is emblematic of her time or made her a pivotal figure in her era. The emphasis is on a "good read," featuring accessible writing and compelling narratives, without sacrificing sound scholarship and academic integrity. Primary sources are included at the end of each biography, alongside study questions and an annotated bibliography, which support the student reader.

https://www.routledge.com/Lives-of-American-Women/book-series/
LIVESAMWOMEN

Barbara Egger Lennon
Teacher, Mother, Activist
Tina Stewart Brakebill

Julia Lathrop
Social Service and Progressive Government
Miriam Cohen

Mary Pickford
Women, Film and Selling Girlhood
Kathleen A. Feeley

Elizabeth Gurley Flynn
Modern American Revolutionary
Lara Vapnek

Dorothea Lange, Documentary Photography, and Twentieth-Century America
Reinventing Self and Nation
Carol Quirke

DOROTHEA LANGE, DOCUMENTARY PHOTOGRAPHY, AND TWENTIETH-CENTURY AMERICA

Reinventing Self and Nation

Carol Quirke

Routledge
Taylor & Francis Group

NEW YORK AND LONDON

First published 2019
by Routledge
52 Vanderbilt Avenue, New York, NY 10017

and by Routledge
2 Park Square, Milton Park, Abingdon, Oxon, OX14 4RN

Routledge is an imprint of the Taylor & Francis Group, an informa business

Library of Congress Cataloging-in-Publication Data
Names: Quirke, Carol, author.
Title: Dorothea Lange, documentary photography, and twentieth-
century America: reinventing self and nation Carol Quirke.
Description: 1 Edition. | New York: Routledge, [2019] |
Series: Lives of american women | Includes bibliographical
references and index.
Identifiers: LCCN 2018043385 | ISBN 9781138394353
(hardback: alk. paper) | ISBN 9780813348599 (pbk.: alk. paper) |
ISBN 9780429028151 (ebook)
Subjects: LCSH: Lange, Dorothea. | Women photographers–United
States–Biography. | Women–United States–History–20th century.
Classification: LCC TR140.L3 Q57 2019 | DDC 770.82–dc23
LC record available at https://lccn.loc.gov/2018043385

ISBN: 978-1-138-39435-3 (hbk)
ISBN: 978-0-8133-4859-9 (pbk)
ISBN: 978-0-429-02815-1 (ebk)

Typeset in Bembo
by Deanta Global Publishing Services, Chennai, India

Printed and bound by Ashford Colour Press Ltd.

For my anchor, Quinn

CONTENTS

FIGURES

SERIES EDITOR INTRODUCTION

Dorothea Lange's haunting photograph, "Migrant Mother," is perhaps the most familiar image of the Depression era. With one snap of the camera, Lange captured both the anxiety and the steely determination to survive that was the story of dislocation and suffering in the wake of the collapse of the American economy. But Lange should be remembered for more than this single portrait. As Carol Quirke shows us, Lange not only took tens of thousands of photos that chronicled the lives of America's poor, she also played a central role in the development of documentary photography. Throughout her life, Lange used the camera to educate, to inform, and to establish, as Quirke puts it, "the relationships between citizens of different regions, means, races, and gender." In this sense, her craft was as profoundly political as it was artistic. Through that craft, Lange revealed her strong support for the welfare programs established in the New Deal. She was an advocate for the women and men of rural America throughout her career.

Quirke traces Lange's career, as she built a successful portrait business in California during the prosperous years before the Depression and later, as she used her camera to support President Roosevelt's policies. In her personal life, Lange flouted many of the rules governing traditional expectations for women. She set out on her own when she was a teenager, exploring New York City with male as well as female friends. She divorced a first husband and married for a second time. Yet she never abandoned her own career during either marriage. However, as Quirke astutely points out, Lange accepted women's traditional work in her everyday life: she did the cooking, cleaning, and arranging of the schedules of her family just as women in the American past—and the present—have always done. It is perhaps ironic that, although she firmly believed that women had an inborn impulse to nurture, Lange herself struggled with motherhood.

In *Dorothea Lange, Documentary Photography, and Twentieth-Century America*, Carol Quirke gives us an in-depth understanding not only of a remarkable woman and a talented and innovative photographer, but also of the impact of the Depression and the political choices made by President Roosevelt's administration. This book, like Lange's photographs, will bring to life an era when government chose to provide dramatic and significant support to the people it served.

In examining and narrating the lives of women both famous and obscure, Routledge's "Lives of American Women" series populates our national past more fully and more richly. Each story told is not simply of an individual but of the era in which she lived, the events in which she participated, and the experiences she shared with her contemporaries. Some of these women will be familiar to the reader; others may not appear at all in the history books, which often focus on the powerful, the brilliant, or the privileged. But each of these women is worth knowing. American history comes alive through their personal odysseys.

Carol Berkin, Editor of "Lives of American Women"

ACKNOWLEDGMENTS

In the 1980s I worked for a women's social justice non-profit, and hung many postcards of women by my desk. Of twenty-some images, three were by or of Dorothea Lange, including her portrait by Rondal Partridge. Lange gave a wicked smile to the camera. Her denim work clothes and fisherman sandals marked her as someone less bound by conventional gender rules, her expression, as someone filled with joy. And yet Lange's camera had the profound ability to convey the harrowing realities of everyday Americans struggling to survive along with the divine present in the everyday.

It has been an honor to follow her footsteps, through one of her homes in California, to her favored Steep Ravine along the Marin County coast, to read her letters to the Farm Security Administration, peruse her interviews, and thrill to the words of the hundreds of Depression-era survivors that she recorded in her field notes. I am so appreciative to Carol Berkin, the series editor of "Lives of American Women," for inviting me to investigate the life of this exacting, expansive, engaged woman.

If writing is lonely work, books are a collective enterprise, and this book has benefited from the support, guidance, and resources of many. SUNY Old Westbury provided two Faculty Development Grants for research; my brothers and sisters in the United University Professions also provided financial support. Old Westbury's American Studies department embraces a social justice mission, and is committed to educating working students. I am sustained by your sense of responsibility to the school and larger community. Thank you Laura Anker, Jermaine Archer, Llana Barber, Aubrey Bonnet, Annu Brewer, Laura Chipley, John Friedman, Mandy Frisken, Karl Grossman, Joe Manfredi, Andy Mattson, Jasmine Mitchell, Sujani Reddy, Samara Smith, Lois Stergiopoulos, and Denton Watson. Margaret Torrell advised me on how to address Lange's disability, for which I'm grateful. Two students in my Depression-era Hollywood course, Stevi Starr and Natalie Maldonado, offered helpful readings of the Dust Bowl chapter. Thanks also to Director of Research and Sponsored Programs, Tom Murphy, Dean of Arts and Sciences Barbara Hillery, Provost and Vice President of Academic Affairs Patrick O'Sullivan, and President Calvin O. Butts for their dedication to public higher education.

So many librarians and archivists enabled this book's research. The Oakland Museum of California, which houses Lange's papers and negatives, was generous with assistance, thanks particularly to Sean Dickerson and Nathan Kerr. Staff at University of California's Bancroft Library were extremely helpful, as were archivists at the Museum of Modern Art. Beverly Brannan and Carol Johnson addressed several online questions about the Library of Congress's rich collection of Lange photographs. This book required answers to arcane queries, and librarians stepped in with answers. Janice Torbet and Tom Carey of the San Francisco Public Library shared demographics on San Francisco in 1910 and 1920, Kevin Hill of the Amarillo Public Library provided me information on 1937 weather patterns, and Danielle Bennett of the Alice Austin House explained Austin's street photography. At Old Westbury, Antonio DiGregorio, Jason Kaloudis, and Heidi Donofrio dealt with hundreds of requests for articles and books over the past few years—this book would not have been completed without their dedication.

Valorie Wilson kindly offered a tour of one of Lange's homes—it was wonderful to enter her bedroom looking out toward the bay, and the basement where she developed her photographs. Dyanna Taylor, Lange's granddaughter by marriage, came to Old Westbury under the auspices of our college's Women's Center, and wowed students and faculty with her American Masters film, a lovely meditation, *Dorothea Lange: Grab a Hunk of Lightning*.

Scholars and editors have provided excellent critiques of versions of this work. Priscilla McGeehon, now of Thames and Hudson, offered advice in the early stages of the book. Nikki Iokimedes of Perseus Books offered a gentle but firm hand as the book came to fruition, and I am grateful for her guidance. Alex McGregor and Kitty Imbert's enthusiasm for gender and history brought the book to its conclusion. The book's anonymous readers pushed me to strengthen the argument and to be firmer in my stance on Lange. Barbara Winslow planned a wonderful panel, "Women's Lives at the Center of the Social Studies Curriculum," for the 2017 Berks; it was lovely to share with other writers in the series, including Cyndi Lobel, Robyn Spencer, Miriam Cohen, Laraine Wallowitz, and Carol Berkin.

Sharing with fellow writers as we move our work into the world is a delight and an honor. Marcella Bencivenni, Evelyn Burg, and Daniel Wishnoff push me to be a better historian, thinker, and friend. Nina Bannett, Nancy Berke, Linda Grasso, and Phyllis Van Slyck broaden my perspective and elevate my prose. It has been a new pleasure to work with Jaqueline Emery, Jillian Crocker, and Sarah Smith. A group of close friends and family helped with that pinch-reading of the final manuscript, and their direction at the end was critical: thanks to Billy Thomas, Jill Strauss, Kate Sampsell, Sheila Quirke, Jeremy Hornik, and Sharon Quirke.

As always, friends and family remain a lodestar. Billy Thomas and Pam DeMetruis, Marcella Bencivenni, Evelyn Burg, Jacqueline Emery, Linda Camarasana, Carolyn Wiebe, Jill Strauss, Jean Halley and Jacob Segal, Janet LeMoal, Sr. Kieran Therese Quirke, Tom and Jeanne Radja, Melissa and James Barnett, Paul and Marcia Radja, Nicole and Calby Mundy, Sharon Quirke and Phil Reece, Michael Quirke, Sheila Quirke, and Jeremy Hornik, thank you. So many thanks to Julian and Sylvia Wolff, who kept me connected to a love of photography and to what is good in life. Their daughters Ronnie and Judy's welcome, especially in Lange's hometown, was affirming.

This book is dedicated to Quinn Cushing—dashing, perceptive, and loved.

INTRODUCTION

As a child in the twentieth century's first decade, Dorothea Lange (1895–1965) learned to make herself invisible. As an adult, she made visible the nation's darkest corners of racism, extreme poverty, and political powerlessness. In between, Lange was a bohemian who rejected convention and sported a green beret and silver bracelets. Friends remember her ascending a San Francisco street with her first husband, Western artist Maynard Dixon; Lange's cape and Dixon's silver-tipped cane, including a stiletto, arrested attention. In San Francisco she established her career as a commercial portraitist, conveying her client's best self, often constructed through the veils of fashion. Lange became internationally known, however, for showing the nation's poor, many barefoot with their clothes in tatters, those facing in her words, "the last ditch."[1]

Lange flouted proscriptions for women, taking advantage of the twentieth century's radically shifting gender roles. As a teen, she enjoyed New York City diversions with men and women friends, breaking prohibitions against men and women's joint socializing. She pursued a career through marriage, divorce, and remarriage. Even so, Lange also did women's traditional work of maintaining everyday life: cooking, cleaning, and arranging things for her family. But Lange struggled with motherhood. Her children found her simultaneously controlling and neglectful, putting her work before them. Ironically, Lange's photographs of mothers and their children compel attention. "Migrant Mother," which some call the most reproduced photograph in the world, promoted maternalist ideology, the view that women have an inborn or natural tendency to nurture, which society and government policy should promote.[2]

While motherhood provoked turmoil for Lange, her paid work led to renown. She took tens of thousands of photographs in her half-century career. She worked for private clients, the state of California, the federal government, and for America's top photo-journal, *Life* magazine. Her photographs were exhibited in the U.S. and abroad, and in 1966 she became the first woman photographer to have a retrospective exhibition at New York's prestigious Museum of Modern Art (MOMA). President Lyndon Johnson commended "the magic of her camera," which "turned mere statistics into compelling human truths."[3] Today, a single image of Lange's might sell for nearly a million dollars. Her evocation of the Depression is how many see this era; her photos are that powerful. Despite such acclaim, Lange struggled to hold on to jobs. Considered one of the New Deal's top photographers, she was fired early on as her supervisor found her too difficult, a criticism often directed at working women.

Lange rarely discussed traditional electoral politics. However, her photos of those ravaged by the Depression are enmeshed in a deeply political project, one still debated today, of the nature of governmental responsibility and care toward citizens' basic needs.

Dorothea Lange, Documentary Photography, and Twentieth-Century America: Reinventing Self and Nation tells the story of a woman whose life was radically altered by the Depression, and whose photography helped transform the nation. In 2017 the WorldCat database lists more than fifty books about Lange, including children's books and exhibition catalogues. Recently Public Broadcasting aired an American Masters film about Lange, and the novel *Mary Coin*, based on Lange's life and that of her most famous photographic subject, Florence Thompson, became a *New York Times* bestseller. Hundreds of scholarly essays, aesthetic commentaries, and news articles explore Lange and her photography. Lange's life and art continue to fascinate as her photographs inspire and disturb, nearly a century after the Depression has passed.

Dorothea Lange, Documentary Photography, and Twentieth-Century America explores the interplay between Lange, who helped develop documentary photography, as it came to be called in the 1930s, and the New Deal–sponsored welfare and administrative state. The lens of "care work," a concept articulated by sociologists and political theorists informs the analysis. Care work, the emotional and physical nurturing of people, often devalued, is traditionally considered women's work. Lange's photography can be considered a form of care work.[4] She engaged fully with her subjects, and brought them, their needs, vulnerabilities, and strengths, to the attention of other Americans. Her photographs established relationships between citizens of different regions, means, races, and genders. Like other photographers, Lange illuminated the devastation of the Depression; but Lange's photographs are unique in their ability to direct an empathetic response from viewers. Unlike Russell Lee's subjects, who seem jocose and happily engaged in community activities, or Walker Evans's crystalline images, where serene sharecroppers are subsumed into Evans's abstract, balanced design, or Arthur Rothstein's photographs which monumentalize the subjects, making them heroes in the drama of the Depression, Lange's subjects impress themselves upon us. Lange identified the challenges rural Americans faced, and she showed them confronting these challenges. One senses an inner tension as her subjects' minds are at work, assessing the conditions they face. Lange's subjects project a tenuous, but palpable endurance. Many beckon viewers with a fierce regard. They are recognized by Lange's camera eye, and the print allows us to recognize her subjects' circumstances and engage in dialogue with them. Documentary photography, Lange's "ammunition" as she once referred to it, had a history of illuminating social distress in order to address it. Lange helped solidify the aesthetic in the Depression, becoming a leading practitioner.

Documentary photography's definition was and remains ambiguous. Near the end of her life Lange complained that the documentary "isn't a good name, [but] it sticks to it. I don't like it, but I haven't been able to come up with a substitute." She remarked that others, such as Beaumont Newhall, MOMA's first curator of photography, were similarly perplexed by the term. Walker Evans, who worked with Lange for the U.S. government, concurred, "My thought is that the term 'documentary' is inexact, vague, and even grammatically weak."[5]

The problems with defining the documentary are multiple. The term arose from the notion that photographs were documents, like a report card, a passport, or a birth certificate. In the nineteenth century, in the first decades of photography's development, the medium was considered a "mirror with a memory," in famed essayist Oliver Wendell Holmes's encapsulation. Photographs reflected back the factual. Matthew Brady's Civil War photos, George Barker's photographs of Niagara Falls, Timothy O'Sullivan and William Henry Jackson's photographs of the awesome West, and even mugshots were all considered truthful records. Berenice Abbott, who photographed New York cityscapes in the 1930s, maintained, "I have yet to see a fine photograph which is not a good document." For Abbott photographs were "rich in information...actual source material." The photograph was evidence.[6] Early examples of photography intended to provoke social reform, such as Jacob Riis's 1880s photographs of New York City tenements, or Lewis Hines's 1910s child laborers, relied on the photograph being accepted as factual.

But the documentary photographs of the 1930s were more. Newhall said that the documentary must "persuade and convince," it "informs and moves us." This description implies that the photograph contains an element that exceeds pure facts. But what is that quality? Roy Stryker, Dorothea Lange's supervisor in the New Deal, contrasted news photographs, which he called noun and verb photographs or simple facts, with the documentary, which he described as adverbs and adjectives. Cultural historian Warren Sussman believes the documentary has a supplemental effect; it "makes it possible to see, know, and feel the details of life, to feel oneself part of some others' experience." William Stott's classic 1973 study of the 1930s maintained that "emotion counted more than fact" in the documentary. Lange described her work more charitably as a negotiation between expression and fact. "A documentary photograph is not a factual photograph per se." Denying any "real warfare...between the artist and the documentary photographer," she thought the documentarian expressed and recorded, pushing the viewer to ask, "What is it really?" Here Lange returned to the idea of the documentary photograph as truth, though we can see that the documentary photograph seeks to affect, persuade, or motivate in some way, resulting in an inherent tension or ambiguity within documentary practice.[7]

The documentary aesthetic that Lange and others developed in the 1930s implied not only a shared visual rhetoric, or way of communicating, but also a specific subject matter: the tragedy of American citizens overwhelmed by the Depression. In 1939, art critic Elizabeth McCausland lauded the documentary, "After the usual diet of the art world-cream puffs, eclairs and such the bitter reality of these photographs is the tonic the soul needs." She admired their grim truths, and suggested that "In them we see the faces of the American people... We might also see (if we were completely honest and fearless intellectually) the faces of ourselves." McCausland, an astute contemporary, suggested the documentary provoked reflection by the viewer about the relationship between the viewer and the subject—this was a social relationship.[8]

Lange's photographs can be breathtaking, but she perceived her camera as "a tool of research," part of a larger investigative process. From her second husband, agricultural economist Paul Taylor, she learned about social science research and the power of the written word, which became critical to her inquiry. "Upon a tripod of photographs, captions and text we rest themes" that "evolved out of long observations in the field." For Lange, the photograph was not enough; it required other supporting materials. Lange was a careful listener, and she transcribed her subjects' words closely. Read together, the words of thousands of dispossessed cut deep.

Also critical for Lange was "the file," as it came to be called at the agency where she worked, the Resettlement Administration, which became the Farm Security Administration (RA/FSA). The file divulged understanding in the thousands of photographs and additional information that the archive contained. Lange contrasted her work to that of earlier photographers, Lewis Hine and Jacob Riis, whose work also explored the lives of the underprivileged and marginalized. She thought these photographers "made collections...but they didn't do documentary photographs." In comparison to their "series and sequences," she argued, "the documentary thing is a little different because it's filed and cross-filed in its pure state, and it's buttressed by written material and by all manner of things which keep it unified and solid." Her supervisor at the RA/FSA wanted to create "an encyclopedia of American life," and Lange's statement suggests their shared belief that amassing visual and textual details could promote comprehension.[9]

Few disagree about the federal government's role in advancing the documentary aesthetic in the 1930s. Under the government's aegis, the RA/FSA hired Lange and other photographers as it broadened its responsibilities toward average Americans, amplifying the federal government's administrative and regulatory structure to enhance its care for citizens. Today, millions of Americans depend on programs initiated during the New Deal, such as Social Security, Medicare, Unemployment Insurance, Disability Insurance, and other forms of welfare, or social insurance as historians and policy makers call it. These programs remain highly contested. Lange's photographs provoked dialogue with Americans about the possibility of our nation developing programs that "care": for the earth, for those who work it, and for those who struggle to subsist upon it.

Once we accept that photographs make arguments, we can see the camera as an instrument for caring, for identifying who needs care, or those with cares or burdens, for showing what happens when care is neglected, and for provoking care by eliciting empathy. Empathy and caring entail the courage to see suffering: to attend to it, and to imagine an alternative solution. This book explores how Lange heeded citizens' cares with a commitment to bettering their situation. In the 1980s and 1990s scholars have criticized the documentary for being sentimental, staged, designed to make middle-class viewers feel better about themselves, or enacting a form of control upon those who are photographed. These analyses depend in part upon binaries that see feeling or emotion as opposed to fact or reason. Lange's photographs fused both, imbuing them with power. Critics of the documentary, including of Lange's work, have also minimized the historical challenges of establishing welfare and social insurance for American citizens. Lange reinvented her photographic practice in times of rapid social change and crisis, and her camera observed these times, forming part of how we understand them today, but her photographs also contributed to the nation's growing welfare state. *Dorothea Lange, Documentary Photography, and 20th Century America* explores the roadblocks politicians, reformers, and activists encountered in expanding the state to support people.

In addition to archival research at the Oakland Museum, University of California's Bancroft Library, and the Museum of Modern Art, This biography relies on a wealth of scholarship. It is especially indebted to Milton Meltzer's *Dorothea Lange: A Photographer's Life* (1978) and Linda Gordon's Bancroft Prize-winning biography, *Dorothea Lange: A Life Beyond Limits* (2009). Gordon's work explores how gender shaped Lange's life, and how gender and race shaped the welfare state that Lange helped build. Gordon argues that Lange was, "a photographer of democracy, and for democracy," whose inclusive eye expanded notions of citizenship while identifying lapses from the nation's democratic ideals. Also informing this study are Jan Goggans' *California on the Breadlines: Dorothea Lange, Paul Taylor and the Making of a New Deal Narrative* (2010), which charts the challenge of upholding the home as a Depression-era ideal; Elizabeth Partridge's multiple analyses and edited collections, particularly *Dorothea Lange: A Visual Life* (1994), which draw on her and her family's close connections to Lange; Richard Steven Street's *Everyone Had Cameras: Photography and Farmworkers in California, 1850–2000* (2008) that places Lange's photography in a century-long project of social activism and representation; and Anne Whiston Spirn's *Daring to Look: Dorothea Lange's Photography and Notes from the Field* (2009), which details the gendered nature of reception to Lange's photography.

Chapters One and Two of *Dorothea Lange, Documentary Photography, and Twentieth-Century America* follow Lange from her childhood in Hoboken, New

Jersey, to the time she spent in New York City as an adolescent, and then to her early adulthood as she gained a career. Chapter Three shows Lange leaving her family and traveling across the country, where she established her portrait studio in San Francisco as a bohemian who chummed around with other artists, enjoyed parties on the Pacific Coast, and married one of San Francisco's most colorful artists. She built a thriving business, becoming one of San Francisco's top portraitists. When the Great Depression hit Lange and her husband hard, she responded by going out into the street with the tool she knew best, the camera. Chapter Four explores how she grappled with representing the Depression. Lange persevered, contributing to the emerging documentary aesthetic, and her courage in leaving her first marriage, which had become conflict-riven, and coming to love a second man, who nurtured her aspirations, are Chapter Five's subjects.

Chapter Six follows Lange in her work for Franklin Delano Roosevelt's New Deal, which transformed the role of government in Americans' lives. Roosevelt believed the nation-state had a role in guaranteeing citizens' security. Toward this end, his administration initiated governmental programs to build the nation's infrastructure, nurture the environment, and offer relief and even jobs to those in need. Lange's most famous photographs were the result of one such program, which intervened in the agricultural economy on behalf of the most marginalized agricultural workers.

Chapters Seven, Eight, and Nine track Lange as she worked for the RA/FSA from 1935 to 1939, using her camera to depict struggling Americans from the Gulf of Mexico, to New York City, across the Deep South, Midwest, Great Plains, all the way to the Pacific Northwest. Chapter Seven details Lange's exploration of the South with its sharecropping system, a consequence of Reconstruction's failure, Chapter Eight considers her understanding of the environmental disaster of the Dust Bowl, and Chapter Nine examines her ongoing relationship to California's industrial agricultural system. Each region had distinctive relationships to the land and the people who labored it, and Lange, ever attentive to "how a man stands in the world," investigated the historic roots and social realities of agriculture in each region.

Chapter Ten contextualizes Lange's work and family life within the Depression's economic turmoil, which pressed against women's traditional roles. Women's intimate lives were affected, and their economic roles shifted as more women worked to make ends meet. Ironically, New Deal welfare programs legislated women's second-class citizenship by providing support based on the ideal of the male breadwinner. Similarly, mass culture, movies, magazine articles, and even Lange's photographs idealized traditional notions of home and motherhood.

Lange did not stop photographing once the Depression was over. Chapter Eleven examines her heartbreaking images of the Japanese American internment in 1942, her investigation of the emerging defense industry, and the social dislocation caused by World War II. Chapter Twelve explores Lange's attention to Cold War affluence and overdevelopment. In her final years, Lange directed her lens widely to peoples around the globe, and focused it narrowly upon her own family and intimate life.

Lange's photographs probed. Her skill at portraiture allowed her to pull out her subjects' inner turmoil over the external distress they confronted. She detailed the extraordinary poverty, dislocation, and powerlessness they withstood without patronizing her subjects. She approached them as equals. Near the end of her life, she wondered if "we could dare look at ourselves." In taking photographs, Lange pushed viewers to ask questions about their values and their relationship to the world around them. Could Americans live with children with no home walking the roads? Could they stand to see mothers and children drinking dirtied water beside their tent? Could they face the formerly enslaved, who sixty years after slavery had ended were still toiling a hard, eroded land? Could they abide encountering a grandmother, whose prized rocking chair sat open to the elements on a muddy field? Could they look without concern at the college-educated tramp, who set up his home in a California field, his pots and pans hanging from trees, the plates held up on fruit crates? Would they accept the sight of three generations of Japanese Americans being labeled with luggage tags, to be interned? Would Americans examine their wounding of the earth in the name of progress?

Lange invited us to look with her, at her subjects, and at ourselves, which is why her photographs continue to provoke nearly a century after she took them.

Notes

1 The bibliography provides the relevant scholarship and oral histories that this biography draws from. Chapter endnotes identify specific citations from scholarship or archives. "The Last Ditch," from MOMA exhibitions, 789.27.

2 Seth Koven and Sonja Michel define maternalism as "ideologies that exalted women's capacity to mother, and extended to society as a whole the values they attached to that care role: care, nurturance and morality." In "Womanly Duties: Maternalist Politics and the Origins of Welfare States in France, Germany, Great Britain, and the United States, 1880–1920," *The American Historical Review* 95, no. 4 (October 1990): 1076–1108.

3 Museum of Modern Art, "Press Release for Dorothea Lange Retrospective," January 24, 1966, accessed on July 9, 2011, available at: http://www.moma.org/docs/press_archives/3581/releases/MOMA_1966_Jan-June_0015_8.pdf?2010.

4 Warren Reich, "History of the Notion of Care," at *Encyclopedia of Bioethics*. Rev. ed. (New York: Simon & Schuster Macmillan, 1995), 319–331; http://care.georgetown.edu/Classic%20Article.html; Alison Jaggar, "Feminist Ethics," in *Encyclopedia of Ethics*, edited by Lawrence C. Becker, and Charlotte B. Becker. 2nd ed. Routledge, 2001, 528–539; Paula England, "Emerging Theories of Care Work," *Annual Reviews of Sociology* 31 (2005): 381–399; Joan Tronto, *Moral Boundaries: A Political Argument for an Ethic of Care* (New York: Routledge, 1993); and Tronto, *Caring Democracy: Markets, Equality, and Justice* (New York: New York University Press, 2013). Reproductive labor is the term, also used to describe women's unpaid labors, typically in the private sphere or home, though recent intersectional analyses show how paid reproductive labor is often done by women of color, in and outside the home. Barbara Ehrenreich and Arlie Russell Hochschild, *Global Woman: Nannies, Maids, and Sex Workers in the New Economy* (New York: Metropolitan Books, 2003); Paula England, Michelle Budig, and Nancy Folbre, "Wages of Virtue: The Relative Pay of Care Work," *Social Problems* 49, no. 4

(2002): 455–473. With the term "care work," political theorists and sociologists explore the links between labor, often women's reproductive labor, and the state.

5 *Dorothea Lange: The Making of a Documentary Photographer*, conducted by Suzanne Riess in 1960-1961, Regional Oral History Office, The Bancroft Library, University of California, Berkeley, 1968, 146, hereafter, ROHO-UCB, Riess interview, available at: http://digitalassets.lib.berkeley.edu/roho/ucb/text/lange_dorothea__w.pdf. Jerry L. Thompson and John T. Hill, eds. *Walker Evans at Work* (New York: Harper and Row, 1982), 238.

6 Oliver Wendell Holmes, "The Stereoscope and the Stereograph," *The Atlantic* (June 1859); Berenice Abbott in *A Guide to Better Photography* (New York: Crown Publishers, 1941).

7 On Newhall, Sussman, and Stott, see Stott, *Documentary Expression and Thirties America* (New York: Oxford University Press, 1973), 30, 8–9; Roy Stryker and Nancy Wood, *In this Proud Land, America 1935–1943 as Seen in the FSA Photographs* (New York: New York Graphic Society, 1973), 8; and Riess interview, 158.

8 James Guimond, *American Photography and the American Dream* (Chapel Hill, NC: University of North Carolina Press, 1991), 109.

9 Stott, 214; Reiss Interview, 155.

1

DOROTHEA LANGE AND TURN-OF-THE-CENTURY AMERICA, 1895–1912

Dorothea Lange had two childhoods. The first childhood was a sheltered one, with two parents, in a seemingly loving household. Her family circle included a younger brother, a grandmother, aunts, and uncles. She enjoyed school, and her parents introduced her to theater and music. Her second childhood was one of loss. Polio disabled her when she was seven; five years later, her father abandoned the family. Her mother struggled as a single parent to raise her children. Lange became unanchored. Out of these two childhoods Lange made herself.

Lange's first years resembled the lives of many middle-class girls at the turn of the century. Lange was second-generation American, her parents both children of German immigrants who had arrived around the time of the Civil War. They lived in Hoboken, New Jersey, across the Hudson River from New York City. In the 1890s when Lange was born, the U.S. brimmed with immigrants. In major cities such as Boston, Chicago, and New York, four out of five people had at least one foreign-born parent, but in the inhospitable plains of Nebraska or Minnesota, and in small mill and mining towns, immigrants were a substantial, sometimes predominant presence. Unlike many immigrant children, however, Lange's early years were comfortable, even privileged.[1]

Lange's maternal family had arrived in steerage, which guaranteed a berth, but not food for the transatlantic journey. They remained shamed by their lowly circumstances, but were soon conveyed to economic stability and middle-class status through their trades. Lange's paternal grandparents, the Nutzhorns, were grocers and property owners. Lange's paternal grandfather was a man of substance who sat on local church and trade boards. Because Hoboken was the terminus for German shipping lines, the majority of residents shared her family's ethnicity.

Lange's parents met in this thriving immigrant city, and their lives prospered in tandem with it. Lange's mother, Johanna (Joan), had a lovely voice and sang soprano in a church choir well enough to command payment for her services. Before her marriage Joan Lange worked as a library clerk, suggesting a degree of independence for a woman of that era. Lange's father, Heinrich (Henry) Nutzhorn, attended a liberal arts college in Wisconsin at a time when just one percent of the population received a college education. He soon practiced the law, and was admitted to the New Jersey bar at twenty-three years of age.[2] Joan and Henry married in 1894, and Dorothea Margaretta Nutzhorn was born one year later. The Nutzhorns lived in a fine brownstone. Soon after Lange's birth, the family moved to nearby Weehawken. Perched on the Hudson River Palisades, Weehawken provided panoramic views of Manhattan, the nation's metropolis. Lange's mother quit her job to care for her daughter and maintain their home, though the family also enjoyed a maid. In 1901 Lange's brother, Henry Martin, or Martin as he would be called, was born. Six years his senior, Lange identified as her brother's keeper throughout her life.

Despite her immigrant roots, Lange perceived herself as American. During her childhood, many leading figures recoiled at the new immigrants surrounding them, believing them a threat to their Anglo-American nation. Novelist Henry James visited Ellis Island and left shaken at having to share his "American consciousness and patriotism" with the "inconceivable aliens" he saw there. Many Americans gave credence to ideas of race and racial hierarchy, which appeared natural to them. The "white race" was divided into higher and lower orders. Anglo-Saxons from Great Britain or Germany such as the Langes sat at the top of such hierarchies. Southern Europeans, Italians and Greeks, and the Jews and Slavs of Eastern Europe, who emigrated in great numbers at the turn of the century, were decidedly lower. Such racial and ethnic thinking saturated public culture. Writing for the middle-class readership of the journal *Century*, a top political economist stated, "Slavs are immune to certain kinds of dirt. They can stand what would kill a white man." Businessmen shared tips on "Americanizing" their immigrant workforce by teaching them how to chew food and brush their teeth. Even Progressive President Theodore Roosevelt implored native white women to bear children to protect "Old Stock" Anglo Americans. Women's refusal would result in "race suicide."[3] As an adult, Lange fought for an egalitarian nation that rejected racism, but she retained a belief in ethnic difference.

Immigrants, whether privileged like Lange's family, or desperately seeking new prospects like so many others, were drawn to the U.S. because of its economy, which flourished after the Civil War. Mammoth industries, such as steel and oil, made the nation an economic powerhouse. Other industries grew apace. Southern blacks and Eastern European immigrants filled jobs in Chicago's meatpacking industry; Italians quarried granite in the hills of Vermont; Welsh and Scots pulled coal from the earth in Illinois and Pennsylvania; Irish and Greeks mined in Montana and Colorado; and Europeans and South and East Asians worked the West Coast canning industries. Across the river from Lange's home, in nearby New York City, the garment trades were well established by 1900, along with other light industry such as umbrella manufacturing, food production, and publishing. Hoboken boasted shipbuilding as its primary industry, but there were also makers of wooden pencils and Hostess baked goods. Jobs were plentiful in this industrial economy, though employment was insecure; layoffs were frequent, wages grossly inadequate, and accidents common.

Industrial expansion fed urban growth in Lange's Hoboken and nationally. In a twenty-year period surrounding Lange's birth, from 1889 to 1909, Hoboken's population of manufacturing workers tripled. In a circular process, cities and their growing populations further developed the local and national economy. Five years before Lange was born, about one-third of the nation's population lived in cities, the other two-thirds in rural areas. Five years after her birth, in 1900, two out of five lived in cities, and in 1920, by the time she was a young adult, the nation had become a nation of towns and cities rather than farms. Joining immigrants, such as the Langes and Nutzhorns, were native-born Americans, who fled farms and rural towns for urban opportunities.[4]

Urban growth made American cities combustible. Cities lacked the complex structures of governance required to meet the needs of exploding populations. Public health programs, municipal sanitation, and welfare support for the poor, the disabled, and the unemployed were limited. There was not enough housing, and growing tenement districts repelled middle class and elites, who feared to enter them. Political corruption was endemic, a reality best encapsulated by one New York City official who described his own graft as "I seen my opportunities and I took 'em."[5]

Lange's father entered this tumult. He was ambitious, and served as a "freeholder" or Hudson County board member. At twenty-seven, he was elected a Republican representative to New Jersey's state legislature. He ran as a Progressive, fighting the excesses of unregulated capitalism and urban political "machines" that managed, often for their own benefit, industrialism's turbulence.

The Nutzhorns' class status cushioned Lange; her early childhood seemed tranquil. Her parents cared for her material well-being, and her extended family indulged her youthful interests. While immigrant urbanites were building a whole new commercial culture of dance halls, vaudeville, amusement parks, and nickelodeons, the Nutzhorns immersed themselves in a classical "high culture." On both sides of the Atlantic, elite and bourgeois Americans and Europeans enjoyed operas by Verdi, symphonies by Mozart and Beethoven, novels by Austen and Tolstoy, and Shakespeare's poetry and plays. Lange remembers her parents laughing at her youthful attempts to read the bard's *A Midsummer Night's Dream*, and her father lifting her atop his shoulders to enjoy an outdoor performance of the play. Her mother brought her to classical concerts in fine Manhattan churches, and filled their home with books and music.

Lange's family also raised her to appreciate craftsmanship. Her maternal great-uncles were lithographers or printers. In interviews as an adult, Lange reminisced about her uncle's lithographers' stones; the stones' purity, she said, spoke to her.

Lange also recollected her grandmother, Sophie Lange, a hard woman, who drank too much and had an acid tongue. But her grandmother was a skilled dressmaker, and the wooden table in her home was filled with the pricks made by her pattern cutting wheel. Lange found this beautiful. She admired the table's utility, which helped bring the wonderful silk garments her grandmother designed into the world. Lange also loved the scarred table, like her uncles' lithographers' stones, for its sheer abstract presence. Lange believed her grandmother understood her fixation with beauty long before she herself did. She remembered her grandmother saying, when Lange was only six or seven years old, that she had "line in her head." Lange thought her grandmother recognized her absorption in "cool, clean," uncorrupted things. They shared a commitment to that which was "finer," that which had been worked with attention to detail.

This childhood idyll ended when Lange was seven; her second childhood began. Lange's parents thought she came down with a cold or the flu. She recovered, then suddenly could not move her legs, and finally became entirely paralyzed. Poliomyelitis (polio) was the culprit. The disease most often hit children, typically with stealth, as it did with Lange. This enteric disease enters through the mouth, breeds in the small intestines, and then attacks the central nervous system, destroying the motor neurons that contract muscles. Before the 1920s, the most unfortunate died, as the diaphragm ceases to maintain lung functioning. In addition to paralysis, polio also causes unbearable pain. When Franklin Delano Roosevelt contracted it in 1921, he could not bear to have the breeze blow over his legs, it hurt so much.[6] Immobilization was then the most common treatment. Physicians were unaware that robbing the patient of the use of their working muscles often worsened their condition. Lange was lucky; she regained the use of her limbs. The illness nonetheless marked Lange physically and psychologically. Her right foot became twisted—it was constantly flexed downward and inward and could no longer be lifted, a condition called drop foot. For some period, she wore special shoes with attached metal braces that reached to her upper thighs to keep her from falling. Local children called her "Limpy." Decades later, her son claimed not to notice her limp, but a friend believed she wore it like her silver bracelets and her beret. Her limp formed part of Lange, but it did not obtrude. Lange complained little, and her vigor astounded others, but polio shaped her self-identity. As she said in an oral history six decades after the disease struck: "[N]o one who hasn't lived the life of a semi-cripple knows how much that means. I think it was perhaps the most important thing that happened to me, and formed me, guided me, instructed me, helped me and humiliated me… I have never gotten over … the force and power of it."

Lange's bout with polio nurtured her independent streak and generated an antipathy toward her mother on whom she was utterly dependent. During the illness's acute phase, Lange's mother would have had to meet all of her needs: to feed her, turn her over, help her onto a bedpan, and bathe her. Such dependence would feed despair or even the dislike of her mother that she articulated. Lange later explained that her disdain stemmed from her mother's insistence that Lange "walk as well as you can" around others. Lange felt diminished by her mother's obsequiousness around doctors, and thought her mother shamed her to save face.

Photos can tell us much, but they can equally veil the truth. A cameo portrait of Lange when she was eight or nine years old shows a girl with her hair pulled back in a large bow, a tight smile, and bright piercing eyes looking directly at the viewer. Her brother stands in front of her, his head canted toward his sister. Both are bedecked in their Sunday best. Martin Nutzhorn wears a suit coat with a sailor collar, and Lange a gathered frock, perhaps of silk or bombazine, with a lace collar. They look contented and cared for; no mark of Lange's ailment asserts itself. This projected image was rent just a few years later when Henry Nutzhorn abandoned his wife, twelve-year-old daughter, and six-year-old son in 1907. Scholars believe he embezzled his clients' money, but details are hazy as his crime was never prosecuted. Authorities never found him, as Nutzhorn changed his name and crossed the Hudson and East Rivers, landing in a Brooklyn neighborhood. Desertion was then a crime, so Nutzhorn could have been imprisoned for leaving his family, as well as for financial misdeeds.

Nutzhorn fled when public awareness of what were called "poor man's divorces" was on the rise.[7] Uncommon before the Civil War, the divorce rate nearly doubled in the late nineteenth century. But divorce was expensive. Economic dislocations and greater geographic mobility led those without means to just leave marriages. Desertion became the focus of a whole new field, social work, which developed in part to address growing poverty rates in post-Civil War America. While some economists, social workers, and Progressive reformers believed that laissez-faire capitalism's low wages, particularly for widows, and unemployment caused poverty, others were convinced that poverty had individual causes, such as male desertion. To control the morally lax, "shiftless" men who refused to support their children, these reformers promoted tough criminal sanctions.

Lange's family was torn apart by her father's disappearance just as Lange reached early adolescence, a time when individuals are highly sensitive to social disapproval, in an era when that censure was a matter of intense public discussion. This must have intensified her pain. Further eroding Lange's equilibrium was her relationship with her mother. Joan Nutzhorn periodically met with her husband for many years. Nutzhorn never told her daughter about her continued connection to Lange's father until she became an adult, but family silences can communicate as strongly as words. Lange must have sensed an ambiguity, an unspoken reality, which contributed to her sense of her mother's weakness. Lange only set eyes on her father when she was nineteen. Subsequently, she only saw him episodically, then lost all contact when she was twenty-three years old. This loss was grievous. With loved ones she spoke sparingly of her bout with polio, but she never discussed her father's abandonment. Her second husband and children did not even know his name.

Nutzhorn's desertion set off a cascade of consequences for Lange's family. Evicted from their Weehawken home for non-payment of rent, the family moved to Lange's grandmother's home. Her grandmother had an outsized personality, in equal parts "temperamental" and "talented," and she had begun to drink more. Verbally and physically abusive, her grandmother made Lange a target for her wrath. Lange believed her mother buckled under her grandmother's will, and she failed to protect her daughter, further corroding relations between mother and daughter. Lange also blamed herself, seeing her younger brother as easygoing and herself as "quarrelsome." At an age when children assert their independence, the twelve-year-old Lange was plunged into a new environment, with an economically, spatially, and psychologically constricted space.

Lange could not acknowledge her mother's strengths, but Joan Nutzhorn kept the family together. She found a position as a librarian paying far higher wages than was typical for a woman. Her work lessened the family's financial dependence on Lange's grandmother, aunts, and uncles. Joan Nutzhorn had few options, as minimal outside resources or charity existed for those without work at the century's turn. Federal programs to help poor families, such as Temporary Aid to Needy Families (TANF), or welfare as it is often called, did not exist. Neither did Food Stamps, or Unemployment Insurance. With the exception of ethnically organized mutual benefit associations, which had limited resources, most welfare programs were organized by churches, cities, or counties, and often employed a punitive approach. Deserted women such as Joan Nutzhorn were forced to sue their husbands for financial maintenance. The wife had to go to court to get a warrant against the husband, and she had to identify a policeman to serve the warrant. If the woman won her suit, she alone was charged with enforcing it. If the husband did not pay, she had no recourse. This era's new social work and judicial infrastructure were better equipped to keep cities or counties from having to support the poor than to keep women and children from poverty. By finding work, Lange's mother escaped such snares. Nutzhorn brought Lange with her each day to her library position in New York City to keep her daughter out of the range of her grandmother's simmering rage. Nutzhorn adeptly navigated financial and familial difficulties.

Lange had been an able student in New Jersey, but her education now began a downward spiral, and she experienced an extraordinary sense of isolation. She attended Public School No. 62 in Manhattan, in the heart of, in her words, the "sweatshop, pushcart, solid Jewish, honeycomb tenement district." She believed herself the lone Gentile among some 3,000 Jewish students. Years later, she recalled the moxie of her youthful peers; she thrilled at their will to succeed, this "savage group," full of "overwhelming ambition." Lange embraced all kinds of people in her life's work, but she often discussed them in stereotypic terms. Her words echo the Irish immigrant poet, Lola Ridge, who described "the sturdy ghetto children" as "lusty, unafraid." Some Americans despaired of the new immigrants in their midst, but others, like Lange and Ridge, instead perceived vitality.[8] Lange thought she lacked her Jewish peers' drive and was thus disadvantaged. She did not participate in her progressive school's many extracurricular activities. Instead, she left school and walked the streets of lower Manhattan. Three days a week, she joined her mother at work at the Chatham Square Library, sitting in the break room, where she dawdled, read books that caught her fancy, and looked through the windows into the tenements, where she watched observant Jewish women in dark-haired wigs and men in yarmulkes. When her mother worked late, Lange walked by herself from Manhattan's East Side to the Hudson River on the island's far western perimeter, where she took the ferry home.

Lange traversed the poorest sections of the city, areas that middle-class adults feared visiting. She later described these walks as "preparation" for her photographic career. Two decades before, police reporter and amateur photographer Jacob Riis had worked in this neighborhood. He attempted to show "How the Other Half Lives," in his words, which suggested the immigrant poor lay outside the social fabric. He photographed Jewish Americans, who he deemed, stereotypically, as tough bargainers and whose young women were "houris" or virginal beauties, "scheming" Chinese Americans who pushed opium, and "picturesque," exploited Italian Americans, who were quick with a knife. Riis's photographs, and those of his companion photographers, Richard Hoe Lawrence and Henry Piffard, were seen in magic lantern shows, akin to slide-shows, which accompanied Riis' lectures and sermons. Riis thought illuminating the slums, or letting "in the light where it was so much needed," would aid his campaign to tear them down and replace them with parks and playgrounds. Press photographer Jessie Tarbox Beals and "social photographer" Lewis Hines also photographed the neighborhoods Lange crossed. Both were directly tied to reform efforts; Hine believed photographs a "lever for social uplift." Today, Riis, Tarbox Beals, and Hine are called "documentary" photographers, although that term did not exist until the 1930s.[9]

These photographers bore witness to a uniquely heterogeneous city. Lola Ridge, who had arrived in New York as Lange made her lonely walks, wrote of Hester Street's squalor, with oppressive heat "heaped like a dray/With the garbage of the world." Lange remembered the alcoholic men who congregated in this district. She stepped over those who had fallen across the sidewalk and became skilled at making herself inconspicuous, in making "the kind of face that eyes go off." She also learned how to enter into a situation without making others uncomfortable, while learning how to be comfortable in varied situations with many kinds of people. Lange was no longer cocooned in a middle-class German American community. As distinct from the ordered neighborhoods of Weehawken, or even Hoboken, New York pulsed with color. She was transfixed, as were many artists at the turn of the century, by the mixtures of peoples in New York's most densely populated neighborhood. The "Ashcan School" of painters, such as Robert Henri, John Sloan, and George Bellows, depicted a crowded world of pushcarts, dingy crowded storefronts, and neighborhood denizens. As Ridge described in her poem "The Ghetto," the neighborhood was "Jostling, pushing, contriving,/Seething as in a great vat.../ Astounding, indestructible/Life." The immigrants' vitality attracted and repelled. But the aural and visual cacophony of the ghetto, of hundreds of thousands of people compressed into this small plot of Manhattan land touched Lange's senses.

Ridge described the pushcart vendors purveying "Coral beads, blue beads,/Beads of pearl and amber, Gewgaws, beauty pins, Bijoutry," and these sights heightened Lange's sense of patterns, light, and color. And she certainly saw, as Ridge did, bodies dangling over fire escapes and sprawled over stoops, a human landscape.[10]

In Lange's first childhood she had enjoyed a life of comfort in a homogeneous community that reflected an affirming image of her family to her. But at twelve years of age, Lange navigated a strange new world. She was without a father, the target of her grandmother's abuse, an isolated girl thrust into a new culture, and always with the difference that her limp brought her. Harsh transitions. Lange describes herself as "solitary" in this period. "I wasn't actively unhappy, but dully behind it all, I went through it. Nobody knew how I was, what the color of my existence was." All around her thrummed life, but she was not part of it. These experiences ultimately nurtured Lange's focus and vigor, her willingness to strike out for her own vision in her personal relations and in her art.

High school proved even more difficult for her. In the early twentieth century, studying past grammar school was unusual, and Manhattan had only three high schools. Wadleigh High School, in upper Manhattan, was for girls. Lange's mother, in an indication of her resourcefulness, contrived to get her daughter admitted. The other girls attending Wadleigh did so to become teachers or white-collar workers, careers Lange found abhorrent. She majored in Latin, an academic area of study, but she performed poorly. She did better with creative subjects such as English literature, drawing, and music.

At Wadleigh, women took themselves seriously. Some remember the teachers as "starchy New Englanders," graduates of elite women's colleges. Wadleigh had its own suffrage group, which included English teacher, Henrietta Rodman, who campaigned for gender equality. Rodman was a member of Greenwich Village's Heterodoxy, a feminist group that attracted activists and thinkers. Rodman also founded the Feminist Alliance, which established apartments with communal kitchens and a day care for the children of working women. In Lange's last year at high school, Rodman appeared in the *New York Times* for protesting the firing of another teacher for "gross misconduct." The crime: not reporting her marriage to the Board of Education. The Board's bylaws prohibited married women from being "appointed to teaching or supervisory positions." Women also lost their jobs if they became pregnant. Rodman had herself hidden her marriage, believing it would keep her from rising within the school system. Rodman called the Board of Education's practices "mother baiting," and claimed the Board wanted to kick mothers out of the schools. For that, the Board fired her. It would have been difficult to miss such ferment, but Lange never discussed the social upheaval surrounding her. She made little mark at Wadleigh, only graduating high school because her physics teacher was willing to "upgrade" her, turning a failing grade into a passing one, thereby gaining Lange's eternal gratitude.[11]

Lange earned a high-school diploma, but her degree should have been in observation. In high school she was a truant, spending much time "bumming around." She estimated she cut classes at least half of the time, carrying her books as she wandered the streets, so no one would know. Lange had walked the ghetto during junior high. In high school she walked the breadth of the city, through Central Park, down New York City's long avenues all the way from the top of Central Park to the Battery, nearly ten miles, and through the city's world-class museums and libraries. She found a companion in another Wadleigh student from Hoboken, Florence "Fronsie" Ahlstrom. Lange and Ahlstrom spent a lot of time looking at pictures. Lange was a promiscuous looker, taking in fine photography in studio windows and portfolios in the public library and the commercial advertisements of New York's blossoming consumer culture.

Lange's truancy made her a "bad girl," in her words. Unwilling to follow the rules, she made up her own. She acknowledged being neglected and lost, yet she described this period as deeply productive. The anonymity of the city, the capacity to simultaneously participate in and be separate from the unending flow of events, gave urban onlookers, including Lange, a deep education. In seeing New York City, she came to possess it.[12] Lange also possessed a bit more of herself, as she came to know her own desires and not be bound by conventions or propriety. Her childhood traumas fed her waywardness but also gave Lange courage to try new paths.

Lange once shared an anecdote about looking through a window at the meadows of Hackensack, New Jersey, near Hoboken. A window is a framing device, like a camera's viewfinder. She remembered the criss-crossing wash lines that intersected with the fences that defended tenement backyards, the red brick lines of the tenements themselves, and beyond, the meadow in the late afternoon light. She remarked on its beauty to a companion who replied, "To you everything is beautiful." According to Lange that comment "made me aware that maybe I had eyesight;" she became conscious of her openness to unexpected visual grace. Ironically, the wash lines of tenement districts form part of the modernist art canon, that body of artwork arising in the late nineteenth century that broke convention by taking the everyday, the disregarded, the laboring classes, as its subject. Riis and Tarbox Beals photographed such clotheslines, as did Hine. Paul Strand's "Geometric Backyards" abstracted the domestic labors of women, the wash, animated in sunlight and breeze, into pure art. Berenice Abbott and Ralph Steiner, two contemporaries, also photographed urban laundry lines. Lange never mentioned earlier photographers' work. But she understood what was latent within herself and within the world around her. She soon acted on that knowledge.

Notes

1 Most details about Lange's youth from, Reiss interview; see Bibliographic essay for more.
2 Gunapala Edirisooriya, "A Market Analysis of the Latter Half of the Nineteenth-Century American Higher Education Sector," *History of Education* (January 2009), 115–132; and John Thelin, *A History of American Higher Education* (Baltimore, MD: Johns Hopkins University Press, 2011).

3 Henry James, *The American Scene*, (London: Chapman and Hall, 1907), 84–85; Thomas G. Dyer, *Theodore Roosevelt and the Idea of Race* (Baton Rouge, LA: Louisiana State University Press, 1980), 146–147; Gail Bederman, *Manliness and Civilization: A Cultural History of Race and Gender, 1880–1917* (Chicago: University of Chicago Press, 1996); On hygiene, David Montgomery, *Workers Control in America: Studies in the History of Work, Technology, and Labor Struggles* (Cambridge: Cambridge University Press, 1979), 40.

4 *Historical Statistics of the United States, 1789–1945* (Washington, DC: Bureau of the Census, 1959), 29, B145–159, available at http://www2.census.gov/prod2/statcomp/documents/HistoricalStatisticsoftheUnitedStates1789-1945.pdf; Mary Procter and Bill Matuszeski, *Gritty Cities* (Philadelphia: Temple University Press, 1978); David Nasaw, *Children of the City: At Work and Play* (New York: Oxford University Press, 1986); Michael McGerr, *A Fierce Discontent: The Rise and Fall of the Progressive Movement* (New York: Oxford University Press, 2005).

5 *Plunkitt of Tammany Hall: A Series of Very Plain Talks on Very Practical Politics, recorded by William L. Riordon* (New York: McClure Phillips and Company, 1905).

6 David Oshinsky *Polio: An American Story* (New York: Oxford, 2005); and Anne Finger *Elegy for a Disease: A Personal and Cultural History of Polio* (New York: St. Martin's Press, 2006).

7 Anna Igra, "Likely to Become a Public Charge: Deserted Women and the Family Law of the Poor in New York City, 1910–1936," *Journal of Women's History* 11 no. 4 (Winter 2000): 59–81; Martha May "The Problem of Duty in the Progressive Era," *Social Service Review* 62 no.1 (March 1988) 40–60; Michael Willrich, "Home Slackers: Men, the State, and Welfare in Modern America," *Journal of American History* 87 no. 2 (September 2000): 460–489.

8 Lola Ridge, *The Ghetto and Other Poems* (New York: B.W. Huebsch, 1918).

9 Jacob Riis, "Flashes from the Slums," *The Sun*, February 12, 1888; and *How the Other Half Lives* (New York: Charles Scribner's Sons, 1890), 129; Bonnie Yochelson and Daniel Czitrom, *Rediscovering Jacob Riis : Exposure Journalism and Photography in Turn-of-the-Century New York* (New York: W.W. Norton, 2007); Lewis Hine, "Social Photography; How the Camera May Help in the Social Uplift," Proceedings of the National Conference of Charities and Correction, Buffalo, New York, June 9–16, 1909, Alexander Johnson ed., (Fort Wayne, IN: Press of Fort Wayne, 1909); 355–359. Kate Sampsell-Willman, *Lewis Hine as Social Critic* (Jackson, Mississippi: University of Mississippi Press, 2009); Alexander Alland, *Jessie Tarbox Beals, First Woman News Photographer* (New York: Camera Graphic Press, 1978) and Beverly Brannan, "Biographical Essay," available at: https://www.loc.gov/rr/print/coll/womphotoj/bealsessay.html.

10 Rebecca Zurier. *Picturing the City: Urban Vision and the Ashcan School* (Berkeley, CA: University of California Press, 2006).

11 "Aided Mrs. Edgell: Married Herself," March 19, 1913; "Henrietta Rodman Loses on Appeal," June 9, 1915; "Try Miss Rodman for School Satire," December 23, 1914, all *New York Times*, (hereafter *NYT*).

12 For a discussion of the urban flaneur who enjoys the city's anonymity and heterogeneity, see Nancy Berke, "Electric Currents of Life: Lola Ridge's Immigrant Flaneuserie," in *American Studies*, 51 n. 1–2 (Spring/Summer 2010): 27–47.

2

"I KNEW IT WAS DANGEROUS TO HAVE SOMETHING TO FALL BACK ON"

Finding the New Woman, Finding Herself, 1912–1918

Dorothea Lange's preoccupation with observing brought her to a career, though like many young adults she wandered before she claimed her path. Her father's absence, her mother's demanding work schedule, and her grandmother's death in 1914 left Lange free to experiment. She did so at a time when all kinds of people—workers, artists, political radicals, women—questioned the most established truths and created vibrant alternative cultures. In New York City and its vicinity, an electric movement of organized labor held pageants and parades in a quest for economic equality. While she was still at Wadleigh, in 1909, tens of thousands of garment workers came out on strike, many of them young women like Lange, who thrilled to Clara Lemlich's call for a general strike to protest long workdays, low pay, and abysmal work conditions. Two years later, these workers and their allies mourned the loss of 146 garment workers with the 1911 Triangle Shirtwaist Factory fire. During Lange's adolescence, women also demanded seismic shifts in their social roles. In the 1910s the suffrage leaders harangued the public in Union Square. In 1915 New York City hosted the largest suffrage march, a line three miles long of women garbed in white. The *New York Evening World* wrote of the crowd's economic diversity, "Some whose names are to be found all through the Social Register marched side by side with working mothers with babies in their arms."[1] Women wanted more than the vote; they also questioned their relegation to the private, domestic sphere. This challenge, begun in the antebellum era, had accelerated toward the end of the nineteenth century. These "New Women," as they were called at the century's turn, went to college, developed professional careers, and challenged strictures on women's public socializing with men. Lange still lived with her family in Hoboken, but she now entered into New York's bohemian enclaves and its elite corners, following in many New Women's footsteps, and ultimately establishing herself in a trade.

As she graduated high school in 1912, Lange had told her mother she wanted to be a photographer. Joan Nutzhorn, struggling to raise a family alone, was not enthused. She wanted Lange to have "something to fall back on." At first, Lange complied. Joan Nutzhorn's life impressed on Lange the value of financial independence. She and her best friend Florence Ahlstrom entered the New York Training School for Teachers. Teaching, nursing, and social work were white-collar careers open to middle-class women; their choice was typical. Three of four women who pursued advanced training chose, or were channeled into, the first two professions. The public world was opening up for women in the early twentieth century, but it opened slowly.

A few decades before Lange's 1895 birth, Americans had debated the decency of women attending college. The opposition was intense. One Harvard University medical professor even argued that the rigors of college study could stop women's menstruation, making them infertile. Others feared a college education would threaten women's social role as mothers. Prior to the Civil War, few colleges allowed women's enrollment; it took nearly two centuries after Harvard opened its doors in 1636 for women to first attend college in the U.S. Women's college enrollment increased after the Civil War, but after graduation they had few places to utilize their knowledge and talents. Unlike working-class women who had labored outside the home for nearly a century, it remained unseemly for middle-class women to do so. The famed social reformer and peace advocate, Jane Addams, would win a Nobel Peace Prize in 1931 for linking social justice demands to international peace efforts, but when she completed college in the 1880s, she struggled to pursue her studies and did not know what to do with her education. Addams' frustration at not being able to use her degree for useful employment led to an emotional breakdown.

College-educated women such as Addams ultimately built the settlement house movement of the late nineteenth century. Perceiving a great failure to meet the needs of the dynamic cities so crowded with immigrant poor, these women decided to pitch in. Their "municipal housekeeping" relied on notions of women's moral and nurturant nature. Using a model pioneered in Britain, men and women set up homes in poor neighborhoods. They provided services such as day care and health care, even bathing facilities. Settlement houses became critical public spaces for political and economic reform. Settlement house workers advocated against exploitative tenement sweat shops and child labor. As social researchers, they surveyed the city with maps, photographs, and demographic data to push for safer worksites and better sanitation and ventilation in homes. By 1890 there were over 400 settlement houses in the U.S. Some settlement house reformers and economists founded the field of social work. This new profession was one way that middle-class women broke out of the private, domestic sphere, by taking responsibility for welfare in the public realm. They also took poverty out of the moral realm, considering it society's failure.

Each day Lange met her mother at the Chatham Square Library, within blocks of several settlement houses. The communities bustled with activity; women such as Eleanor Roosevelt and Frances Perkins (later Franklin Roosevelt's Secretary of Labor) worked or volunteered here. But Lange never commented on women's social action. Her mother eventually worked in this field, diminishing it perhaps in her eyes. Not long after Lange graduated from high school, Joan Nutzhorn left the New York's library system to work with juveniles trapped in New Jersey's Hudson County's criminal justice system. In Lange's oral history she described her mother as "reliable and good, responsible, compassionate," with an "integrity" that "no one ever tried to break." But then she continued, "I don't think she threw light on any areas as the result of her presence." It was an interesting judgment, since Lange would become recognized for "writing with light," a metaphor for photography.

Lange took advantage of the new social roles New Women carved out for themselves, although not all New Women were as sober or socially concerned as the college-educated reformers. The term, coined in the late nineteenth century, became a catchall phrase used into the 1920s, for women who sought independence from earlier social norms. As one *New York Times* writer stated in 1920, "the New Woman of the [18]90s seems old-fashioned today." In the 1890s the women in Charles Dana Gibson's mass-market illustrations were considered New Women. Gibson Girls appeared as illustrations in magazines such as *Life*, *Collier's* and *Scribner's* that were found in middle-class parlors. It could be difficult to ascertain if the Gibson Girl was a woman at leisure, hiking or biking along, a college graduate and professional woman, or a working woman. She dressed casually but well, in a shirt-waist that expressed her can-do attitude. This blouse mimicked male attire and replaced low décolletages or bustles, earlier fashion that sexualized the female form.[2]

Gibson's drawing, "The Reason Dinner Was Late," which appeared in 1912 in *Life*, while Lange was making her way in the world, suggests an ambiguous relationship to women's shifting social roles. Gibson drew a group of apron-clad servants crowding around the kitchen table. One of the servants sketched a police officer who appeared a regular guest. Gibson's admiration for the budding artist was evident in the woman's youth and beauty. Yet her drawing of the officer was so primitive that it suggested she had limited talent. Gibson's title conveyed the servant's inattention to her domestic duties. This ambiguity toward the Gibson Girl paralleled the public's attitude toward New Women. They were celebrated for their independence, yet scrutinized, even chastised, for failing to comport themselves according to traditional gender standards. Women attended college in 1910 at only slightly higher levels than they had four decades before, when Jane Addams faced such obstacles in charting her life's direction. More women sought entry to elite, male-dominated professions such as law or medicine, but professional associations often restricted their admittance. Some schools employed overt quotas limiting the number of women students; other schools relied on social censure to curb their entry.

FIGURE 2.1 Charles Dana Gibson, "The reason dinner was late," *Life*, 24 (October 1912).

© Cabinet of American Illustration, Prints and Photographs Division, Library of Congress. LC-DIG-cai-2a128630.

Lange must have felt constrained as she first took the safer route and acquiesced to her family's wishes, attending the teachers college. Like nursing, social work, and librarianship, teaching mirrored women's assumed nurturing role within the family, and little challenged the gender order. Lange's decision was socially acceptable and economically secure. High-school graduation was becoming the norm for white Americans in the early twentieth century, and as the nation's population swelled, so did its need for teachers. By 1910 nearly three-quarters of U.S. teachers were women.[3] Lange had been a lackluster student and so it says much about the demand for teachers and women's limited choices that she considered teaching an option.

Even as Lange quelled her mother's fears by attending college, she simultaneously pursued her desire to develop her "eyesight," and become a photographer. She believed her walks in New York had nurtured her love of the visual world. Not only was the city full of people from all over the globe, but also full of the marks of modernity: department store windows, billboards, movie marquees and posters, and magazine stands. The controversial "Armory Show" opened in 1913, during Lange's visual apprenticeship, and it exploded traditional notions of art and beauty, advancing a radical modernist aesthetic. Many compare this artistic avant-garde with the political ferment of the era.[4] If Riis, Hine, and Sloan recorded city slums, other artists exulted in New York's lively nightlife, its heterogeneous populations, its living, breathing steam machines, and its technological prowess. They embraced that which was modern, even ugly, and broke from centuries-old realist forms of representation, toward fractured and abstracted imagery.

There are many reasons the camera would have appealed to Lange. Photography seemed to require less training than drawing, painting, or sculpture. And it required little in start-up costs, only enough funds for a camera and a darkroom. Because of its newness, the field of photography was more fluid and open, with fewer barriers to women's entry, unlike other highly organized professions such as law, or even art, which typically required attendance at an academy.

Many white, middle-class women grabbed cameras and entered the public world as photography became popularized as a recreational and professional activity. Technological advances simplified the medium, and by the nineteenth century's end, urban camera clubs had sprung up. Women were a distinct minority within these clubs, but they became avid photographers. They exhibited their work, attended lectures, and learned tips from fellow amateurs. Some became celebrated. Tarbox Beals, who had been commissioned by New York charities to depict the ravages of tenement life, was known as the first female press staff photographer, and an official photographer at the 1904 St. Louis World's Fair.[5] Tarbox Beals set up shop as a freelancer in New York City in 1905, while Lange was in grammar school. Alice Austen, an amateur, published her New York City street photographs. Another photographer, Gertrude Kasebeir, frustrated by the limits of motherhood and her marriage to a conventional businessman, began photographing in her forties. First, she explored her domestic life, and then the Coloradan Native Americans with whom she had lived as a child. The mass-market *Everybody's Magazine* published her photos.

In 1913 the *New York Times* featured an article about the camera opening new professions for women, pointing to the pioneering Tarbox Beals and Kasebeir. Arguing that a woman with "imagination and the capacity for taking infinite pains" could become a photographer, the *Times* claimed that photography required less time and less expense to build one's skill than painting. And because of the magazine revolution at the century's turn, these "jill-of-all-trades" could fill the burgeoning publishing industry's need for visual content. According to the *Times,* women could photograph everything: flowers, New England homes, and babies. While these domestic themes fit women's assumed concerns, Tarbox Beals had of course taken celebrated photos of Teddy Roosevelt's Rough Riders.[6]

The mass consumer culture that matured as Lange did also make the photographer's trade an enticing option for Lange. Many of today's consumer brands were founded at about the time Lange was born. Singer Sewing Machines, Hershey

Chocolate, Quaker Oats, and Coca-Cola quickly became the backbone of the twentieth-century American consumer economy. Photography contributed to this growing economy. Photos advertised consumer products, and photographing itself became a mass consumer activity. In the late nineteenth century, several entrepreneurs, the most famous of them being George Eastman of Rochester, New York, built a mass market of photographers by making photography more convenient. Eastman's coup was the Kodak camera, which formed part of a distribution system that took the developing process out of the hands of the photographer, and put it into his company's hands. Eastman manufactured the film and the camera, which he sold to photographers, who then sent them back to get their film developed and their photos printed. In short, Eastman established a vertical monopoly. Eastman expressly marketed the camera to women, believing that he could build a consumer base by convincing Americans that picture taking was easy. His ads relied on gender biases. If a woman could snap a photo, anyone could. Eastman's "Kodak Girl," a pleasing New Woman who appeared in the company's advertising campaigns, was active; she traveled. One scholar called her a "superhero in skirts," who "bounded" as if "all the world were her runway." The winsome Kodak Girl who followed her pleasures was everything Lange could not

FIGURE 2.2   Eastman Kodak Brownie camera advertisement, circa 1900.

be: fully embodied, untethered to duty or to economic dictates. The Kodak Girl would have appealed to a young woman who felt as if she were being forced into a profession not of her choice.[7]

Lange was not a dreamer though; she acted on her desires. On one of her many walks she encountered one of New York City's top portrait studios and she climbed the stairs to find work. Arnold Genthe's studio, on Fifth Avenue and 46th Street, lay in the heart of New York City's elite retail district. She asked Genthe, a German immigrant, for a job. One of Genthe's portraits of modernist dancer Isadora Duncan attracted her. Since her first encounter with Duncan at New York's Metropolitan Opera House when she was a young adolescent Lange had been entranced with the dancer.

The infamous modern dancer touched Lange's heart at the deepest level, she had seen her dance many times and she believed Genthe's portraits made her "mysterious and beautiful."[8] Duncan made dance acceptable, and the classical Greek garb she wore contributed to the sense that she was making art, not entertainment. But Duncan spurned respectability in many ways, which was part of her appeal to Lange and to many modernists and feminists; she represented yet another kind of New Woman. Duncan disregarded Victorian strictures for dress,

FIGURE 2.3   Arnold Genthe, "Isadora Duncan," circa 1900.

© National Portrait Gallery, Smithsonian Institution, NPG.76.73.

movement, and sexuality. Duncan's Grecian gowns flowed off her body, allowing for her novel, "natural" movement. She wore no corsets, and her feet were bare except for golden sandals, and typically she wore her hair free. Most scintillating to many, including Lange, was Duncan's unwillingness to accept limits on women's expectations. Duncan wrote, "I do not believe in putting chains and a padlock on life. Life is an experience, an adventure. It is an expression." Duncan articulated Lange's desire not to stagnate in a conventional life. Duncan believed respectability caged women. Lange must have thrilled to Duncan's charge, "You were once wild here. Don't let them tame you."[9]

Lange openly admired Duncan, but she never commented on Duncan's belief that women had the right to their own sexual expression. Duncan was one of the more famous denizens of New York City's bohemian Greenwich Village, who broke the sexual double standard, and proclaimed women sexual beings who should enjoy their bodies and their sexuality as much as men. Elite women, socialists, anarchists, feminists, and other radicals also questioned the binds upon women's sexuality. The anarchist Emma Goldman advocated for free love and women's sexual expression in her essay, "Marriage and Love." For Goldman, marriage was "an economic arrangement, an insurance pact." Women got the worse in this bargain, she believed, as marriage condemned women to "life-long dependency" and "parasitism."[10] Lange was not a free-love advocate, but enjoyed greater interpersonal freedoms as a result of radicals' critique of sexual boundaries upon women.

Working "girls" also broke bourgeois boundaries and were another kind of New Woman that Lange encountered in her walks through New York. Their need to labor challenged the notion that women must be confined to the home. The commercial culture that they built mixed men and women at leisure in dance halls, nickelodeons, movie theaters, and amusement parks such as Coney Island. By the time Lange roamed New York's streets, working girls participated in public amusements without fear of a lost reputation. New York's Ashcan Artists, who depicted immigrant tenement life, and who often illustrated for *The Masses*, were enamored of these women, and represented them at work, at demonstrations and strikes, and thronging New York's commercial amusements. Lange could have been one of these women. As Lange filled in the contours of whom she would become, the divided spheres of the nineteenth century, its ideology and its reality, were fraying past repair. College-educated women and working girls took jobs and made careers that brought them economic and social independence. Radicals, feminists, artists such as Duncan, and young working women crossed former lines of propriety in leisure activities and sexuality.

When Lange made her way past Genthe's portrait of Isadora Duncan into his studio, she made a momentous decision. She fused her fascination with imagery with a quest for a meaningful career. And she made a smart decision, for Genthe was a master. He portrayed figures of political importance, such as Presidents

FIGURE 2.4 John Sloan, "The return from toil," *The Masses* 4 (July 1913).

© Tamiment Library and Robert F. Wagner Labor Archives, New York University.

Theodore Roosevelt and Woodrow Wilson, the world-famous actresses Eleanora Duse and Sarah Bernhardt, Hollywood stars Mary Pickford and Greta Garbo, and writers Jack London and Edna St. Vincent Millay. Before establishing his New York studio, Genthe worked in San Francisco, where he was renowned for portraiture and for documenting that city's Chinatown and the 1906 San Francisco earthquake, which destroyed his studio. He relocated to New York in 1911, as New York was the nation's publishing capital.

Lange learned much from Genthe. She called him a roué, an "unconscionable old goat," for his attentions to women. But she believed that he "loved women," and his regard relaxed sitters, resulting in stronger portraits. According to Lange, "even if it was the plainest dame, when he photographed her, he understood her." From Genthe, she learned to make her subjects feel comfortable. She gained tangible skills as well: how to create an inviting studio space that attracted elite clients, how to administer a studio, and expertise such as making proofs from glass plates, "spotting" photographs by covering blotches in the print with ink, or retouching negatives with an etcher's knife.[11] Each morning Lange took classes at the Teachers College, but she scurried to work for Genthe afterward. When she failed her student teaching, ostensibly the children walked out of the classroom from a fire escape, photography beckoned.

While grateful to Genthe, Lange's ambition and curiosity led her to apprentice with a series of other commercial photographers. We know about these jobs through Lange's memory, although by the time she described her early years, she was hazy on detail. Her next job was with Armenian émigré Aram Kazanjian, a celebrated portraitist of Broadway and international opera stars, such as Enrico Caruso. Kazanjian taught her to drum up business by calling on his former clients and reaching out to prospective "cold" clients. She then moved on to a woman studio-owner, Mrs. Spencer-Beatty, who contracted out her studio work to other photographers and printers. When a freelance photographer quit on short notice, Lange took his place. One client's limousine, replete with footman, ferried Lange to a job. This was an adventure. She enjoyed use of a large format, 8x10 camera, that provided more detailed images. Lange was elated; her skills were growing. She could now call herself a camera operator. She perceived her brash willingness to accept this challenge as "sheer luck and gall."

That same audaciousness led Lange to invite an itinerant photographer into her home to help her learn how to print photographs. She referred to him as a "loveable old hack" and mentor in later interviews; his name is unknown. He had made his living in Europe as a portraitist, but in her New Jersey neighborhood he sold his services door-to-door. Lange cleaned out the chicken coop in the family's back yard, turning it into a darkroom. He gained a workspace, and she gained an education in setting up and running a darkroom. She also worked with Charles H. Davis, a portraitist of Broadway and opera stars. Davis had been one of Fifth Avenue's top commercial photographers at the turn of the century, but his career tumbled when his last wife won their home and studio in legal proceedings. Davis enjoyed dining with Lange and introducing her to his theater and opera acquaintances. Lange found Davis's photographic style mannered, but she must have felt flattered by his adult attention and savoir-faire.[12]

From working with these photographers Lange learned about photography as a career and a passion, which she furthered by enrolling in classes with Clarence H. White, most likely in 1917. White was one of the few photographers then offering professional lessons, and he encouraged women photographers. In 1924 he published the article "Photography as a Profession for Women," which promoted women photographing in medicine, architecture, museums, libraries, photojournalism, and commercial photography, although he believed women "particularly qualified" to do family portraits in the home. His recommendation ironically promoted gender divisions, for even as White argued against them, he retained the notion that women were linked to the domestic. Nonetheless, he stood out from his peers. The era's most recognized art photographer, Alfred Stieglitz, dismissed White's women students as "half-baked dilettantes—not a single real talent."[13]

White and Stieglitz's fight was partially over aesthetics. Both began as pictorialists who sought to elevate photography from a mechanical process to artistic status. They manipulated the processes of picture taking and printing to emphasize the producer's artistry. Obscuring the scientific roots of photography and the realism that is photography's forte, they played with soft focus, papers that altered the image, special printing processes, and painting or drawing on the print, or scratching it, to imbue the photograph with an atmosphere that connoted craftsmanship. As artists, the pictorialists were neither the gentlemen and women photographers who experimented with the medium early on, nor were they George Eastman's Kodak snap-shooters. White passed on to many students, including photographers Margaret Bourke-White, Doris Ulman, Laura Gilpin, and Ralph Steiner, a deep respect for the image. Lange believed him a "gentle, inarticulate" soul, but she was a less than diligent student, just as in high school.

Lange established her independence in her living arrangements as well as her career. She shared an apartment with another young woman, though we have no record of where the apartment was located or her roommate's name. Lange had many male companions, not just the portraitist Davis, but also a sculptor, and then a professional printer. All three men were significantly older. Lange claimed these relationships were not romantic, but it is impossible to know. With John Landon, the printer, she visited New York's Pleiades Club, where Mark Twain had been a member. The club hosted elaborate, mixed-gender dinners, that catered to "bonvivants and ministers to the mind intellectual and artistic" at the Hotel Brevoort, where Isadora Duncan also enjoyed visiting.

Lange's mother had wanted her to be financially independent. However, Lange told an interviewer near the end of her life: "I knew it was dangerous to have something to fall back on." She thought the idea of settling in a career for security "detestable." She rejected the safe route of becoming a teacher and reached for something different. Lange's time and place helped her. She joined New York City's bustle. It was a modern city—alive with new skyscrapers and grand suspension bridges such as the Brooklyn Bridge, electric lighting and its growing commercial culture of amusements. Feminists, labor radicals, socialists, anarchists, Wobblies, and other free thinkers made New York their stage. Lange made her way through this city—a New Woman who took college courses, a working woman who learned a "trade" by apprenticing to Manhattan's top commercial photographers, and a woman at play who enjoyed the new openings for heterosocial leisure.

Notes

1 Bain Brothers, "Breaking in Suffrage Speakers," Bain Brothers, 1913, available at: http://www.loc.gov/pictures/item/97510684/; *New York Evening World*, October 23, 1915, 1.

2 "Fiction that Shatters Old Standards," *NYT*, October 31, 1920; See the Library of Congress's superb online exhibition, "The Gibson Girl's America: Drawings by Charles Dana Gibson," available at: https://www.loc.gov/exhibits/gibson-girls-america/.

3 Thomas Synder, ed. *120 Years of American Education: A Statistical Portrait* (Washington, DC: National Center of Educational Statistics, 1993), 14, 29.

4 Nat Herz, "Dorothea Lange in Perspective," *Infinity* 12 no. 4 (1963): 8; Martin Green, *New York 1913: The Armory Show and the Paterson Strike Pageant* (New York:

Scribner, 1988), 4. Milton Brown, *The Story of the Armory Show* (New York: Abbeville Press, 1988).

5 C. Jane Gover, *The Positive Image: Women Photographers in Turn-Of-The-Century America* (Albany, NY: SUNY Press, 1988); and Brannan, "Tarbox Beals."

6 Barbara Michaels, *Gertrude Käsebier: The Photographer and Her Photographs* (New York: H.N. Abrams, 1992); and "The Camera Has Opened a New Profession for Women— Some of Those Who Have Made Good." *NYT*, April 20, 1913. Such articles were common. See also: Southern Pines, NC *Free Press*, August 9, 1901; *Washington D.C. Evening Star.*, December 27, 1914, 5, Lincoln County (OR) *Leader.*, November 16, 1900; Lincoln Nebraska *The Commoner*, July 21, 1911, 8; and *The Washington Times*, January 24, 1917, 10, which reported on a Clarence White lecture about women and photography.

7 Susan Strasser, *Satisfaction Guaranteed: The Making of the Mass Market* (New York, Pantheon Books, 1989), 102–106; and Nancy West, "Her Finger on the Button: Kodak Girls, Snapshot Nostalgia, and the Age of Unripening," *Genre* 39 (Summer 1996): 77–79.

8 Herz, "Dorothea Lange," 10.

9 Arnold Genthe, *Twenty Four Studies* (New York: Mitchell Kennerly, 1929); Isadora Duncan, *My Life* (New York: Liveright, 2013 revised ed.) or Elizabeth Francis, *Secret Treachery of Words: Feminism and Modernism in America* (Minneapolis: University of Minnesota Press, 2002.)

10 Chad Heap, *Slumming: Sexual and Racial Encounters in American Nightlife, 1885–1940* (Chicago: University of Chicago Press, 2009); Emma Goldman, *Marriage and Love* (New York: Mother Earth Publishing Association, 1911), available at http://www. gutenberg.org/ebooks/20715.

11 Arnold Genthe, *As I Remember* (New York: Reynal and Hitchcock, 1936).

12 "Photography and the American Stage," at http://broadway.cas.sc.edu/content/ davis-and-sanford, designed by David Shields, author of *Stills* (Chicago: University of Chicago Press, 2013).

13 Bonnie Yochelson, "Clarence H. White: Peaceful Warrior," in *Pictorialism into Modernism: The Clarence H. White School of Photography*, edited by Marianne Fulton (New York: Rizzoli, 1996); and "The Clarence H. White School of Photography," at https://www.moma.org/interactives/objectphoto/assets/essays/Yochelson.pdf; and Clarence White, "Photography as a Profession for Women," *American Photography* 18 no. 7 (1924): 426–432.

3

LOVE AND WORK

Tangled Negotiations, 1918–1929

Lange and her friend Florence Ahlstrom (Fronzie) sought adventure; they decided to take a trip around the world against their parents' wishes. Lange later described herself as "wanting to go as far away as I could go." Like many youth, she wanted to "test" herself. "Could you or couldn't you?" she asked. Instead of a continental tour, the two headed west, presumably for Asia. World War I was tearing apart much of Europe as of June 1914, and the U.S. had entered the conflict in January 1917, pushing the women westward. Their desires may have been stoked by the travel impulse that circulated throughout popular culture in news stories, memoirs, popular magazines such as *National Geographic*, and the moving pictures. A generation before, journalist Nellie Bly had taken her famous trip around the world in seventy-two days for the *New York World*, a Pulitzer tabloid known for its sensationalism. Theodore Roosevelt's daughter, Alice, made headlines in 1905 when she joined a diplomatic mission to East Asia. Bly's and Roosevelt's exploits thrilled young women like Lange and Ahlstrom. Asia and the Pacific appeared exotic, with unusual flora and fauna and peoples less touched by Western ideas.[1] Their choice speaks to Lange's willingness to move outside conventional paths.

Ahlstrom and Lange were independent; they made it difficult for their parents to help them. Both girls met their parents' objections by saying they had work experience to keep them afloat. Ahlstrom worked for Western Union, the international telegraph monopoly, and thus she could find a job anywhere in the world. And Lange traveled with a camera; she could take her trade with her.

The pair set off by boat in January of 1918, but they were first confined to New York Harbor. Authorities feared Germans might sink the boat. Their ship finally took them to New Orleans, where they toured. Lange remembered carrying their heavy suitcases; they did not have enough money to pay porters. They then headed further west, by the Southern Pacific Railroad, for a visit near the border town of El Paso, Texas, and then a New Mexican ranch. They tarried a few days in Los Angeles, home to the nation's moving picture industry. But Ahlstrom and Lange headed out again almost immediately for San Francisco in Northern California.

The glittering city was the west's metropolis until Los Angeles's population surpassed it, just after Lange and Ahlstrom arrived. It was a far different city than Lange's New York. San Francisco's fantastic beauty, with towering hills over an expansive bay, made it a world-class city. It was an "instant city," growing explosively after the Gold Rush. Finance fueled its expansion: the city was made by gold, then silver, and the railroads. San Francisco was also a western entrepôt, hosting the headquarters of companies in shipping, food processing, and oil, along with other extractive industries. When Lange arrived it had been rebuilt following the 1906 earthquake. Its downtown boasted skyscrapers and "substantial stone-clad buildings," with "plate glass windows for window shopping."[2] It was incredibly heterogeneous, with immigrants from Europe, Asia, and Central America. *Care-Free San Francisco* (1912), published just a few years before Lange arrived, described the "dozen tongues, a dozen grades of color, a dozen national costumes—miner from the desert, cowboy form the range, chekako or sourdough from Alaska." Such guides specialized in making cities unique destinations for tourist consumption, but the U.S. census shows San Francisco as the most ethnically diverse major city from 1870 through 1890. And unlike New York, San Francisco was a workers' city with one of the most powerful labor movements in the nation. Organized labor was in equal measure progressive and reactionary, and its race-based unionism pushed California, and then the nation, to exclude non-white labor from jobs and Asians from citizenship. San Francisco is known as "tolerant," with great social fluidity, but that view ignores how the city's expansion required international flows of labor and U.S. imperialism.[3] To two young white women like Lange and Ahlstrom however, the city offered possibility.

On their first day in San Francisco, May 18, 1918, someone "picked" all their money from Ahlstrom's purse. Friends later said that both young women were crushed.[4] The facts suggest otherwise. The two left the Young Women's Christian Association (YWCA) where they had been staying for the Mary Elizabeth Inn, a home for girls. This Methodist home, still in operation today, had been founded only four years before Lange and Ahlstrom arrived at its doors. The home's founder, Lizzie Glide, sought to provide a safe space for working girls. Anxieties over the forced prostitution of young women, or the "white slave trade" as it was then called, were on the wane, but for several generations cities and large towns created refuges such as the YWCA to safeguard women by providing moderately-priced housing and moral direction.[5] Lange described their cubicle rooms as prisonlike, and she remembered the Deaconess passing through the hallways, sniffing for cigarette smoke. They were evicted several days after they arrived, for smoking and burning an ironing board cover. Rules would not constrict two women who had just crossed the country intent on making their way in the world.

Lange and Ahlstrom landed on their feet. Ahlstrom suggested they give the University of California at Berkeley a "whirl," but Lange insisted on looking for work. That first day Ahlstrom was hired at Western Union and Lange found a position at a local shop on San Francisco's main commercial thoroughfare, Market Street. Marsh and Company sold an odd mix: luggage, umbrellas, stationery, and photographic supplies. They also took orders for photofinishing. Unlike the fancy studios that Lange had worked at in New York City, Marsh's was strictly commercial and the photos printed there were largely mundane. Even so, Lange later claimed she received important lessons in looking by seeing all the snapshots that passed through her hands at Marsh's. She observed the intimate connections people establish through photographic imagery.

Lange's spell behind the counter introduced her to people who changed her life. "Extraordinary things happened to me over that most unpromising counter," she later said. Many artists and photographers doing commercial work went to Marsh's. That's how she met Roi Partridge, an illustrator who worked for the billboard agency Foster and Kleister. Lange enjoyed the advice of Partridge and other photographers. She subsequently developed a lifelong relationship with the Partridges: Roi, his wife, modernist photographer Imogen Cunningham, and their children. Cunningham had been taking photographs since 1901, had worked for Edward Curtis, the famous photographer of Native Americans, and had won a grant to develop her printing skills in Dresden, Germany. Like her husband, she pursued commercial photography to pay the bills. Cunningham's early work was soft-focused and romantic like that of Clarence White. Later, however, Cunningham joined modernists who rejected this aesthetic as false, and had instead sought a direct or "straight" use of the medium. By 1919, Cunningham was already taking startling close-ups of natural objects such as agave plants, aloe leaves, and magnolia blossoms, which emphasized shape, form, line, and light. Though nearly a century old, the timeless simplicity of Cunningham's photos make them seem contemporary, even today.

In this new environment, with a new set of people around her, Lange remade her life. A "big heavy curtain" lay between her life in New York City and her life in San Francisco, she said years later. To Lange, it seemed as if her youth in New York, "happened in another century." No longer Dorothea Nutzhorn, she took her mother's maiden name and became Dorothea Lange; thus, she shed ties to her father. Lange challenged herself in other ways. She had seen a woman with a limp in an elevator, she confided to her new friend Cunningham. She would learn to dance, something she had never done because of her limp. Perhaps she was thinking of the "peculiar grace" of her idol, Isadora Duncan. Lange and Roi Partridge paid for ballroom dance lessons in a studio Lange established not long after arriving. Joining them was Maynard Dixon, a Western illustrator and painter, visitor to Lange's studio, and a close friend of Partridge and Cunningham. Lange's determination to not just move but to dance, her vivaciousness, and her commitment to her craft would capture Dixon.[6] Lange was constructing a self and a life, it would seem, as if from scratch.

FIGURE 3.1   Imogen Cunningham, "Agave Design 2," circa 1920s.

© Imogen Cunningham Trust.

Lange built close friendships with other unusual men and women and nurtured professional relationships. She joined the San Francisco Camera Club, which she later described as full of "old fogies to whom [photography] has been a hobby." But the club gave her access to the most up-to-date publications on photography, an inside knowledge of local resources, and importantly, a darkroom where she could develop her negatives and enlarge prints. In 1920 she also became a founding member of San Francisco's Pictorial Photographic Society. Most importantly, she cultivated new friends and associates who nourished her career. She met Alma Lavenson, who took landscape and industrial photographs of California, and whose work graced *Photo-Era* magazine's cover nearly a decade before Lange shifted to recording the world outside her studio. Lange also met Consuelo Kanaga, an Oregonian who became a *San Francisco Chronicle* reporter, then photographer, highly unusual positions for a woman. For Lange, Kanaga was a "terribly attractive, dashing kind of girl," who was "way ahead of her time." Kanaga lived in a Portuguese workingman's hotel as the lone woman tenant. Lange believed Kanaga made her own rules, living as she wanted, "unscathed." Today, Kanaga is known for her searching portraits of African American life under *de jure* and *de facto* Jim Crow. She captured people's interiority: "Most people try to be striking to catch the eye. I think the thing is not to catch the eye but catch the spirit."[7] Lange remained friends with Kanaga until the end of her life. With Cunningham, Kanaga, and Lavenson, Lange found unconventional women as role models for her new life. She and Ahlstrom also enjoyed the company of Joe O'Connor and Jack Boumphrey, two men from the Camera Club. The meeting was fortuitous as Boumphrey loaned Lange 3,000 dollars to open a studio.

Lange was only twenty-four, but she was keen to strike out on her own. She found a lovely space at 540 Sutton Street, in an elite shopping district, within walking distance from San Francisco's modernizing downtown. She shared a building with the Hill Tolerton engraving and prints gallery. The location was excellent as Hill Tolerton's patrons could see Lange's work. Her space was through the back, the darkroom downstairs. The studio's ambiance was romantic. It had a fireplace and a large black velvet sofa with flowers that Lange arranged behind it. Friends referred to the sofa as "the matrimonial bureau." Its French doors opened out onto a courtyard with a pool and fountain. In the late afternoon, Lange's assistant lit a huge Russian samovar of tea for the guests who gathered there into the evening. The assistant, Ah Yee, a beautiful Chinese American woman, greeted customers, did photo work, and also cleaned. It is impossible to know if Lange was making a strike against San Francisco's racism, or adding a note of exoticism to her studio when she decided to employ Yee. Lange enjoyed Yee's marvelous laugh and her "absolute sense of the ridiculous." Lange's studio was so homey, visitors brought shortbread and other treats for their visits.[8]

Lange contributed to the artful atmosphere by sometimes garbing herself in a Fortuny gown. In an era when women's bodies were constrained with corsets, the Spaniard, Mariano Fortuny y Madrazo, revolutionized fashion in 1907 with his Delphos gown. The dress fell in a column that moved with the body; it did not enforce curves through a corset. Like Isadora Duncan, who wore simple gowns reminiscent of Classical Greek garb, Fortuny's timeless Delphos evoked a strong female figure, unencumbered by hard undergarments, free of society's restrictions. The gowns were made exactingly by hand; the multi-pleated shimmering silk was hand-dyed. The gown remained functional and its look could be altered by moving a cord. The gown spoke to Lange's love of craft and intention, it was luxurious and also suggested her forward-thinking tendencies in shaping her and her studio's image.[9]

Lange consolidated her studio experiences in New York City, soon becoming a popular San Francisco portraitist. Her early portraits seem shaped by her training with Clarence White and Arnold Genthe. They are straightforward, but the light is silky for a gentler effect. Many are close-ups of families, couples, or children. Her photographs of male clients have them poised for action, with lit cigarettes or reading glasses in their hands, though Lange's male artist friends appear more introspective. Some portraits are dramatic. In one, a woman sits in darkness with a shaft of light cutting onto her face, emphasizing her dark eyes, cropped and marcelled hair, and fur collar. Another seems almost like a glamorous, modernist fashion spread, with a woman in a lovely evening gown standing in an open

French doorway. The sunlight reflects her front and back into each of the door's glass panes. Portraits of Lange's well-heeled clients formed part of a tradition leading back centuries, of nobility and later the upper classes being able to present their best selves to the outside world through an enactment of self, first for a painter, and then for a photographer's eye.[10]

Lange believed she did not pander to her clients' needs or make fawning portraits, though as a "tradesman," she believed her vision was secondary to the clients. In short order, she built up an impressive array of clients, including the lumber barons of Seattle, the Weyerhausers, whom she traveled to Washington State to photograph. She also had clients from Salt Lake City and Honolulu. One darkroom assistant remembers being dumbfounded when at a client's summerhouse, his and Lange's shoes went missing the next morning. Unbeknownst to Lange and her assistant the servants had taken their shoes for polishing. Lange noted that many of her early clients were San Francisco's Jewish elite, in her words, the city's "merchant princes," whose patronage of the arts and cultural institutions made the Bay metropolitan area "warm and beautiful."

Lange toiled passionately through the weekends and into the evenings to establish her business. As she worked below in her studio's darkroom she heard the footsteps of those who visited the studio above. One day she heard sharp clicks. The sound came from the high-heeled cowboy boots of Maynard Dixon, whom she would soon marry. Lange was at first wary of him. Dixon had a tempestuous romantic life that he carried into their relationship. And Dixon's magnetism intimidated. He was twenty years older than Lange, had established himself as one of San Francisco's most popular illustrators when Lange was still a toddler, and cut a sharp figure in the San Francisco arts and culture scene.

Unlike Lange, who came from the urban, immigrant East Coast, Dixon was a child of the West, with family roots leading back to the Confederate South. Dixon's family left their Mississippi plantation after the Civil War for California. They landed in Fresno, largely populated by Mexican Americans and transplanted Southerners. Born in 1875, Dixon's California was "the West" of frontier myth, a land of few people and awesome nature. He told Lange of traveling with his father by wagon through the sublime Yosemite Valley. Western photographer, Carleton Watkins, had taken mammoth plate photographs of Yosemite years before, contributing to its being named a national park, today the nation's most visited. But in the 1880s, Dixon and his father could pass through the valley as they pleased; it was their own private Eden.

From a young age, Dixon set out to capture the essence of the land he was raised in. Lange remembered him as "being magnetized by it." As a boy he loved to draw. Chronic asthma often confined him to bed with little to do, leaving him time to develop his artistic talents. Like Lange, Dixon was ambitious, and at sixteen he sent his drawings to the premier Western illustrator, Frederick Remington, who encouraged his aptitude. In Dixon's early twenties, in 1899, he was named head illustrator for William Randolph Hearst's *San Francisco Examiner*.

The *Examiner* published the work of some of the West's greatest authors: Jack London, Ambrose Bierce, and Frank Norris, each of whom made as their subject an America centered in the west. Dixon contributed to the nation's media revolution that made everyday events more visual to mass consumers, mostly urbanites. Despite Dixon's success he grew frustrated, calling his job, "wage slavery." He left the *Examiner* permanently not long after, and returned to his favorite occupation, taking long sojourns into the outdoors in search of artistic subjects.

Being outdoors, in motion, outside of "civilization" engaged some deep part of Dixon, even as Dixon maintained himself by selling the West. He painted murals for the Southern Pacific Rail Road's Tucson train station; the railroad was central to western settlement. He also drew advertisements for Coca-Cola and Standard Oil, and covers for major publications like *Sunset* magazine, along with numerous news and book illustrations, including the popular cowboy series, *Hopalong Cassidy*. His *Sunset* cover of an Apache warrior was printed as a poster and a quarter of a million copies were distributed. Dixon's career success was linked to the growth of consumer capitalism, which expanded by feeding the American public mythic images of the West. And consumer culture's West remained an untouched frontier, even as the nation developed and incorporated the West into national and global markets, destroying what Dixon so loved.[11]

Dixon's career continued on swimmingly. He and his wife, Lillian (née Tobey) moved to New York City in 1908. The 1906 San Francisco earthquake had a profound effect on Dixon, as it destroyed the vast majority of his canvases and his Western collection of Navajo rugs and pottery. In New York, capital of publishing during this "golden era" of illustration, Dixon at first thrived. He became a member of the National Academy of Design and interacted with some of the twentieth century New York's most famous artists, and also Western celebrity stars such as Annie Oakley and Buffalo Bill. But the Dixons returned to San Francisco in 1912; Dixon missed the West too much. They returned with their daughter, Constance or "Consie," who had been born in 1910. Upon return he took a job at the nation's top billboard agency, Foster and Kleister, where Roi Partridge worked. The firm considered him the best among their stable of artists.

Dixon's personal life was tempestuous, however. While in New York, Lillian Dixon had experienced several breakdowns, exacerbated by drinking. Consie's birth had first joined the couple, but Dixon left his wife when her drinking continued unabated. His daughter remained with his wife, on the condition she would not drink, a condition she had failed to meet for years. It could not have helped that Dixon was engaged in an affair for nearly a decade with the remarkable journalist, playwright and adventurer, Sophie Treadwell. Treadwell had severed the affair before Lange met Dixon.[12]

The romance between Lange and Dixon was brief. They were married within a year, on March 21, 1920. The news covered their engagement and included a large portrait of Lange. Lange and Dixon's wedding coverage suggested their renown. They married in her studio, with a "few branches of flowering peach and hazel," and "glowing candles." One article informed readers that Lange would keep her "identity," by which they meant her own name.[13]

Lange became part of Dixon's circle of San Francisco bohemians. She described him one of the "kingpins," the "most spoiled and enviable." For Lange "the bohemians were the free and easy livers. They were the people who lived according to their own standards and did what they wanted." Bohemianism as a term had not come into usage until the mid-nineteenth century. Its use corresponded with an understanding of artists as nonconformists who rejected middle-class conventions. Dixon, like Lange, was always an iconoclast, as Lange noted later in her life, "When he was with the cowboys he was the sophisticated artist, while when he was with the artists he was the cowboy." As with her, his childhood illnesses had forged in him a strong individualism. Like Lange, he too lost his father, who was institutionalized when he was an adolescent, and also like Lange he was, by nature, a bit of a loner.

Their early years together appeared idyllic and loving. Dixon took her into the West, to California's mountains and coastal area, and she loved them. They moved to a small cottage in Russian Hill, where the bay was visible from their street corner. In 1921 Lange's mother visited with her new husband, and Dixon led them, along with Lange and his daughter Consie, on a voyage into the High Sierra. Consie soon came to live with Dixon and Lange. The next year they visited Arizona where Lange took exquisite photographs of the Navajo and Hopi. Lange met Dixon's friend and mentor, John Lorenzo Hubbell. Hubbell popularized Southwest Native American silver and pottery, and Lange sported a large silver bracelet from this trip for the remainder of her life. In 1923 Dixon left Foster and Kleister, to paint and sell his canvases and murals. Lange's steady income made her the stable breadwinner. She enjoyed caring for her family in this way. Their first child, Daniel, was born in 1925, and John Goodnews, later changed to Eaglefeather, was born in 1928. Dixon gave him the middle name "Goodnews" as Dixon was off on a trip when John was born and received notice of his son's birth by telephone.

Photographs by Lange and her friends seem to indicate a happy family. Lange took a lovely photograph of one of the boys as a baby, cradled in Dixon's arms. And many photos show the threesome, then foursome cavorting on verdant Bay area hills, or inland in the scrubby grass. What the photographs failed to capture was the growing tensions in the family. Over time many frictions developed between Dixon and Lange, and Lange and her stepdaughter. Dixon was used to being independent. His lone responsibility had been his daughter, who he had relinquished to his first wife after their divorce, then boarded out. When Consie moved into their home Lange became the responsible parent. She must have remembered her father's abandonment, and Consie was clearly needy. Her mother, Lillian Dixon, by then an "inebriate, an advanced alcoholic," could not care for her. But Lange and Consie fought, sometimes brutally. Lange had come from a highly disciplined household; Consie felt Lange pushed her to do too many household chores. Once, the two fought so seriously, it became physical. Consie, who was seventeen at the time, moved out. Dixon steered clear of all of this. He was easygoing, in part because he took little responsibility. He could catch his children's fancy with drawings of Native Americans or skinny dip with them in nearby streams. But nearly every year he went off, often for months at a time, to sell his work, or to draw and sketch in the outdoors. Lange was left to her own devices when he was gone; she was responsible for their two children, her stepdaughter, and her business.

Notes

1 Jeanette Roan, *Envisioning Asia: On Location, Travel, and the Cinematic Geography of U.S. Orientalism* (Ann Arbor, MI: University of Michigan Press, 2010); Tessa DeCarlo, "Gibson Girl in New Guinea," *Smithsonian*, 37 no. 1 (April 2006); Mary Suzanne Shriber notes that 1,765 books of travel were published in the United States between 1830 and 1900, in *Writing Home: American Women Abroad, 1830–1920* (Charlottesville, VA: University of Virginia Press, 1997), 2; and Laura Wexler, *Tender Violence: Domestic Visions in an Age of U.S. Imperialism* (Charlotte, NC: University of North Carolina Press, 2000).

2 Jessica Ellen Sewell, *Women and the Everyday City: Public Space in San Francisco, 1880–1915* (Minneapolis, MN: University of Minnesota Press, 2011); Daniel Cornford, *Working People of California* (Berkeley, CA: University of California Press, 1995); Roger Lotchin, "The Darwinian City: The Politics of Urbanization in San Francisco Between the World Wars," *Pacific History Review* 48 no. 3 (September 1979), 357–381; R. W. Cherny and W. Issel, *San Francisco 1865–1932: Politics, Power and Urban Development* (Berkeley, CA: University of California Press, 1986), 23.

3 Chekako is a slur for a wage-earning frontiersman; sourdoughs stayed in Alaska over the winter. *Cosmopolitan*, 45 no. 5 (October 1908): 670, and http://www.npr.org/templates/story/story.php?storyId=6061648; Allan Dunn, *Care-Free San Francisco* (San Francisco, CA: A.M. Robertson, 1912) available at: http://www.sfgenealogy.com/sf/history/hbcare1.htm; Barbara Berglund, *Making San Francisco American* (Lawrence, KS: University of Kansas Press, 2007).

4 Therese Heyman interview of Chris Gardner and Homer Page, August 26, 1975, at the Oakland Museum of California, (hereafter, OMCA, Gardner and Page interview). Both were photographers in their own right, and Lange's assistants and friends. Gardner accompanied Lange during the 1940s Japanese American internment.

5 The Inn still exists, http://www.meinn.org/; "Women Find Solace at Mary Elizabeth Inn," *San Francisco Gate*, April 19, 2010.

6 Reiss interview, 76–77; Oral history interview with Imogen Cunningham, June 9, 1975, Archives of American Art, Smithsonian Institution, at https://www.aaa.si.edu/collections/interviews/oral-history-interview-imogen-cunningham-12850.

7 Susan Ehrens *Alma Lavenson: Photographs* (Berkeley, CA: Wildwood Arts, 1990); Barbara Head Millstein and Sarah Lowe, *Consuela Kanaga: An American Photographer* (Seattle, WA: University of Washington Press, 1992), 17.

8 ROHO-UCB, Susan Reiss, interviewer, Theodore Bernardi, Donn Emmons, Roger Sturtevant, 1975–1978, available at: https://ia601409.us.archive.org/32/items/landscapearchite01thomrich/landscapearchite01thomrich.pdf.

9 Victoria and Albert Museum, "Delphos Dress," http://collections.vam.ac.uk/item/O362552/delphos-dress-mariano-fortuny/ and Cathy Horyn, "Liberating Pleats," *NYT*, December 23, 2012.

10 Over 20,000 Lange photographs are available through the www.Calisphere.org, California's Digital Library linking the University of California with state archives

and museums. Any image with an LNG comes from the OMCA. Referenced photos include: LNG5825, LNG5830, LNG5840, and LNG5814.

11 Daniel Hagerty, *The Life of Maynard Dixon* (Layton, Utah: Gibbs Smith, 2010); and Haggerty, *Desert Dream: The Life and Art of Maynard Dixon* (Layton, Utah: Peregrine Smith Books, 1993).

12 University of Arizona, "Illustrated Biography of Sophie Treadwell," available at: http://www.library.arizona.edu/exhibits/treadwell/ilusbio.html.

13 Dixon Papers, UCB, b85f101.

4

"TO GRAB A HUNK OF LIGHTNING"

A Radical Change of Focus, 1929–1934

Lange took an unexpected turn that made her, ultimately, a world-famous photographer. She had dabbled in other forms of photography such as local scene and landscape in the 1920s. But in the early 1930s, as she neared forty, Lange turned her camera on the Depression as she encountered it in the Bay area. The city's lemon light illuminated a harsh and growing poverty born of unemployment. Using the sensitive eye she had employed as a portraitist, she left her studio and photographed those traumatized by the Depression. She testified to their pain. There was no financial inducement for taking such photos. People did not understand them. No career path or community of photographers existed for what she sought to record. Lange became a leading contributor to this new aesthetic that did not yet have a name, but would become known as "the documentary" by the decade's end.

In the popular imagination, the Great Depression begins with a bang, marked by the stock market crash of October 29, 1929, sometimes called Black Tuesday. The reality was slower and harsher. Despite glossy consumerist fantasies which circulated in Hollywood movies and mass-market magazines such as the *Ladies Home Journal*, *Time*, and *Collier's*, the 1920s vaunted prosperity eluded millions of Americans. Hints of the economic disaster began in the mid-1920s, as the farm economy and housing market dropped precipitously. Unemployment was never less than ten percent after 1923 and most workers lost a month's worth of wages each year from illness or layoffs. In some industries, such as steel, workers made lower wages in 1929 than they did in 1892. The nation kept few statistics about workers until the New Deal, but historians now believe that an astounding forty percent of Americans lived in poverty. Many citizens were "working poor," who spent untold hours at work for subsistence wages. The era from 1922 to 1929 was seen as an era of abundance, but seventy percent of the income increase went to the richest one percent, and only fifteen percent to the bottom ninety percent.[1] Lange's success as a portraitist to San Francisco's elite, depended in part on such concentrated wealth.

The Great Depression exacerbated Americans' economic insecurity. Once the stock market crashed and investment narrowed, U.S. Gross National Product (GNP) fell by one-third. Corporations cut wages, then their workforce. Throughout the 1930s unemployment averaged twenty-five percent, although it was far worse in mill-towns and single industry towns such as tire-making Akron, Ohio, or shoe-making Lawrence, Massachusetts, and also among African Americans. California fared better in the 1920s through the early Depression, though the state's migrant workforce lay on a permanent bottom. Farming, California's premier industry, stalled out, and in the earliest years of the Depression farmers let food rot in the fields in the hopes that less produce would raise prices. John Steinbeck's famous *Grapes of Wrath* described a scene of coordinated destruction: "Carloads of oranges dumped on the ground. The people came for miles to take the fruit, but this could not be. How would they buy oranges at twenty cents a dozen if they could drive out and pick them up? And men with hoses squirt kerosene on the oranges." Near Los Angeles farmers spilled 12,000 gallons of milk every day into the sewers. It did not pay to market it, as prices had dropped so low.[2]

Because art is often perceived as a luxury, Lange and Dixon's livelihoods suffered. Dixon was particularly affected. He had built a thriving mural business, painting in private homes, high schools, corporate offices, and hotels. His fabulous mural of Califia, the Queen of California and other warrior goddesses embellished San Francisco's fashionable Mark Hopkins Hotel. In 1928 Maynard was working on his largest ever mural, a fourteen by sixty-nine-foot mural for California's State Library. In early 1929 he and Lange traveled together to Phoenix several times as he painted a mural for the "Jewel of the Desert," the modernist Biltmore Hotel. But commissions dried up after 1929. Dixon still painted, but sold only twenty of the two hundred-some canvases and sketches he produced in the four years after 1929.

Lange's thriving portrait business also diminished. In 1932 Lange earned a third of what she had made the previous two years. In 1931, believing that the Depression was straining her already difficult relationship with Dixon, she decided that they should take a trip with their children to his beloved Southwest. Lange and Maynard bought an automobile and set out to Taos, New Mexico. "The outside world was full of uncertainty and unrest and trouble and we got in that car and we went and stayed there," she said.

Taos was an artists' mecca, where avant-garde poets, novelists, painters, and sculptors had established a community in the early twentieth century. Mabel Dodge Luhan provided Dixon a studio as she had done for dozens of other artists over the years. Dodge Luhan, who "radiated... tentacles and influence" was temperamentally opposed to the disciplined, self-effacing Lange. This "Queen of the Southwest," a Buffalo, New York-born heiress, was married and widowed before twenty-three. Known for her sexual escapades with men and women, she had married twice more before settling in Taos in the late 1910s. Dodge Luhan claimed to avoid the public eye, but she engaged in private intrigue quite publicly. She had an affair with her gynecologist, and with the Harvard-educated "romantic revolutionary" and journalist, John Reed, who was eight years her junior. Once she settled in Taos she commenced an affair with Tony Luhan, a married Native American man. In the twentieth century's first decade, Dodge Luhan established a salon in Florence, Italy, for artists and expatriates; in its second, she contributed to the Provincetown, Massachusetts, arts scene and rallied with radicals, Wobblies, and socialists; and in 1912 she established her second salon at 23 Fifth Avenue at the northern edges of New York's Greenwich Village. Noted for its trademark chandeliers, white walls and white bearskin rug, the salon's most critical component was people. Dodge-Luhan brought together a "magnetic field" of poets, dramatists, jazz musicians, anarchists, socialists, reformers, psychoanalysts, philosophers, society ladies, and suffragists. Lange had traversed the Village's streets at the same time that Dodge-Luhan mounted her salon. Lange was an outsider, Dodge Luhan, the ultimate insider.

Dodge Luhan later launched the creative community in Taos that was more than a decade old when Lange, Dixon, and the children arrived. Dodge Luhan bought up property and several adobe homes to lend to the artists and bon-vivants who clustered around her, including such giants as painters Georgia O'Keeffe and Marsden Hartley, and authors Willa Cather and D.H. Lawrence. Many of her guests perceived Native Americans as more authentic than white Americans; they saw them as closer to the earth, with a simpler, more communitarian way of life. These views were similar to those elite white New Yorkers who embraced the culture of African Americans in Harlem as more vital than ordinary middle-class white life, or artists who perceived Maine fisherman or loggers as truer folk.[3] Lange's husband shared Dodge Luhan's fascination with Indians and the Southwest. He too romanticized the West, though it's unlikely he shared Dodge Luhan's mysticism toward Native American life.[4]

Lange, more practical, was less taken in by the region and its adherents. She remembers "a very good time for me," an enriched period for her and her family. But she described the poverty she witnessed, rather than New Mexico's majesty. She recalled, "living by barter. Indians, Mexicans, poor whites, natives, all would come to that square in Taos on Saturday afternoons and bring their produce, their red beans and pinto beans, their piñon nuts, their dried corn, some weaving, flour, eggs, lamb, hides, and there they bartered." She remembered the people "all bundled up" and the fact that night arrived with the poor "still...bartering." The material world of humans in social interaction, the circulation of goods and how survival unified heterogeneous groups touched her. An invented past did not appeal; she did not seek refuge in an identity of a people ostensibly closer to the earth.

Dixon and Lange's family spent eight months in Taos. These were productive months for Dixon. But most of Lange's time was spent easing her husband's life, "keeping everything smooth and being happy and making it an enjoyable time." Setting up home with Dixon and her children after months apart appealed to her. But she alone left friends and business; Dixon had both with him. Dixon often withdrew with male companions as he scouted new places to paint, abandoning the family. Lange's attention to "keeping everything smooth" is a form of labor that feminist theorists call "emotional labor." This work is often unrecognized and undervalued. Lange considered it natural that she served Maynard's needs. Lange also did the household's "reproductive labor," the monotonous, everyday chores, also devalued, that are required to maintain private family life and public economic life. She did not question that her role was to make family meals and clean. These were hefty duties in Rancho de Taos, for their romantic adobe house had no toilet, running water, or electricity. Lange cooked by making a fire and by carrying water into the home from a well. There was no radio entertainment, not even a clock that could tell them the time. Toward the end of their stay it was very cold, and, "the gloves, the galoshes, the wet clothes—you put them on and you take them off." Here Lange described the repetitive nature of her domestic labors.

Lange knew these labors kept her from her craft. She noticed the famous modernist, Paul Strand, on his way to work when he visited Taos. She considered him a "sober, serious man with a purpose," who was fully committed to his photography as art. She acknowledged gender limits when she contrasted herself with him: "that thing that Paul Strand was able to do, I wasn't able to do. Women rarely can, unless they're not living a woman's life." Lange accepted traditional female care work, even as she reckoned with the cost on her artistry.

In the late fall of 1931, they left Taos because mountain cold and snow made daily life too difficult. Lange maintained the trip rejuvenated, but she and Dixon could not rekindle their earlier happiness. Ironically, not long after they returned, a *San Francisco News* reporter penned an article featuring Lange, entitled: "Their Other Halves, Mrs. Maynard Dixon: Artist Wife of Artist Proves Temperamental Theory Is All Wrong." Advancing the argument that men and women could both be artists within a relationship, the article reported that Lange saw her "chief job" as seeing "that his [Maynard's] life does not become too involved—that he has a clear field." She sought to provide Dixon "freedom from the petty, personal things of life." But their life together did not cohere. Lange told the *News* reporter that she and Dixon had to board their children, "to work out the overwhelming experience of their trip." It seems more likely that life with Dixon and the Depression overwhelmed.[5]

In Lange's words, "the outside world was in smithereens," with the "terrors of the Depression," making people "shocked and panicky." Once they had returned to San Francisco, they stripped their lives down. They gave up the home that they had rented and Lange and Maynard each lived in their respective Montgomery Street studios. Their children were boarded out several hours from San Francisco. They could not visit every week. Decades later, Lange articulated her painful decision to send them off when Daniel, the eldest, was only seven and their youngest, John, was four. "I carry these things inside, and it hurts me in the same spot that it did then." Her children were devastated by the separation and the wounds remained fresh well into their adulthood. Lange describes how hard the decision was for her, how she "had the boys put in school," how she "thought that financially" she had better. Her remembrance implies Dixon's absence from such difficult decisions.

Today, boarding out children would be unusual, but it was not uncommon in the early twentieth century. In the late nineteenth century East Coast reformers shut down "baby farms," which provided foster care, but they flourished in California. Because the U.S. had limited welfare systems and virtually no public child care, parents sometimes had little choice. They might decide to board their children if a father injured himself on the job, or became disabled, or was an alcoholic or deserted, and the mother worked. Or if the mother died and the father's work kept him from child care the father might board the children. A study of the Ladies Relief Society of Oakland, California near Lange's home, found that nearly every child had at least one living parent; the parents just could not maintain their household.[6] Lange's decision paralleled the choice other families made when they were stretched to the limit, lacking financial resources or the capacity to care for growing children.

It is too easy to nostalgically read backward a solid nuclear family, but historically family life, particularly for those lacking economic security, has been quite fluid. Lange and Dixon traveled in elite circles, but their professions as artists left them economically marginal. Lange's son Daniel was furious at her for abandoning him just as Lange had been angry at her mother for being emotionally dependent on Lange's grandmother. Lange gave priority to her work and her relationship with Dixon when she sent off the children, but their finances were so dire that choosing to board them seemed a reasonable choice.

Lange and Dixon's marriage continued to unravel however. A favored photograph of Lange's was of her husband's hands. Often she caught the hand curved, fingers curled, or stretched outward. More often his hand held the brush that made him famous. She had taken photos of her elegant husband early in their relationship; her photos of him holding their babies reveal a tender relationship between man and child, and photographer and subject. But in later years, it was almost as if in representing her husband, his métier came first, even before the man himself. Portraiture requires a relationship between the sitter and the photographer. It is possible that Dixon no longer shared his self with Lange's camera eye, or that she could no longer look.

Dixon was a trickster and a skewerer of pretensions and he publicly humiliated Lange. She loved to host dinner parties at their home for friends and clients, and he once taught a child a lewd poem to recite for guests. Another time he snagged a pair of women's underwear on his cane, brandishing them before visitors. After another grand entrance, he went off stage to the kitchen where he pretended to retch from the meal. Dixon's willingness to wound Lange suggests animosity or a lack of maturity or both. Perhaps he enjoyed Lange as a young woman who was enamored with him and his artistry. It might have been difficult for him to reckon with a woman who had strong, perhaps rigid ideas of what a proper life was for their family.[7] By the early 1930s, Lange's marriage was at a breaking point.

As the Depression continued, its wounds deepened. No federal safety net existed for the poor. Cities and private charities offered limited relief, typically to women and children. But the need was so great, municipalities could not keep up. *Time* reported that, "By 1932, only 1/4 of unemployed families received any relief... Cities, which had to bear the brunt of the relief efforts, teetered on the edge of bankruptcy. By 1932, Cook County (Chicago) was firing firemen, police, and teachers (who had not been paid in 8 months)." When FDR came into office, in February of 1933, over a thousand municipalities had defaulted; there simply was no money to pay creditors. Twenty-four mayors besieged Washington D.C., asking the new president for a billion dollars a year to stave off bankruptcy and help the sixty-five million citizens in their care, including orphan children and widows. In Los Angeles, nine in ten who needed aid did not receive it; those who received aid got nickels and dimes.[8]

Lange felt the economic sinkhole deepening, and she and Dixon both supported the new president. President Herbert Hoover had been ill-equipped to deal with the economic crisis. Hoover recognized that there was no such thing as a pure "laissez-faire" market, that the state had, from colonial times, fostered U.S. economic and industrial growth. He had strengthened the Department of Commerce to enhance consumer spending, and he promoted the Reconstruction Finance Corporation Act, which provided loans to state and local governments and businesses to keep disaster at bay. Hoover supported business welfare, but bowing to notions of self-reliance, he rejected using the state to guarantee citizens' welfare. One business leader said the poor "do not practice the habits of thrift and conservation," instead, they "gambled away" their savings. Hoover himself, who in his 1929 inaugural address had promised to "remove poverty still further from our borders," would call those who relied upon government welfare programs, "lazy parasites."

And so things got worse. By the 1932 presidential elections, one quarter of working Americans had no job; four months later, one-third were without work. Makeshift encampments across America were called "Hoovervilles" for a president who would not acknowledge Americans' distress. People lived in cardboard boxes, and under pieces of tin; some lived in caves, or water mains, or dug themselves into holes. Major cities such as New York, Washington D.C., or St. Louis had thousands living in such communities. Oakland, California's third largest city had "Pipe City," on its waterfront. Hundreds sheltered within cement sewer pipes that the city could not afford to lay. City leaders did not want itinerants grouped there, but the owner of American Pipe Company insisted they be allowed to stay.[9] Two million people rode the rails. Novelist Nelson Algren wrote about the nation's "vast army of America's homeless ones," trudging ever onward in the hopes of food or a place to rest their heads. Railroad "bulls" or security and police could be savage to the tramps who rode the rails; municipalities sprayed their garbage with poison to "let you starve healthily;" and vagrancy, or being so poor that you could not afford shelter, could land you in jail or work camps. Soup lines ran like "centipedes" along city streets. Even those who had set aside money might hurt. By March of 1933, one in five banks had folded, 9,000 in all.[10] The government had no regulations for banks to ensure citizens' security, so nine million Americans lost all of their life savings.

The ideology of self-reliance promoted by businessmen and governing politicians was shared by many; citizens internalized society's blame. Yet other citizens began to reject these views, which came to seem out of touch, even inhumane, in the face of such widespread distress. Americans started challenging notions of laissez-faire, claiming that the government must do something to provide security and care in the face of the staggering levels of unemployment. Some organized. Residents in Seattle's self-governing Hooverville had their own "mayor" and post office. Across the Midwest farmers banded together, often under the Farmers' Holiday Association and organized "penny auctions," where locals kept anyone from bidding on lands or equipment, so that their neighbors could retain their property. Nebraska, South Dakota, and Minnesota enacted moratoriums on farm foreclosures as a result of such activism. The Unemployment Councils, allied with the Communist Party, tried to prevent evictions. Council members stood with families when the sheriffs came and if this confrontation failed, activists returned peoples' possessions to their apartments once the sheriffs left. Los Angeles hosted a cooperative movement so strong it fed hundreds of thousands of people in 1932. Members of that city's Unemployed Cooperative Relief Association coordinated with Unemployment Council members to stop evictions, and to turn on electricity and gas after utilities had turned them off. There were hunger marches, and citizens overran city halls and state legislatures.[11] At the national level, World War I veterans marched on the White House in the famous Bonus March to get their "bonus" pensions early.

Lange and other cultural producers began creating new aesthetics and new artistic forms in response to the economic crisis. She had already decided in 1929 that people were her métier. She described being in the midst of a storm, out in the California countryside, "and right in the middle of it, with the thunder bursting and the wind whistling it came to me that what I had to do was to take pictures and concentrate upon people, only people, all kinds of people, people who paid me and people who didn't." Her attempts to branch out artistically had frustrated her. "I tried to photograph the young pine trees there, and I tried to photograph some stumps, and I tried to photograph in the late afternoon the way the sunlight comes through some…skunk cabbage, with big pale leaves and the afternoon sun showing all the veins." Such photography was then in vogue in San Francisco. Her friend Imogen Cunningham had continued her precise studies of nature, another friend, Edmund Weston, was photographing nautilus, artichokes, and bell peppers, and Ansel Adams was isolating Yosemite Park's stupendous Half Dome. These photographers came together in 1932 for a self-organized group exhibition under the rubric "f64." F64 refers to the aperture opening on the camera that allows for a clear and highly detailed photograph. F64's informal "manifesto" proclaimed they wanted to feature the "best contemporary photography of the West," through "purely photographic methods." They rejected pictorialism, which retained mass popularity as an aesthetic movement. Lange took another tack, deciding to, "photograph the people that my life touched." People were her "area;" with people she "could freely move."

Her later descriptions sound dramatic and decisive, but she was experimenting, working in a way few had done before. Standing in the sunny southern exposure of her second-floor window on Montgomery Street, she waited for her prints to darken so she could evaluate them. From the window Lange could see "the flow of life." Her studio lay at a crossroads; she was,

> surrounded by evidences of the Depression… Up from the waterfront it came to that particular corner, that junction of many different things. There was the financial district to the left, Chinatown straight ahead, and the Barbary Coast and the Italian town. The unemployed would drift up there, would stop, and I could just see that they did not know where next.

Watching them she felt a great tension, a "discrepancy between what I was working on in the printing frames and what was going on in the street," that could not be "assimilate[d]." Lange was herself at a crossroads, though she may not have known it. She believed that relinquishing her children to the care of another made it possible to take these pictures. She was both goaded "by the fact that I was under personal turmoil to do something," and freed from the time constraints of domestic life, and she felt she must attempt to represent the tragedy many were facing.

So Lange left her studio. At first she ventured out with her brother, Martin. The former merchant marine and construction worker was garrulous and enjoyed accompanying her. Though Lange had walked New York City's poverty-stricken Bowery in her youth, in San Francisco she interacted with elites and artists. She was uncertain how to approach her subjects; her trade was taking studio portraits. Typically clients had thought about what they wanted out of their photo session, had dressed well and made themselves up, and were presenting a face to the world that they wanted seen. As a portraitist, she had all her tools at hand and her space to direct. But in the streets Lange could not control the lighting, or the space, or who or what moved in and out of the frame. She was small, and she feared the "jostling about in groups of tormented, depressed and angry men, with a camera." Her large-format, 4x5 camera was difficult to carry and she thought someone might try to take it or hit her from behind. Most significantly, she had to establish a relationship with her subjects in a brief window of time, typically spontaneously.

She was uncertain about the meaning of this new work. She placed her photographs on her studio walls, and clients would ask "What are you going to do with it." Even so, in this early period of experimentation, she composed one of her most famous photographs, "White Angel Breadline," recognized for its expression of Depression-era isolation and despair. It shows a man with head turned down, standing against a waist-high set of crude lumber rails. His mouth is pulled downward in a grimace, his fedora is not sharp but dirtied and soft, his hands clench one another and reach out toward the viewer. A cup, apparently empty, sits on the rails between his arms. The light captures the stubble on his chin and his clasped hands. Behind him are the backs of many men. Only two other faces can be seen in the background; even as he is pinned in a crowd, the man broods alone. Asked about this photograph years later, she said: "there are moments such as these when time stands still and all you do is hold your breath and hope it will wait for you." Her job was to "get it organized in a fraction of a second on that tiny piece of sensitive film." She believed the man in the photo illuminated what was happening in the world around her, but did not yet know what to make of it. This new work vitalized her, "I went out just absolutely in the blind staggers. I had something to do." In her words, she kept at it, "pretty much without interruption."[12] Dixon was touched, writing in his diary that "Lange begins work photographing Forgotten Man." Lange believed her project inchoate, but Dixon thought he had witnessed a shift in her artistry.

Lewis Hine and Jacob Riis had taken photographs clearly intended, in Hine's words, as a "lever for social uplift," to confront crowded urban tenements, sweatshops, and child labor. News photographers such as Jesse Tarbox Beals and freelancers for the Bain News Service had also taken photos of urban poverty, harsh living conditions, the charitable dispersal of food and shoes to poor children, and Bowery "bums" and bindlestiffs crowding "hobo conventions."[13] Their photos were published just as photography became a more crucial part of the news. Lange was moving toward something different.

As Lange pursued her photographic investigations, the political and cultural landscape was changing around her. Franklin Delano Roosevelt had campaigned against Hoover in 1932, pledging "a new deal for the American people." Moneyed scion of Hudson River elites, Roosevelt was a politician less wedded to causes than to solutions. His wife Eleanor, who had worked in the College Settlement on the Lower East Side's Rivington Street before her marriage, was more committed to righting injustices. New York State, which Roosevelt had governed, was a pioneer in regulating capitalism's more ruthless aspects. For decades, New York City had been a center of Progressive reform efforts and women's activism. Elite and working women agitated for regulation, and passed novel legislation in 1890 for women factory inspectors to oversee work conditions, a win for women and for workers. The New York City Triangle Fire, which killed 146 workers, led to fire safety regulations and ultimately maximum hour legislation. Workmen's compensation was passed in 1914, and in 1915 widowed mothers were provided small "allowances" to help raise their children.

In 1930 New York State passed "old age relief," a precursor to Social Security. An overwhelmed and paralyzed charity system led the state to experiment with providing emergency poor relief in the early 1930s.[14] Roosevelt was vague about how he would right the economy, but he won the 1932 national election in a landslide. Lange and Dixon celebrated his victory.

Today, presidents are assessed by their first hundred days; FDR set this measure in his whirlwind attempts to confront the Depression. He tried many tacks. A bank holiday restored confidence in banks and financial regulations. The Civilian Conservation Corps (CCC) put a quarter of a million unemployed youth, mostly urbanites, into rural areas and national parks to build park infrastructure and help conserve the land by planting trees. The Rural Electrification Administration (REA) brought light to rural homes and farms, ninety percent of which lacked electricity nearly fifty years after American cities were electrified. The Works Progress Administration (WPA) built post offices and bridges, and employed artists to develop plays, write tourist guides about each state, conduct oral histories of former slaves, and make murals and sculpture, ultimately employing more than eight and a half million people. Importantly, Roosevelt believed he must reach the man that Lange depicted in the "White Angel Breadline," "the forgotten man at the bottom of the economic pyramid." Roosevelt promoted legislation that facilitated labor union organization, funded massive public works project across the nation in the Public Works Administration (PWA), and provided direct relief to citizens. Roosevelt's commitments were inconsistent, he encountered much resistance, and the nation's economic devastation was deep. But the New Deal "alphabet soup" of initiatives comprised revolutionary shifts toward a federal welfare, regulatory, and administrative state that institutionalized the state's care for U.S. citizens. Lange would become part of these governmental efforts.

Lange continued to probe the question "what are you going to do with this kind of thing?" Over the next two years, she had "gone down with the dregs," gaining greater "confidence" in going out onto the streets and determining what she wanted to say with her camera. She took photographs of men reclining on plots of grass, or smack in the middle of the street, or huddled against walls in stoops or alleyways adjoining commercial thoroughfares. In one photograph, a man sits on a wheelbarrow against a blank expanse of cinderblock wall; he is turned in on himself, shutting out the world. The light in this photo is so bright, it interrogates. He is a dark figure, his face replaced by his workman's cap; he cannot look into this light, this world. Lange said that whereas before she would have taken his portrait, now "I wanted to take a picture of a man as he stood in his world—in this case, a man with his head down, with his back against the wall, with his livelihood, like the wheelbarrow, overturned." Lange showed "man as he stood in his world." This was a relationship, a social relationship, which she sought to pin down with her exacting camera eye.[15]

The pull of the streets took Lange away from her paying work and she thought perhaps she could set "limits… and get it out of her system." So she decided to

FIGURE 4.1   Dorothea Lange, "Man beside wheelbarrow," San Francisco, 1934.

© The Dorothea Lange Collection, the Oakland Museum of California. Gift of Paul S. Taylor.

document a May Day demonstration of the unemployed. "I will set myself a big problem. I will go there, I will photograph this thing, I will come back, and develop it. I will print it, and I will mount it and I will put it on the wall, all in twenty-four hours. I will do this, to see if I can just grab a hunk of lightning that is going on and finish it." Communist Party-sponsored May Day celebrations flourished during the Depression as the Party's message appealed to ordinary workers and activists. By going to the May Day parade, Lange was looking at the world with a new lens. She grappled with how to photograph those in the streets. A portraitist engages with the individual, perhaps with the individuals' family, friends, or colleagues. But Lange was seeking to define how citizens' economic difficulties and their activism drew them together as social beings.

Lange did "grab a hunk of lightning," celebrating activism as few other major photographers have. In one photo, Lange stood below the speaker and his micro-phone, monumentalizing his act of public outreach. His mouth is open, nearly in a snarl, as he exhorts the crowd. Her vantage point is akin to what rally-goers might have experienced; Lange makes the viewer part of the activism. In another photo, two young men stand with upraised fists. One is white, the other Asian. One holds his left fist up, the other his right. To the side another protester's arm nearly thrusts through the picture frame. Both chant in unison. Lange depicted an unusual act of interracial solidarity. Other photos from this rally present participants with the self-possession of Lange's paying clients. One dashing woman appears to be a Hollywood working girl. Her rapt attention to the speaker and the set of May Day journals clasped in her arms evidence her commitments.

Lange's best-known image from this period of intense labor activism examines the police, who have been dispatched to uphold the social order. Lange's photograph is ambiguous. Most of the crowd of men look off to their right. Many carry picket signs against "press slander," Hitler's Nazis and "imperialist aggression," and the strong graphic quality of the English and Japanese script attracts attention. But several men look out at the viewers, drawing them into the protest. The policeman is the star of the composition—he spans almost the entire vertical frame of the photo from top to bottom. Because he is closest to the viewer, he is larger than the men behind him. He stands casually, almost at rest though his attention, sharply drawn to his right, parallels the glances of other protesters on the street. His profile, emphasized by his cap, points in the same direction. His hands are clasped at his belly, and yet his feet are planted, and he seems poised to spring into action if need be. His uniform's side stripe, brass buttons, and gleaming badge highlight his role in the crowd. This photo provokes, pushing viewers to ask: what role should police have

FIGURE 4.2   Dorothea Lange, "May Day listener at rally," circa 1934.

© The Dorothea Lange Collection, the Oakland Museum of California. Gift of Paul S. Taylor.

FIGURE 4.3 Dorothea Lange, "Street demonstration—San Francisco," 1934.

© The Dorothea Lange Collection, the Oakland Museum of California. Gift of Paul S. Taylor.

at a civil protest? Do police protect? What are they trying to contain? Will violence occur, and from where or from whom will it originate? The persistence of such questions to this day explains the image's continued pull.[16]

In January of 1934, as Lange continued to photograph these new themes, she and her husband, Maynard Dixon, moved once again, this time to 2515 Gough Street. Lange and Maynard brought their sons home, and Lange gave up her portrait studio. She sent out a change of address card, stating she did "photographs of people." On it, she included a quotation from the sixteenth-century philosopher-scientist Francis Bacon: "The contemplation of things as they are, without substitution or imposture, without error or confusion is in itself a nobler thing than a whole harvest of invention." Lange was making a claim for the "real;" she wanted to capture the world as it was, and document the economic tragedy around her rather than aestheticize it or make it beautiful.

Notes

1 José Gabriel Palma, "The Revenge of the Market on the Rentiers: Why Neoliberal Reports of the End of History Turned Out to Be Premature," *Cambridge Journal of Economics* 33 no. 4 (July 2009): 4.

2 John Steinbeck, Chapter 25, *Grapes of Wrath* (New York: Viking Press, 1939); Jonathan Rowe, "Entrepreneurs of Cooperation," *Yes!*, (Spring 2006), available at: http://www.yesmagazine.org/article.asp? ID=1464.

3 Lois Palken Rudnick, *Mabel Dodge Luhan: New Woman, New Worlds* (Albuquerque, NM: University of New Mexico Press, 1984); Ronald Steel, *Walter Lippman and the American Century* (Boston: Little Brown, 1980), 50; Donna Cassidy, *Marsden Hartley: Race, Region and Nation* (Durham, NC: University of New Hampshire Press, 2005), 87–93.

4 Keith Bryant, "Atchison, Topeka and Santa Fe Railway and the Development of the Taos and Santa Fe Art Colonies," *Western Historical Quarterly* 9 no. 4 (October 1978): 437–454.

5 Anna Sommer, "Their Other Halves: Mrs. Maynard Dixon," *San Francisco News,* February 11, 1932.

6 Marta Gutman, "Adopted Homes for Yesterday's Children: Intention and Experience in an Oakland Orphanage," *Pacific Historical Review*, 73, no. 4 (November 2004): 581–618; Kenneth Cmiel, *A Home of Another Kind: One Chicago Orphanage and the Tangle of Child Welfare* (Chicago: University of Chicago Press, 1995); Susan Whitelaw Downs and Michael W. Sherraden, "The Orphan Asylum in the Nineteenth Century," *Social Service Review,* 57 (1983): 273–290.

7 Gardner and Page interview, OMCA.

8 *Time Magazine*, "Mayors Without Money," June 5, 1933: 13; and "Municipal Bankruptcy, June 12, 1933: 23; and Rowe, "Entrepreneurs."

9 Jaclyn Casem, "Pipe City's Dreams: Oakland, California and the Great Depression," at http://www.museumofthecity.org/project/pipe-citys-dreams-oakland-california-and-the-great-depression/; and James Munsey, "Oakland's 'Sewer Pipe City,'" *The Nation* 136 no. 3525 (January 25, 1933): 92–93.

10 William Leuchtenberg, *Franklin D. Roosevelt and the New Deal, 1932-1940* (New York: Harper Torch Books, 1963), 261; Arthur Schlesinger, *The Coming of the New Deal* (Boston: Houghton and Mifflin, 1959), 275; Eric Foner, *Story of American Freedom* (New York: W.W. Norton, 1994), 205; Nelson Algren, "Somebody in Boots," in Harvey Swados, ed., *The American Writer and the Great Depression* (Indianapolis: Bobbs-Merrill Company, 1966), 319–348.

11 Laura Renata Martin, "California's Unemployed Feed Themselves" Conservative Intervention in the Los Angeles Cooperative Movement, 1931–1934," *Pacific Historical Review*, 82, no. 1 (February 2013): 33–62.

12 "White Angel Jungle," Found San Francisco available, at http://foundsf.org/index.php?title=White_Angel_Jungle.

13 "Bain Collection," Library of Congress, available at: http://www.loc.gov/pictures/collection/ggbain/.

14 See Katherine Kish Sklar, *Florence Kelley and the Nation's Work* (New Haven: Yale University Press, 1995), 142, 171-236; David Von Drehle, *Triangle: The Fire that Changed America* (New York: Grove Press, 2003); Nathaniel Fehnsterstock, *History of New York Social Welfare Legislation* (New York, E. Thompson and Company, 1941).

15 Ironically, this photograph is much stronger than her "Five workers against concrete wall, Industrial District, San Francisco, 1933," where the men sit miniscule against the wall. San Francisco Museum of Modern Art.

16 Correspondence, OMCA, indicate the photograph is from 1933. http://www.museumca.org/picturethis/pictures/may-day-1934-%E2%80%93-crowd-labor-rally; http://content.cdlib.org/ark:/13030/ft5k40045v/?query=1934&brand=calisphere.

5

"WORDS WOULD NOT BE ENOUGH," 1934–1935

As Lange contemplated "things as they are," other artists in the 1930s similarly pursued art forms that explored social injustice and the lives of common Americans. The federal government supported more than ten thousand artists in this period. It commissioned artists to fill public spaces such as post offices or federal courthouses. Others received monetary relief, as the artists could not find work. The federal government sustained twentieth-century cultural masterpieces such as Berenice Abbott's *Changing New York* documentary, Ben Shahn's murals for the Bronx Post Office, "Resources of America," a paean to industrial and agricultural workers, the thousands of interviews by the Federal Writers Project of enslaved people, San Francisco's Coit Tower murals, Marc Blitzstein's *The Cradle Will Rock,* and the restoration of Tlingit totem poles throughout Alaska. Now internationally recognized authors and artists who had New Deal sponsorship include Zora Neale Hurston, Mark Rothko, Stuart Davis, Philip Guston, Jackson Pollock, Arshile Gorky, Richard Wright, Willem De Kooning, Milton Avery, and Jacob Lawrence.[1] Lange's husband, Maynard Dixon, was hired in the spring of 1934 for one such project. The Public Works of Art Project (PWAP) commissioned him to paint canvases of the Boulder Dam (renamed the Hoover Dam), a massive infrastructure project that employed thousands of men. Lange's brother, Martin, found work at the dam. Dixon lived with the workers and expressed their desperation in his mural. Dixon soon returned to his lifelong involvement with Western landscapes and genre. But Lange permanently redirected her camera, remade her life, and helped to remake the world around her.

Preoccupied with documenting the contours of the Depression, Lange also sought out labor's mobilization. San Francisco churned with labor and populist activism. Its unemployment, which had mirrored the national average in 1930, skyrocketed in 1931. Nearly a third of Bay area workers had no job.[2] This economic distress heightened people's anxieties and anger. In confronting their circumstances, Bay-area citizens drew on a history of organization and mobilization. A labor stronghold since the nineteenth century, in San Francisco more workers had "enjoyed the eight hour day" than anywhere else in the U.S. San Francisco's citywide labor federation was so strong, and its union membership rate so high, that it was known as the nation's premier city for organized labor.[3]

FDR's 1933 National Industrial Recovery Act (NIRA) galvanized the labor movement nationally, making 1934 a volatile year with city-wide uprisings in Toledo and Minneapolis, and an industry-wide textile strike affecting nearly half a million East Coast workers. In San Francisco, on May 9, 1934, longshoremen went on strike, joined within weeks by other maritime workers, seamen, and teamsters. The strike continued throughout June, leading employers to bring in scab labor under police protection. In July, two picketers and a bystander were killed, prompting 65,000 workers to come out in a general strike. Public transport workers, butchers, cooks, laundry workers, machinists, and construction workers joined in the labor action and brought San Francisco to a standstill. It was the largest municipal general strike in U.S. history.[4]

Lange captured events with her camera. She took photos at strike rallies, where men were tense and coiled for action, and she took portraits of California labor leaders. She photographed Tom Mooney, socialist and former Wobbly. Mooney became a worldwide cause célèbre in 1916 when a bomb killed ten during a World War I "preparedness parade." He was convicted of planning it, but even President Woodrow Wilson believed he had been railroaded. She also photographed Andrew Furuseth. The centenarian sat in profile, eyes closed, eagle hooked nose curved in one direction, neatly combed silver hair in another. Furuseth led the International Seamen's Union of America (ISU), which had fought "shanghaiing," the vernacular term for the coercing of men into sailing, one of the maritime industry's more egregious labor practices. Furuseth pushed for the Seaman's Act of 1915, maritime workers' "Magna Carta," which required that workers be provided adequate food and lifeboats, along with limits on hours worked. Ignominiously, Furuseth also had participated in the anti-Chinese movement that culminated in the 1882 Chinese Exclusion Act. Lange kept multiple images and stories about Furuseth in her files, including his response to government threats of an injunction against the seamen: "They can't put me in a smaller room than I've always lived in. They can't give me plainer food than I've always eaten. They can't make me any lonelier than I've ever been."[5] Furuseth's thoughts mirrored the committed resistance that Lange strived to explore in her photography.

Lange's new direction caught the attention of those outside her art circle, including the agricultural economist, Paul Taylor. An innovative scholar, Taylor wondered how others represented "the social effects of the Depression." He had previously pioneered the study of Mexican immigration to the U.S. He spoke directly to migrant laborers, capturing their perspectives on work and life. Other social scientists thought his approach overly "personal" and unscientific, but he was unrepentant. He believed his methods got at truths that the social sciences were incapable of measuring. "By the time you statisticians know the numbers, what I'm trying to tell you about in advance will be history, and you'll be too late." Richard Steven Street, scholar and photographer of California's agricultural economy has referred to Taylor as "one of the towering figures in California intellectual life. You cannot write the history of agriculture and farm labor without referring to him." As part of Taylor's innovations, he bought himself a professional Rollei camera to record migrants' lives.[6]

Taylor was writing an article about San Francisco's general strike when he encountered Lange's photographs at an Oakland gallery's exhibition put together by f64 photographer, critic, and curator, Willard Van Dyke. Taylor described "this striking array of relevant photography by Dorothea Lange whom I had never heard of." Taylor was struck by a "very powerful photograph…of a radical speaker before a microphone," and he decided to see if he could get the reform magazine *Survey Graphic* to publish the photograph with his article. *Survey Graphic*, begun in 1909, was a leader in publishing photography for Progressive reform, and it had promoted Lewis Hine's photography in the 1910s. Its editors agreed with Taylor about Lange's photographs.[7] This was her first national attention, and soon afterwards Van Dyke advanced Lange's reputation by writing about her work in *Camera Craft*, identifying her "deep sympathies for the unfortunates, the downtrodden, the misfits among her contemporaries." Lange told Van Dyke that she worked like "an unexposed film," letting herself be open to what she saw. Her metaphor suggested one of documentary photography's premises, seeing reality without prejudice or embellishment, though of course all images are mediated by their makers. Van Dyke couldn't commend her photographs enough, comparing her record to that of the great Civil War photographer, Matthew Brady.[8]

A second investigative project of Taylor's brought Lange into his orbit. Taylor's Iowa roots gave him an appreciation for the communal reciprocity of small family farms. The Depression made cooperatives and joint economic and social efforts attractive to citizens for the economic security they promised. California's cooperative movement was especially strong, with nearly a hundred thousand members. Oakland's Hooverville had its own Unemployment Exchange Association (UXA) where those too poor to pay for housing lived together and bartered their work, such as making soap, repairing autos, canning food, or even providing dental work. Van Dyke asked if Taylor might help him and his colleagues photograph the UXA. Photographers wanted to capture social distress, but were also anxious about taking photos of those on the edge, fearing that the poor would not like their photos being taken. By this point, Lange already had several years' experience taking photos on San Francisco's streets, but she joined her friends Van Dyke and Cunningham. Such collaborative work would have been a rare treat.[9]

Lange and Taylor met for the first time on this two-day outing in late September of 1934 and each became enthused with the other's commitments and work methods. Lange was "very interested in the way in which [Taylor] got the broad answers to questions without people really realizing how much they were telling him. Everybody else went to bed while he was still sitting there in that cold, miserable place talking with those people." Taylor was equally impressed with Lange, who he observed, was "quiet, intent on her work." He noticed her ability to take photographs "on the wing, quick, with the minimum time to focus and adjust the instrument." He remembered her first photograph, "the back of a man standing, resting on his axe as a man would rest on a cane, facing the forest preparatory to going to work with the axe. It is the expression of that man's back that is telling." Lange was a quick study, and she had an uncanny ability to express relationships in a simple image of a man's back: the man's exhaustion, his connection to the work that must be done. Both Taylor and Lange took much solace in their work; both sought to ameliorate the Depression's injustices through their professional skills. Taylor brought numbers and narratives to bear on agricultural laborers' tragedy to develop policy solutions, and Lange embodied migrant labor's suffering and endurance in photographs. They recognized a shared mission.[10]

Taylor and Lange continued working together. In November, Taylor hosted an exhibition at UC Berkeley that featured the photographs of the UXA cooperative. And Lange sent Taylor a copy of her portrait of labor leader Andrew Furuseth. In offering a gift, Lange opened herself up and became vulnerable; she gave him a material object that she had created, imbued with their common values, without knowing how Taylor would receive it. This small gift marked Lange's growing attachment to Paul Taylor.[11]

Soon Taylor invited Lange to join his investigative team for California's new Division of Rural Rehabilitation, under the State Emergency Relief Act (SERA). The University of California gave Taylor leave from his professorship to become the Division's Field Director. This was not unusual. For a generation, activists and academics had participated in and studied state and local efforts to address a variety of injustices, from urban and rural poverty, to industrial disease and workplace safety, to work conditions, and maternal health. As with social work, many academic fields that we take for granted today, economics, sociology, and political science, only became part of the university curricula during the lifetimes of Taylor and Lange. Researchers and faculty brought their scholarship and expertise to bear on society and its problems. The moralism of an earlier age, that perceived poverty as a mark of individual unworthiness, was replaced, at least in some quarters, with an awareness that unemployment was intrinsic to the modern economic system, that poverty had social causes, and that the government could and should mitigate social distress.

Taylor and Lange joined forces in working to enhance governmental forms of security and caring for citizens and California's farm crisis cemented their close working relationship. Addressing the farm crisis was one of Roosevelt's first priorities; under Calvin Coolidge and Herbert Hoover farm income had dropped by half from 1926 to 1932. Hoover's attempts to get farmers to voluntarily cut back on production had little success. As Roosevelt was inaugurated in 1933 rural America's prospects had plummeted further; forty percent of farms went under that year. Agricultural prices dropped so low that farmers took desperate measures, dumping their agricultural products as others starved for lack of food. Farmers came to blows; some conflicts resulted in death. In 1932 Midwestern farmers blocked other farmers from bringing cattle and grains to distribution centers such as Sioux City or Omaha. In 1933 New York and Wisconsin dairy farmers who dumped or tainted their milk forced other farmers to do the same. Local sheriffs bombarded them with tear gas and bullets and several were killed in these fracases.[12] Conditions were worse in California, where large-scale agriculture dependent upon migrant labor predominated. Though the state's population was eighty-eight percent white in 1930, its agricultural workers were immigrants, from Europe, many Asian nations, and Mexico, though hundreds of thousands of migrants from the Plains soon joined them. Growers cut wages with the Depression because labor was so plentiful. They could. Workers who had made seventy-five cents an hour picking cantaloupes were told they would take a fifth of that, and if they did not like it, they could move on. As a result, California experienced major agricultural strikes: in lettuce, cherries, grapes, peaches, pears, sugar beets, tomatoes, and cotton.[13]

Roosevelt had to stabilize the freefall of agricultural prices, stem the resulting tide of farm bankruptcies, respond to the suffering of migrant agricultural labor, and confront the overwork and over-speculation of the land. FDR brokered the 1933 Agricultural Adjustment Act (AAA), which allowed the federal government to set prices, offer generous financial incentives to limit production, and provide mortgage relief to stave off foreclosure. California's SERA hired Taylor just as the federal government implemented the AAA. Taylor's colleagues thought he had a striking ability to find workable political solutions, and he saw photography as critical to such solutions.

Lange joined Taylor's team in the spring of 1935. Taylor and Lange convinced the program coordinator, Lawrence Hewes (an elite, young Republican who'd lost his financier job) to hire Lange as an investigative photographer. Hewes said, "under the bright spell of Dorothea's gay personality" he found it possible to cut "red tape," though he brought her on as a "stenographer." Stenography, or taking dictation, typically by shorthand, was a gendered job category for women. Hewes explained it, "Paul was insistent that somehow he and Lange would have to go to Nipomo" to investigate the status of several hundred migrant families who had come to pick peas when weather destroyed the crops. "An endless cold rain fell on desperate families cooped up in ancient Model T Fords or crouching under makeshift shelters of blankets and tarpaulins. They had come to the end of the line." People had no beds, no toilets, no food, or "gas for their old jalopies."

Lange and Taylor thought they could do something; that they could push the state to help. Taylor and Lange showed how this crisis, "a major catastrophe," transcended "state and local boundaries," with California being "the leading edge of a large regional migration of destitute rural people from the drought-blasted cotton fields of Arkansas, Texas, and Oklahoma." The two traversed California that spring, documenting the trauma of the Earth's dispossessed in photos and in surveys, focusing primarily on migratory labor and their living conditions. When Hewes moved to the federal government's RA/FSA, he brought word about Lange and Taylor's investigations to national leaders addressing the farm crisis.[14]

Lange's photographs made a powerful claim. "Jack Neill: 'Migratory Fruit Tramp'" shows a former University of Montana student who was reduced to living beside the Peulah Creek. He had organized his kitchen outdoors, using fruit crates as table and pantry. Iron pans hung on prongs on the heavy pole to the side. His tent looked like a backdrop to a studio photograph. "Young Family Eating by Car," shows a father squatting, his children on either side with their plates and bowls. They lacked even a cloth to separate their meal from the dusty ground. Many photos show the drought refugees sitting in the dust, or under a tree on their fine wooden rocking chairs. The rocker was the last item linking them to their former stability. No longer in a parlor, or on a porch, it now lay vulnerable to the elements, awaiting the rain and the dust. One elderly woman spoke of panning for gold in the American River, nearly a century after the Gold Rush. She had her rocker, but no bed to sleep in. Lange showed "Refugees detained at the California Border," a whole family stuck in their car at the state line where they were refused admittance. In another photograph, a family of twenty-two camping in Bakersfield, California had no money or water. Some refugees' things spilled out of cars, off the top of truck beds. Others managed to organize everything tight upon their trucks and cars, creating an impossible order out of the chaos of economic life. One Mexican American field laborer told Lange, "I have worked all my life, and all I have now is my broken body." The sun sculpted his face and his frail body beneath his chambray work shirt. "Plantation Under: Texas Travelers," showed an older black couple in their late fifties or early sixties (see Figure 8.2). The man crouched beside a giant billboard which provided the only shade in the searing bright sunlight, the woman stood, hands held outward in supplication. [15]

Taylor insisted that Lange's photographs appear in bound reports for his agency superiors, believing that her photos would convince them to fund camps for the rural refugees. In his view, "knowing the conditions and reporting them in a way to produce action were two different things…*words* would not be enough" (italics his).[16] Lange's husband, Maynard Dixon, made the bound reports more attractive with handwritten captions and hand-drawn maps of the regions Lange and Taylor traveled through. Taylor and Hewes funneled these to Washington, and into the hands of Roy Stryker, who was directing the Historical Section of the Resettlement Administration (RA/FSA), established in April of 1935.

As Lange and Taylor traveled across California they developed a close rapport. Lange remained taken with Taylor's passion for his work. He drove his research expeditions hard, caring little about his crews' physical needs for food or rest. His sole motivation was getting the work done. Her husband, Dixon, was equally passionate about his work, but he excluded Lange, pursuing painting with male companions or alone. Taylor, conversely, opened his project up to any who would fight with him. On the road Lange and Taylor passed a notebook back and forth between them, writing captions and logging data that would form part of their investigative record for change. Once their travels were over, Taylor often visited Lange's home on Gough Street to catch up on work they were completing.

In this ferment, Lange and Taylor fell in love. Their letters, diaries, or interviews do not reveal when their working relationship became an affectionate one. But that summer their regard turned to intimacy, and they decided to marry. Taylor described it: "Attraction and accomplishment met." Dixon seemed astonished; he wrote in his diary "tragic interlude: divorce." Friends such as Imogen Cunningham and radical photographer, emigré Hansel Meith, both Lange's friends, were startled, even censorious, when Lange brought Taylor by to introduce him. The children were told of their parents' divorce in a rush. Lange's relationship with her children, then seven and ten, became difficult, at times entirely torn.[17] Like Lange, Taylor was married, to Kathleen Schuster Taylor, and they had three children, Katherine, Ross, and Margaret. Taylor's wife saw herself as a modern woman and had insisted on an open relationship. She had had multiple affairs, which Taylor experienced painfully. Their relationship had been rocky for years.

Lange and Taylor's union was a joyful one. Unlike Dixon, who criticized Lange, Taylor found Lange's attention to their home and family circle a sustaining aspect of his life. There were often tensions with children, particularly as they matured, but Lange built a home life for Taylor, his children, and her own that became the center of all of their lives until her death.

Lange's first husband built up the myth of the West from close detail; her second husband used documentary detail to show how that myth was fantasy. Her first husband pulled her down; her second husband built her up. In cementing a relationship with Taylor, Lange found a companion who accepted her ambition and nurtured it. As she experimented, she had a companion who opened doors for her. More importantly, she stood side by side with someone who modeled the interactions with the dispossessed that she sought with her camera. Her talents, already established by 1935, flourished.

Notes

1 Excellent works about New Deal era art include: Gerald Markowitz and Marlene Park, *Democratic Vistas: Post Offices and Public Art in the New Deal* (Philadelphia: Temple University Press, 1984); Karal Ann Marling, *Wall to Wall America: Post Office Murals in the Great Depression* (Minneapolis, MN: University of Minnesota Press, 2000); Roger Kennedy, *When Art Worked: The New Deal, Art, and Democracy* (New York: Rizzoli, 2009).

2 The Cliometric Society, "Unemployment Relief Distribution in the Bay Area During the Depression," available at: http://www.cliometrics.org/publications/unemployment.htm.

3 Daniel Conford, *Working People of California* (Berkeley, CA: University of California Press, 1995), 7.

4 *California in the 1930s: The WPA Guide to the Golden State* (Berkeley, CA: University of California Press, 2013, reprint of 1939): 95–108; Paul Taylor and Norman Leon Gold, "San Francisco and the General Strike," *Survey Graphic*, 23, no. 9 (September 1934): 405; Bruce Nelson, *Workers on the Waterfront* (Urbana, IL: University of Illinois Press, 1988).

5 Furuseth file, Lange, v 2 OMCA; and Furuseth photo, LNG5255.

6 Paul Taylor, "From the Field," *Land Policy Review* (January 1942), 233; Anne Loftis, *Witness to the Struggle: Imagining the 1930s California Labor Movement* (Reno, NV: University of Nevada Press, 1995), 86; Richard Steven Street, "The Documentary Eye," *California Magazine* (May/June 2009), http://alumni.berkeley.edu/california-magazine/may-june-2009-go-bare/documentary-eye.

7 Beginning in 1897, the publication was first entitled *Charities and the Commons: A Weekly Journal of Philanthropy and Social Advance.* The title change indicates a shift from helping the poor through philanthropy or alms-giving, to understanding and fighting poverty's social roots. As the editors wrote in 1909, "not by the name of charity do most men call the movement we stand for." They received letters saying the earlier title appeared "undemocratic," and one professor active in social work wrote saying, "among workingmen there is no antithesis in the English language that is more established than that between charity and justice," 21 no. 3 (March 27, 1909): 1251–1253.

8 Willard Van Dyke, "The Photographs of Dorothea Lange," *Camera Craft* 41 no. 10 (October 1934): 461–467.

9 Jan Goggans, *California on the Breadlines: Dorothea Lange, Paul Taylor, and the Making of a New Deal Narrative* (Berkeley: University of California Press, 2010), 8, 38–47; Paul S. Taylor and Clark Kerr, "Whither Self-Help?" *Survey Graphic* 23 no. 7 (July 1934): 328.

10 Paul Schuster Taylor, *A California Social Scientist* Volume I: Education, Field Research, and Family, 1973. Interviewed for the Earl Warren Oral History Project in 1970 by Suzanne B. Riess, UCB-ROHO, hereafter Taylor interview, 118–119, 122–125; available at: http://www.oac.cdlib.org/view?docId=ft5q2nb29x&brand=oac4&doc.view=entire_text.

11 Goggans, *California Breadlines*, n 67, 287.

12 Gilbert Fite, "Farmer Opinion and the Agricultural Adjustment Act, 1933," *The Mississippi Valley Historical Review* 48 no. 4 (March 1962): 656–673; Herbert Jacobs, "Wisconsin Milk Strikes," *Wisconsin Magazine of History* 35 no. 1 (Autumn 1951); Sandeep Vaheesan, review of Bill Wenders, *The Politics of Food Supply: U.S. Agricultural Policy in the World Economy* in *ASEAN Economic Bulletin*, 27 no. 2 (August 2010): 241–243; Paul Abrahams, "Agricultural Adjustment During the New Deal Period, The New York Milk Industry: A Case Study," *Agricultural History*, 39, n. 2 (1965): 92–101.

13 Kevin Starr, *Endangered Dreams: The Great Depression in California* (New York: Oxford University Press, 1996), 67.

14 Lawrence Hewes, introduction to Taylor interview.

15 Fruit tramp, LNG35159.1; Family by car, LNG35217.2; Woman with rocker, LNG35230.1; Refugees at border; LNG35248; Kern County migrants, LNG35175.1; Chaos, LNG35212.1; Mexican worker LNG35024.1; Billboard LNG38229.1. The Mexican laborer is located at the Library of Congress, Prints and Photographs Division, Washington, DC, LC-USF34- 001618-C [P&P]. All Lange photos in this collection will be identified with an LC prefix. Lange took this photograph in June under California's SERA.

16 Taylor interview, 126–127.

17 Sturtevant interview, 10; Theresa Heyman interview of Daniel Dixon, hereafter Dixon interview, n.p. OMCA.

6

"THESE THINGS ARE A PRESSIN' ON US"

Dorothea Lange as Government Photographer, 1935–1936

Lange's attempt to see "things as they are" was the animating idea behind an important new movement in photography.[1] Provoked by the Depression and nurtured by the New Deal, dozens if not hundreds of photographers felt compelled to record history in progress. There was a vitality to this photography. Maynard Dixon, Lange's first husband, recounted how she entertained a New York photographer, probably Consuela Kanaga. The visitor told them, "Photography is going to save the world."[2] Lange did not lead this movement of photographers, but became one of its most famous practitioners. She and Paul Taylor had succeeded in getting her a government job, cementing her place in history. In September 1935 Lange became an official photographer for the U.S. government under the Resettlement Administration, later folded into the Farm Security Administration (RA/FSA).[3] She only worked for the RA/FSA for half a decade, taking about 4,000 images for it, a small percentage of its archive. Nonetheless, by the decade's end, she was acknowledged as one of the nation's foremost "documentary" photographers, as the movement and the aesthetic would come to be called. Lange was responsible for some of the Depression's most iconic images; ultimately her engagement with the Depression catapulted her to international renown.

In her new job, Lange crisscrossed the U.S. before a system of national highways existed. She continued to investigate conditions in California, becoming preoccupied with her state's transition from one of wild splendor to a magnet for development. Taylor joined her on many trips. In just five years she also travelled to the Northwest, both Oregon and Idaho, where Midwesterners and Southerners hoping for respite had fled from their overworked land, into mountainous Utah and Wyoming, across the Great Plains, to Oklahoma and Nebraska, through midwestern Iowa and Indiana, and back toward her East Coast roots in New York. Lange returned to the Southwest and visited for the first time the mountainous hardscrabble South and the Deep South of King Cotton where former slaves still toiled in cotton fields.

By joining the RA/FSA, she participated in one of the nation's most interesting experiments in using the camera to build public policy. The RA/FSA's head, Columbia University economist Rexford Tugwell, conceived of and initiated the emergency agency, and he believed that the arts could foster concern for rural Americans. Many New Deal agencies used photography to explore their work and publicize the New Deal, but no other photographers achieved the collective stature of the RA/FSA photographers. The RA/FSA collected some 175,000 black and white photographs, and another several thousand color images, creating our nation's largest, most evocative record of the Depression era. The RA/FSA's Historical Section was formed in May 1935, and was rolled into the Office of War Information in 1941. Tugwell hired Roy Stryker, a former student, as the Historical Division's chief, "to direct the activities of investigators, photographers, economists, sociologists, and statisticians engaged in the accumulation and compilation of reports."[4]

More than twenty men and women photographers worked for the RA/FSA's over its six years' existence, though fewer than a dozen were key participants. Lange and Walker Evans, the agency's two most famous photographers, were also the most experienced. Painter Ben Shahn also took unusually probing photos for the RA/FSA. Other RA/FSA photographers learned under the tutelage of Stryker. Arthur Rothstein, who would go on to be *Look* magazine's photo editor, Russell Lee, Marion Post Wolcott, and John Collier, who had boarded with Dorothea Lange and Maynard Dixon years earlier, all matured under Stryker's direction.

Tugwell, Stryker, and the RA/FSA photographers were part of Franklin Delano Roosevelt's "Brain Trust." Roosevelt's "alphabet soup" of agencies dealt with socioeconomic problems that economists, labor unionists, businessmen, city planners, social workers, policymakers, and politicians had attempted to address since the nation's rapid industrialization after the Civil War. Many of these reformers and activists had worked at the state and local level, experimenting with regulation and government programs that responded to the economy's deficiencies, which mostly affected the most economically disadvantaged, unemployed industrial workers and small farmers, sharecroppers, tenant farmers, and itinerant laborers. They were called FDR's Brain Trust, as college professors figured largely among his administrators and advisors. These reformers had a zeal for their jobs. Even the lowest level government worker felt they had a mission. One man remembered years later. "The New Dealers were different. I'm not only talking about policy people. I'm talking about the clerks, who felt that they were doing was important. You didn't take time out for lunch because of a job that had to be done. You had a sandwich on the desk."[5] FDR and his administration addressed the Depression boldly. Some experiments succeeded, while others failed. The RA/FSA had been Tugwell's idea and like many New Deal agencies, the RA expanded the role of the federal government to address national problems. Taylor believed in the RA/FSA's goals; he thought federal support could sustain California's migrant camps. He did everything in his power to get Stryker to hire Lange.

Like Taylor, Tugwell's history shows how academics and government officials came to focus on the economy as a set of human-made relations that could be altered for the better. As an undergraduate, Tugwell studied with economics professor Simon Patten, at the University of Pennsylvania's Wharton Business School, beginning in 1911. The pathbreaking Patten studied emerging consumer economies and argued that citizens could leave the past's economy of scarcity, or "the pain economy." Mass production made possible, if equitably distributed, a modern economy of abundance, in his terms a "pleasure economy." America's films and magazines sold that pleasure economy, but the Depression indicated how flimsy its promises were. FDR invited Tugwell to Washington to help patch up the farm crises. Tugwell was the strongest advocate within the Department of Agriculture of government planning against "human wastage," how the economy destroyed individuals, families, and even communities. In *The Battle for Democracy* (1935), he wrote: "The cat is out of the bag. There is no invisible hand. There never was. We must be the guiding hand."[6] He rejected laissez-faire solutions and sought government responses to market-driven economic failures.

Tugwell's Resettlement Administration (RA/FSA), founded in April of 1935 by Roosevelt's executive order, comprised multiple programs that were inadequate to their task. One arm of the RA/FSA relocated those who lived on farms with inferior soil, where the land was played out from years of poor farming practices, or where the land was bad to begin with. The RA/FSA also made loans, called "rehabilitation," for farmers to buy small subsistence-based farms. Farmers ultimately paid loans back with interest. Loans also established cooperatives. Minnesota farmers might borrow to build a grain elevator to limit their dependence on monopolistic distributors, or California farmers might buy cows for milk production. Additionally, the RA/FSA developed several greenbelt communities near major cities, which were organized cooperatively and designed with "City Beautiful" principles. These were pet projects of the president's wife, Eleanor Roosevelt. Finally, the RA/FSA operated camps for migrants forced out of the Great Plains who had headed west. RA/FSA programs were so ill-funded that one historian argues it would have taken three centuries for its loans to reach needy farmers. Congressional support remained limited and tilted toward the big growers, hobbling the program from the start.[7] Some programs succeeded nonetheless, pioneering new national initiatives. National leaders deemed the migrant camps that Lange and Taylor had helped conceive and lobbied to expand highly successful. Lange photographed all these efforts, while documenting the dire contours of rural life to help build support for RA/FSA programs.

Tugwell believed the RA/FSA must humanize the farmers' and agricultural workers' struggles so that other citizens could understand what the agricultural sector endured. Tugwell told his associate, "Roy, a man may have holes in his shoes and you may see the holes when you take the picture... There's a lot more to that man then the holes in his shoes, and you ought to try to get that idea across."[8] Stryker took advantage of Tugwell's general charge to forge an ambitious mandate for the RA/FSA's photographers. Lange believed Stryker just loved photographs, claiming, "Roy... is a natural picture-lover, saves pictures like some people save string." RA/FSA photographer John Vachon thought the agency was, "introducing America to Americans." Over time, Stryker envisioned the collection of photographs, or the "file" as they called it, as a historic record of America.[9]

Stryker, Lange's supervisor, was raised on a Colorado ranch and his father, a radical populist, liked to quip "Damn Wall Street, damned the railroads, and double damned Standard Oil." Stryker had left the plains for an Eastern education, where Tugwell became his professor and mentor. Tugwell nurtured Stryker's interest in how economic information is conveyed to students and to the general public. Stryker aided Tugwell with his textbook, *American Economic Life and the Means of Its Improvement* by identifying photographs that best illustrated economic principles, structures of work, and the economy's distribution networks.[10] The textbook project introduced Stryker to Lewis Hine's earlier photographs, particularly the child labor images, that demonstrated that industrialization was not a benign process of progress, but frequently a travesty for workers.

As the Historical Section's director, Stryker set immediate goals. He wrote to Lange early in her employment, "the first purpose of our existence [is] to get as much good publicity as we can for the Resettlement Association." Stryker often asked Lange and other staff to photograph the RA/FSA's relief projects: migrant housing or labor camps designed to help build citizens' skills and joint economic power. In 1935, he sent out about 200 photos a month in the hopes of publicizing RA/FSA work, near the agency's end he was sending out some 1,400 photos monthly. Lange understood photography's public relations value. In February of 1936, she advised Stryker that she was sending "four hard boiled publicity negatives." Even when they were not always the most interesting shots these photographs buttressed support for the RA/FSA efforts.[11]

The RA/FSA's Historical Section became a resource for a picture-hungry public. Stryker promoted the RA/FSA photographers' photos, including Lange's for exhibits, newspapers, periodicals and books. New York City held an International Photography Exposition in 1938, and San Francisco held one not long after. RA/FSA photographs appeared at the Museum of Modern Art, the Cleveland Museum and the Tucson Center for the Arts and Crafts. Photographs even circulated to churches, colleges, and fairs; one exhibit was held at Howard University, another at the Greenwood Presbyterian Church in Indiana, yet another at Nebraska's Franklin County Fair. A quarter of a million commuters would enjoy the RA/FSAs photos as they passed through New York City's Grand Central Station in late 1941. Associated Press's editors visited Stryker, asking for photographs, advocacy organizations sought photos to exhibit at conferences and conventions, and politicians and the new government agencies all sought photographs to help explain American farmers' problems. The major new photo magazines such as *Life* and *Look*, founded in 1936 and 1937 respectively, heightened the craving for photographs. They too wanted to publish government photographs. Lange met with picture agents and agencies during a 1936 visit to New York City. She was "amazed at the interest shown in sociological photography," and bragged a bit to Stryker that they offered "nothing short of the Empire State Building for a good sequence."[12] Stryker negotiated with Lange about which photographs should be sent to which publications, and he also fought for bylines to credit RA/FSA photographers. Previously news photography had been considered a lowly art, not meriting individual acknowledgment, but this changed in the 1930s, in part due to the RA/FSA photographers' extraordinary work.

Stryker communicated his excitement for "an encyclopedia of American life," an expansive project, with Lange and her husband. But he never attempted to convince government officials of his goals; they might have seemed grandiose. With his government sponsors, he remained circumspect and focused on photography's publicity value. Lange, however, shared their enthusiasm for the project, writing to *The Nation*'s editors that the RA/FSA files were "rich," with photos of the economic crisis, and of "contemporary American life" more generally.

Historians have criticized Stryker for being overly directive, but his correspondence with Lange indicates only general guidance on subjects, "the people, the homes, any community pictures and good character pictures," or "the equipment these people use, and the type of life that goes on in the camp." At times he might have a specific need, for "motor camps" or how "Sacramento solved its problem," but he gave Lange broad aesthetic latitude to address such needs. Stryker sent Lange out in the field with directions to "vary the diet" of their representation of American poverty, to get San Francisco slums, Los Angeles slums, even rural slums to expand the file. Lange determined how to do this.[13]

A year into directing the project, Stryker had become adept at navigating Washington bureaucracy. Tugwell was forced to resign in late 1936. He had become a lightning rod for conservatives who rejected Roosevelt's expansion of the government, its direction of the economy, and its development of new programs to address citizens' needs. Stryker however kept the Historical Section going despite budget cuts. In 1937 the RA was folded into a new agency, the Farm Security Administration (FSA), under the auspices of a new farm bill, the Bankshead-Jones Bill. The RA/FSA now had congressional approval.

If Stryker was not aesthetically controlling, he was so in other ways, creating friction with Lange and other photographers. From their initial correspondence, he insisted she send him her itinerary, her contact information, and her estimated budget costs. Lange desperately wanted help building a darkroom, lenses for her camera, and a new camera but Stryker typically told her to wait, ignoring her funding requests.[14] Part of Stryker's concern came from his desire to navigate federal bureaucracy. If photographers submitted claims that the government would not reimburse, he and the project might be questioned. Artists under his supervision were often thousands of miles from his oversight, heightening his anxiety. Lange charted her own course; she wanted "a chance to get in the field, film, gross of paper when I need it and a chemical or two without having to beg, borrow, worry and steal to get it." She insisted that a fixed schedule was impossible as she worked in "uncertain weather covering many miles." Of greatest concern to Lange was Stryker's insistence that all negatives be stored and printed in Washington D.C. Like most photographers, Lange wanted to see her work as she produced it to evaluate whether the photos met the RA/FSA's needs and her own exacting aesthetic standards. She feared that her negatives might "deteriorate if development is postponed," due to harsh weather. And she believed she had "print sense," that she best knew how to print her photographs or to oversee their printing.[15]

Lange and Stryker corresponded regularly that spring of 1936, identifying and prioritizing her projects. In February she visited Hot Springs, over three hundred miles away in California's Northeast corner. The RA/FSA camp sheltered men incapable of manual labor or relief work. The men's average age was fifty; these were the economy's disposable men.[16] In early spring, she revisited the California coast, to Salinas, where lettuce was farmed, and San Luis Obispo and Nipomo, where Filipino American gang laborers worked in Japanese American owned pea farms. In Kern County, she took a photo of a mother and father and their two smiling children standing before their tent in an RA camp. They had fled Arkansas, but Los Angeles police sent them back to California's border where guards refused them re-entry. Depression-era America created a stateless class of refugees. The Arkansas family had to wire home for money, fifty dollars, which as sharecroppers might have taken them months of labor in the fields to garner!

In March Lange visited Utah, where she photographed mining camps, company towns, and Mormon settlements. One person told her: "People jist been settin' here waiting and hopin'." In one photo a Danish Mormon woman decked out in fur collar and sleeves against the harsh mountainous landscape clutched her first "old age assistance" check, or Social Security. Before the New Deal, there were no federal programs for the nation's elderly or disabled. At Consumers, Utah, known as the "Dumping grounds of the West," Lange noted that the coal mines were "owned and controlled by absentee capital in the East." Lange documented people above all else, but Lange's Utah photographs indicate an early interest in people's relationship with the environment. In one photo, a young woman with a toddler on her hip held onto her daughter with her other hand. They slipped on the mud on their way through the town. Snow was everywhere but none of them had on even a coat or scarf.[17] In Consumers, the RA/FSA offered miners loans to build their own homes so that they could leave company-owned shacks. With a plot of land, miners could grow their own food and stop buying overpriced provisions at the company store.

Lange became a master at developing a rapport with her subjects and they shared with her their feelings of despair, resignation, or resolve. She took a photo of an eighty-year-old mother of twenty-two, formerly of Oklahoma, who told Lange, "If you lose your pluck, you lose the most there is in you." Captions such as these insisted on American capacity for survival. Taylor, himself a noted investigator, said of Lange, "Her ear was as good as her eye." She returned to Marysville, California, outside Sacramento. In 1935 she had captured a man slouched over the spare tire attached to the back end of his automobile. He looked so worn, too tired to even pull his foot forward; it bent back in the dust. Another photo from 1935 showed a camp so chaotic it was difficult to identify the human amid the morass of shacks, cardboard boxes, and underbrush. But in 1936 she showcased residents' access to camp facilities like toilets, showers, and laundry through the RA/FSA.

Lange's travel was rewarding, but hard. Her journey in early February took place during the winter. Heavy rain forced her to photograph from the back of her station wagon. She wrote Stryker she had to leave one job prematurely "before the road washed away." She later advised him that she was "done up." Later that year she

FIGURE 6.1 Dorothea Lange, "Bakersfield, Calif. (vicinity). Grandmother of 22 children, from a farm in Oklahoma, 80 years old, now living in a camp. 'If you lose your pluck you lose the most there is in your—all you've got to live with,'" 1936.

© FSA/OWI Collection. Prints and Photography Division, Library of Congress. [LC-DIG-ds-01496] LC-USF34-9857-C.

FIGURE 6.2 Dorothea Lange, "Migrant agricultural worker in Marysville migrant camp (trying to figure out his year's earnings)," October 1935.

traveled through sections of California where the temperature reached 100 degrees each day, this before air conditioning in cars or in accommodations. Lange described "fourteen days" of "successive record breaking heat waves." Lange had other pressures to contend with as well. Stryker wrote her as she prepared to visit the Imperial Valley, "Best wishes for a successful trip and I hope that the cops don't pick you up. Don't let them break your camera."[18] California's large landowners were politically powerful. Some had their own security forces, or could rely on local police forces to enforce their will, even extra-legally.

Lange took a deep and immediate pride in her ability to capture the Depression's agony, the RA/FSA's work was a "real achievement—especially when seen after all that misery of homeless people who I've been meeting and photographing." She passionately believed the RA/FSA photographers could provoke change. Even so, photographing Americans' distress must have felt a solitary endeavor. She pushed to visit the RA/FSA team in Washington, writing Stryker she'd love to "see what the others are doing and where the work for my region would best fit in," asking, "Couldn't I come by car photographing as I travel?" Stryker replied that he wished she could "drop in," but that he was unable to visit the West Coast. Two months later, Lange made her way out East.[19]

FIGURE 6.3 Dorothea Lange, "Migrant workers' camp, outskirts of Marysville, California. The new migratory camps now being built by the Resettlement Administration will remove people from unsatisfactory living conditions such as these and substitute at least the minimum of comfort and sanitation," April 1935.

© Courtesy of FSA/OWI Collection. Prints and Photography Division, Library of Congress. LC-DIG-fsa-8b38193.

Years later Lange described her first encounter with the agency and Roy Stryker, her supervisor. She claimed to find little organization or planning for their work.

> I found a little office, tucked away, in a hot, muggy, early summer, where nobody especially knew exactly what he was going to do or how he was going to do it. And this is no criticism, because you walked into an atmosphere of a very special kind of freedom.

Stryker provided something that was "almost impossible to duplicate or find," latitude and openness. "You found your own way, without criticism from anyone." Lange appreciated this as her own method was intuitive. She worked her way into a situation, believing this organic method "unearthed and discovered neglected problems and situations." Because she visited regions multiple times, her process was iterative. She would take photos; analyze what she had seen and discuss the

FIGURE 6.4 Dorothea Lange, "Utility units at Marysville resettlement camp. Shows sites and units, towels, hot shower, and laundry." California, February 1936.

© FSA/OWI Collection. Prints and Photography Division, Library of Congress. LC–DIG-fsa-8b27145.

situation with Stryker, Taylor, and other colleagues; read about it; and then take more photos. This process may account for the intense focus and observed detail in her photos.[20]

Stryker, so assiduous about budgets and itineraries, freed her to photograph as she wished. And like the lowly clerks who ate at their desks because of their commitment to the New Deal, Lange thought the RA/FSA photographers felt an "elan" because "what you were doing was important." The feeling of being part of something larger felt "contagious," Photographers knew they "had a responsibility." Lange thought the photographers "expanded" to meet these responsibilities: to the RA/FSA, the nation, and the people who they photographed. Unlike the "big shot photographers" from the glossy magazines, *Look* or *Life*, who parachuted in, captured their subjects, and left, RA/FSA photographers were "alone… unknown…and unprepared." They were more privileged than their subjects, but they didn't have large expense accounts from the picture magazines. Lange thought this fostered in RA/FSA photographers a solidarity with their subjects. For Lange, "The U.S. government gave us a magnificent education," creating a structure that gave photographers a slow, "unobtrusive" way to get to know their subjects, and ferret out individual problems which aggregated formed the nation's problems.

From Washington D.C., Stryker sent Lange to record the lives of New York City garment workers, who with RA/FSA support were building an intentional community in rural New Jersey to grow their own food and organize a small factory and retail operation. Lange developed the back story, showing striking workers picketing outside Macy's in Midtown Manhattan, and laborers lunching in the nearby Garment District. She returned to the Lower East Side tenements where she had spent so much time as a young girl, waiting for her mother to finish work at the Chatham Library, and photographed women and children hanging out of the tenement windows and fire escapes. Several photos from a Jewish family's rear tenement window showed a darkened vestibule that looked little different than Jacob Riis' photos taken a half-century earlier. Books, dirtied mops and spindly chairs sat outside; New Yorkers' quest for space made them grab exterior space for their own additional real estate. Laundry stretched from the left corner of the photo frame nearly across to the other side; one is reminded of Lange's reminisces of the beauty of laundry on a line. She had sat in this neighborhood some three decades earlier, daydreaming and staring into nearby tenements. The collapsing space of these photos was her past. Now as a government photographer she recorded it, and moved on.

Lange continued her assignment in Hightstown, now Roosevelt, New Jersey, where two hundred families were to live. Residents contributed toward the construction of cinder-block ranch-style homes designed by Louis Kahn, soon to become a world-renowned architect. Built in a modernist style, these homes were simple, but elegant in conception. Lange's photos emphasized the homes' starkness and openness. In contrast to the small windows of the tenement, Kahn's designs had windows that stretched nearly from floor to ceiling. Residents could look out on the "green belt" connecting each house. Families familiar with living in one of the world's most populated areas now enjoyed grass lawns and blossoming trees. Residents also had land to farm. This experiment, advertised in New York's Yiddish papers, took advantage of long-time Jewish interest in moving back to the land, modernist ideals, and the era's political and experimental fervor. Even Albert Einstein, who worked in nearby Princeton, advocated for Hightstown, which expressed the optimistic New Deal vision linking modernity to social change that continues to evoke collective possibility. One little girl, excited about her first day in the country, exclaimed: "Mama, come here. I got a light. I got this sun for myself."[21]

Notes

1 Unless otherwise indicated, quotes from agricultural workers and owners come from Lange's "Field Notes," transcribed by Zoe Brown, OMCA.

2 Sturtevant interview, OMCA.

3 For clarity, I refer to the Historical Section of the RA, then FSA as the RA/FSA.

4 Wood and Stryker, *In This Proud Land*, 11.

5 Joe Marches in Studs Terkel, *Hard Times: An Oral History of the Great Depression*, (New York: New Press, 2005), 308.

6 On Patten, William Leach, *Land of Desire: Merchants, Power, and the Rise of a New American Culture* (New York: Vintage, 1993 231–244; and Rexford Tugwell, *The Battle for Democracy* (New York: Columbia University Press, 1935), 14.

7 Donald Grubbs, *Cry from the Cotton: The Southern Tenant Farmers' Union and the New Deal* (Little Rock, AR: University of Arkansas Press, 2000), 136.

8 Oral history interview with Rexford Tugwell, January 21, 1965. Archives of American Art, Smithsonian Institution.

9 Stryker and Wood, *In This Proud Land*, 11. Other photographers were less charitable toward Stryker's visual sense.

10 John G. Morris, *Get the Picture: A Personal History of Photojournalism,* Chicago: University of Chicago Press, 2002), 124; Oral history interview with Roy Emerson Stryker by Richard Doud, multiple interviews, 1963–1965. Archives of American Art, Smithsonian Institution; Carl Fleischauer and Beverly Brannan, eds., *Documenting America: 1935–1943* (Berkeley: University of California Press, 1998), 4.

11 John Raeburn, *A Staggering Revolution: A Cultural History of Thirties Photography,* (Champaign: University of Illinois Press, 2006), 144; Lange correspondence to Stryker, from FSA, February 12, 1936, OMCA, hereafter FSA.

12 Nicholas Natanson, *The Black Image in the New Deal: The Politics of FSA Photography* (Nashville: University of Tennessee Press, 1996), 212–213; Lange to James Rorty, *The Nation*, May 29, 1936; Lange to Stryker, January 21, 1937, FSA.

13 *Ibid.*; and Stryker to Lange, January 3, 1936 and January 14, 1936, FSA.

14 Styker to Lange, January 3, 1936, FSA.

15 Lange to Stryker, January 14, 1936; December 31, 1935, and February 12, 1936, FSA.

16 Franklin Roosevelt Fireside Chat, April 7, 1932.

17 Fieldnotes, OMCA; LC-USF34-018750-E; LC-USF34-T01-009027; Lot 511.

18 Stryker to Lange, February 24, 1936, FSA.

19 Lange to Stryker, March 26, 1936, OMCA.

20 Discussion of FSA from Richard Doud, interview of Lange, May 22, 1964, Archives of American Art, Smithsonian Institution, available at: https://www.aaa.si.edu/collections/interviews/oral-history-interview-dorothea-lange-11757.

21 "Perdita Buchan, "When Louis Kahn and Roosevelt Created a New Jersey Utopia," *Curbed,* December 4, 2014, available at: http://curbed.com/archives/2014/12/04/when-louis-kahn-and-roosevelt-created-a-new-jersey-utopia.php; Sora Friedman, "No Place Like Home: The Settling of Jersey Homesteads, New Jersey," *Communal Studies* (1999) 19: 23–48.

7

"THE SORRIEST PLACE IN THIS COUNTRY"

Dorothea Lange and Southern Struggles, 1935–1939

After her work in the Mid-Atlantic states, the RA/FSA's Stryker sent Lange south.[1] There she witnessed a distinctive agricultural poverty shaped by Reconstruction's failure. She documented the region's socio-economic relations of exploitation, and despite her unfamiliarity with the South's history and culture, her photographs command attention. Neither Lange's sympathetic camera nor the RA/FSA's programs could fix the South's grave economic problems. In fact, Lange was capturing the transition of the South from a near-feudal past into a future that proved equally untenable for farmers at the bottom of the agricultural ladder. Lange showed the government hastening that transition. Her photographs conferred great dignity on her subjects, black and white. Her respect for black Southern life came at a time when America's mass culture either erased black Americans from the body politic or presented them as caricatures. Hence, Lange's work should be understood as part of the New Deal's attempt to incorporate all Americans into full citizenship, even if she witnessed more than other citizens were willing to see, or more than her government sponsor could address. Her unparalleled record of Southern poverty and racism probed uncomfortable truths about our nation that remain unresolved.

Roosevelt called the South "the nation's No. 1 economic problem" in 1938, a reality long before he proclaimed it. The region's stagnant economy was characterized by highly unequal social relations, limited landownership rates, and limited industrialization. Harry Hopkins, the federal government's WPA director calculated Southern poverty: "If the combined bank deposits of the United States had been distributed in June 1933 on a per capita basis, every person in the North would have received $419, every person in the West $222, and every person in the South only $81." It was as if Southerners lived in another nation. Because the region had such a large, vulnerable workforce, its agriculture relied on human, not mechanical labor. Southern farming methods could have been used in Germany,

England, or France in the middle ages. Some Southerners held that farming by hand was better than by machine. One landowner told Lange, "I don't think machines will ever pick as clean as hands." Early on in her trip some Virginia farmers asserted they had never heard of the combine harvester, an agricultural implement that had been invented a century before. Some owners would not let black sharecroppers drive tractors; some even refused to let them farm with horses, thinking the horse too sensitive. Instead, mules were used, an animal championed by George Washington in the 1700s.[2]

Southern agriculture was mostly organized under a tenancy system. The former slaves, abolitionists, some military leaders, and government officials had imagined with the Civil War's end that land would be redistributed. "Forty acres and a mule," became the cry, based on Sherman's Field Order No. 15, to redistribute land to the formerly enslaved. Instead, once white Southerners' early attempts to force black labor failed, they established a tenancy system. At the bottom of the system were sharecroppers. They worked someone else's land, and used someone else's farm implements and draft animals to plow the fields and reap the harvest. They had no home, often no food or cash; they raised whatever crops the landowner chose. Tenants, in contrast, leased the land, but used their own farm animals and implements and provided their own seed. They might pay the landowner in seed, or in a portion of the crops which the owner then sold at market. Landowners received two-thirds or three-quarters of monies gained; in Southern parlance, they were on thirds or fourths. The most privileged tenants rented the land, paying in cash. They could lease for multiple years, and plant what they chose. Tenants were more frequently white.

Over the twentieth century Southern farmers became increasingly impoverished. In 1935, three sociologists determined some eight million Americans subsisted in a semi-feudal state; most were Southerners.[3] Sharecropping became more pervasive, fewer farmers moved upwards to tenancy or land ownership. Sharecroppers required credit for their basic needs, clothing, implements, and even food, which indebted them to local merchants and landowners. This debt ate what little profit they had squeezed from the land, so they took credit again. One sociologist claimed the Southern agriculture's credit system "supports agriculture as the cord supports the hanged."[4] Lange met a sharecropper scarred by this system who told her: "$1 from dawn till when you just can't see. Can't make nuthin here and wash county is the wustest place." The President's Committee on Farm Tenancy proclaimed that agriculture provided no ladder up. Instead, "the rungs of the ladder" became "bars" that imprisoned farmers. In the Deep South ninety percent of African Americans were tenants, but white tenancy also grew over the twentieth century. The *New Republic* called tenancy and sharecropping "an economic cancer that should have been operated upon years ago."[5]

White Southerners, particularly the planter class, had passed laws restricting voting rights, which conserved their economic and political control. Grandfather clauses, which denied the franchise to citizens whose grandfathers could not vote, were deemed unconstitutional in 1915, but poll taxes and literacy tests restricted voting for African Americans and poor whites. Virtually no Southern blacks voted, but neither did half of Southern whites. This allowed landowners who controlled account books free to cheat tenants from their proper shares. The owners used "crooked pencils" wrote one Southern Tenant Farmworkers Union organizer. A person who challenged crooked accounts could be killed.[6] Another Mississippi sharecropper told Lange: "They live, but they don't want us to live. Sure we keeps the books. But they sell the cotton." Farmers were not ignorant about what befell them, but they felt powerless to challenge the system. Neither elected officials nor the courts would support them. One Lange interviewee described this stark reality: "If you're a black man they give em what they want you to have. If you say sumpin they run you off or give you a beatin'." Another explained: "I want to tell you sumpin about this delta. Workin' em and taken' all they had wussn if they had been slaves. You can't sue a man, not here on this Delta… You'd better go along quiet and put up with it… don't say nuthin." These sharecroppers described the obstacles to bettering their economic lives. It was so bad that leaders, family members, or those who sympathized with resisters might be beaten, shot, or tortured and lynched. One Alabama man, whose father had been "sold on the block" in Charlestown, South Carolina told Lange: "It's slavery now—they just don't hold a strap on you."[7]

The RA/FSA's Historical Section considered Southern economic woes central to the nation's distress, and so centered much of their documentation in this region. Forty percent of the file's photographs were taken in the South. Although Lange was from California, she took some of her most powerful photographs in this region. Among RA/FSA photographers only African American photographer Gordon Parks took a greater proportion of African American citizens as his subject.[8] Racism lay at the heart of the South's society and political economy. It asserted itself in everyday life, as white women refused to have their clothing cleaned alongside black workers' clothing. Whites used daily humiliation as a form of social control. Defying the racial order could land one in jail. The head of the interracial Southern Tenants Farmers Union claimed that one leader was jailed for "calling a black man 'Mister.'"[9] In the Jim Crow South, *de jure* (legal) segregation, separated blacks and whites at water fountains, public transportation, and schools. *De facto* (literally "in fact" or by tradition) segregation, including labor segmentation, excluded African Americans from a broad swath of job types, and separated them from whites at department stores and leisure spots.

FDR's New Deal had a complex relationship to the South and the constriction of Black Americans' lives. On the one hand, his administration augured a new era for civil rights. Roosevelt denounced lynching at a national church convention and was often photographed with black leaders. He also hired many black leaders, including college founder and women's club leader, Mary McLeod Bethune. Born a decade after the Civil War's end and the child of former slaves, Bethune directed the Negro Affairs Division of the National Youth Administration (NYA), making relief more equitable. FDR appointed the first African American federal judge, William Hastie. FDR had more African American advisors than previous presidents; they were informally called the Black Cabinet. And First Lady Eleanor Roosevelt became a tireless civil rights advocate, goading FDR to do better. Her commitment to challenging racism led Southerners to claim Roosevelt was a communist, or black herself.[10]

On the other hand, the president only tentatively challenged Southern Democrats who upheld a racist order. His political coalition's reliance upon Southern Democrats blunted Roosevelt's challenge to racism. The South voted as a strong, almost impenetrable Democratic bloc. Forty percent of the Democratic Congress was from the South and they controlled half of the congressional committees. FDR condemned lynching in a Fireside Address but he never supported anti-lynching legislation. The Southern bloc insured that the New Deal denied African Americans full access to government programs. For example, the Agricultural Adjustment Administration (AAA) pushed for equal representation of blacks and whites to their proportion in the population, but if local citizens sabotaged "Negro" involvement, the agency provided funding to whites only. And in some areas, for example, the Mississippi Delta, blacks were pushed off the land so whites could redevelop it. Speculators from as far as New York drove blacks from land they had worked since Reconstruction. Residents complained: "It seems like those who are in authority feels that because we are Colored, we should not be rehabilitated, as other citizens. We have worked the land for a number of years, and would like to make it our home."[11] Other New Deal programs also excluded African Americans. The WPA often refused to hire blacks, or fired them when white labor was available. Similarly, the National Industrial Relations Act, which sought to standardize higher wages, and the Social Security Act excluded job categories held by African Americans. By making unionization and access to welfare programs more difficult, white Southern politicians and administrators maintained a vulnerable surplus labor force and weakened the labor movement and the welfare state.[12]

Still, the New Deal did bring succor to millions of African Americans. As one activist stated, the New Deal "was a shot in the arm for Negroes." In 1932 most blacks who could vote, mostly residents in Northern states, voted for the party of Lincoln, but by 1936 there was an extraordinary shift of African Americans into the Democratic party. Historians consider the New Deal as part of a "long civil rights movement" as interracialist organizations such as the Southern Commission on Human Welfare, and black-led organizations like the National Negro Congress and the National Congress of Negro Youth sprang up, challenging African Americans' second-class status.[13]

In 1936 Lange first headed through Virginia and Tennessee to the Deep South of Mississippi and Alabama. She also spent time in Birmingham, the capital of Southern steel-making. She visited an RA/FSA-organized cooperative. By the second week of July, she looped through the Florida panhandle and eastern

Florida, before heading north through Georgia. Her field notes place her in North Carolina, then South Carolina, then back north again. Before she was done, she and Taylor had logged some 17,000 miles.

Lange's record of the South conflicted with its gracious, nostalgic presence in the American imagination. Hollywood movies and popular tunes had served up the plantation myth for decades. Shirley Temple, the popular mop-topped child actress who sang and tap danced herself into America's heart was featured in films set in the plantation South, where blacks happily served whites' whims. In films such as *Jezebel, Show Boat,* and *Gone with the Wind,* white Southerners were portrayed as virtuous and brave and their hierarchical community seemed natural, one that Americans should regard favorably. Stephen Foster's wildly popular folk song, "Old Folks at Home" (Way Down Upon the Suwanee River), written in 1851, was several generations later, in 1935, voted Florida's state song. This iconic American melody's lyrics had been written in an ostensible Southern black dialect. The singer longs "for de old plantation," where he "squandered" many happy days "round de little farm." Mass culture represented elite whites as supreme, a refined gentry and political elite, with their grand land holdings and cultured demeanor, and it rendered poor whites invisible.[14]

Playwrights and novelists offered more unblinking views, while still purveying stereotypic views of the South and its large African American population. And even the Southern Renaissance in literature that probed racism's contours, simultaneously promoted it. *Gone with the Wind,* Margaret Mitchell's bestseller, published the first year Lange went South, won both the Pulitzer Prize and the National Book Award. Once filmed, it won nine Oscars. Americans couldn't seem to get enough of the story of Scarlett, the Southern belle triumphing over adversity with the help of stereotypic servants such as the comical Prissy and Scarlett's ever devoted Mammy. Filmmakers rushed to make similar films.[15]

Lange's camera eviscerated these myths. As Lange knew, the South was not a region in isolation; it had been tied into international economics and national policies since the nineteenth century. In Alabama, Lange showed a young African American farmer leading his ox-driven wagon through town. Behind him sat a Ford showroom with a giant billboard for a sedan with a Ford V-8 engine, a stark note of modernity. Lange's photographs illuminated such contradictions; the interconnections between regional and national economies, backward- and forward-looking realities that pressed on Southern citizens.

Southern farmers were poor, and so was their land. Cotton, which had increasingly defined the South over the late nineteenth century, depleted the soils. But large landowners forced tenants and sharecroppers to tend cotton, often prohibiting them from growing their own food. A sharecropper Lange met in Hinds County Mississippi in 1937 said: "Cotton rules the world;" novelist Richard Wright wrote, "our lives are walled with cotton;" opined the *New Republic:* "King Cotton...has become King Curse."[16]

FIGURE 7.1 Dorothea Lange, "A note on transportation," Eden, Alabama, June 1936.
© FSA/OWI Collection. Prints and Photography Division, Library of Congress. LC–USF34–009625.

Southern life was shaped by other grave challenges: poor housing, diets, health, and education. Most Southern farmers lived in shacks, typically of one or two rooms. Large families crowded themselves in. More than two-thirds of families lived in "congested" conditions, as bad as urban areas. Windows and doors lacked screens and construction was so shoddy that the walls themselves could be seen through. Tenants' housing lacked toilets, or even outhouses. Locals jeered at a New Englander who built an outhouse for his tenants. "Miss, all that a sharecropper needs is a cotton patch and a corn cob." Even toilet paper was considered too much for tenant farmers. Diets were limited, confined largely to cornmeal, molasses and fatback. One of Lange's subjects told her "a piece of meat in the house would like to scare these children mine to death." Insufficient diets led to diseases long banished in other parts of the country: typhoid, malaria, rickets, pellagra, and hookworm. Tuberculosis affected those living in tight quarters.[17] Health care was equally abysmal. In 1936 Lange photographed an African American woman in Hinds County, Mississippi, who tied dimes around her ankle to ward off headaches. She, like most poor Southerners, black and white, could hope for no better medical care. Another hung black beads from her neck to guard against heart troubles. Southerners' educational system was also woefully inadequate. When Lange

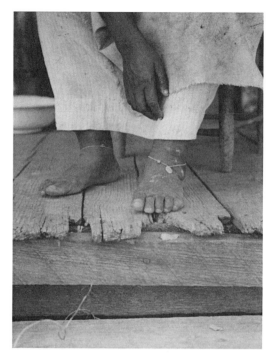

FIGURE 7.2   Dorothea Lange, "Fifty-seven year old sharecropper woman. Thin dimes around the ankles to prevent headaches," Hinds County, Mississippi, June 1937.

© Courtesy of FSA/OWI Collection. Prints and Photography Division, Library of Congress. LC-DIG-fsa-8b32018.

traveled South, most whites could read and write but twenty percent of blacks remained illiterate.[18] One young man explained to Lange: "I don't go to school because I have to plow." Thirteen years old, he had only attained fourth grade. The U.S. Children's Bureau found that nearly three-quarters of Texan and North Carolinian children between six and sixteen worked the fields; they were lucky to receive several months of schooling.[19]

The poorest Southern farmers lacked clothing. One set of parents described their pleasure purchasing a change of clothing for their six children; they had not done so for three or four years. Richard Wright wrote about this disjuncture, "Of a summer night, sitting on our front porches, we discuss how "funny" it is that we who raise cotton to clothe the nation do not have handkerchiefs to wipe the sweat of our brows, do not have mattresses to sleep on; we need shirts, dresses, sheets, drawers (underpants,) tablecloths." The head of the Southern Tenants Farmers Union (STFU), J.R. Butler described black and white tenants' extreme deprivation: "They grow cotton but they dress in flour sacks." One commentator jested that Southern style was based upon what company the flour sack came from.[20]

FIGURE 7.3   Dorothea Lange, "Thirteen year old sharecropper boy cultivating a field," near Americus, Georgia, 1937.

© FSA/OWI Collection. Prints and Photography Division, Library of Congress. LC-DIG-fsa-8b32269.

When Lange first encountered the exploitation of these workers she became infuriated, writing Stryker to seek redress. She had visited an RA/FSA project where several client families had worked the land for a year. They had never been given any accounts of their indebtedness: "the agent says he's too busy." They received irregular checks from the government as the agent, T.E. Yates, pocketed them instead. Yates was proprietor of Bolivar Grocery and Supply Company— General Merchandise, and so Yates squeezed more from them when the families shopped "on credit at the store." Ultimately the agent demanded the client family's cow and mules for payment for outstanding loans. At another RA project in Earle, Arkansas, a family with eight children nearly starved in the summer of 1935. Lange wrote they had "gin tickets to prove" the amount of cotton they had harvested. Their work only benefited the agent, who was "forging their names to government cheques and keeping the money." Lange witnessed exploitative dynamics that had persisted in the South for decades. Unfortunately, new federal New Deal programs could exacerbate these inequalities when administered by white Southern politicians. The government took steps to ensure that sharecroppers received crop reduction funds in 1934 and 1935, but these measures also failed. White Southern officials also used relief to pressure people into working for less.[21]

One of Lange's most famous images encapsulates Southern racial and social inequalities. She shows a Southern plantation overseer with his foot up on the bumper of a car. The Mississippi license plate peeks out between his thighs, announcing his location. He appraises the viewer with a sour expression, his thin lips pressed together. The overseer's eyes, covered by his panama hat, betray little. He is a broad man, and suspenders hold up his pants. On the stairs leading up to the general store sit four African American men. The white man owns the composition; he is in its central spot and he spans the photo nearly from the top to the bottom. Novelist Richard Wright referred to him as the "Lord of the Land." In contrast to the white man's prosperous girth, the African American men are lanky from overwork and inadequate diets; in place of his proprietary stance, they are contained, they fold their legs or arms over their knees.[22]

Lange probed poverty's contours. A portrait of one young man, the son of an illiterate sharecropper who told Lange he was desperate for a high school education, pushes at us with his gaze even today. Will he achieve his dream? Just outside Greenville, Mississippi her photo of a "Negro Church" proffers an austere, vernacular beauty; its brick chimney peels off, toward the ground. She found divinity

FIGURE 7.4   Dorothea Lange, "Plantation owner, Mississippi Delta," near Clarksdale, Mississippi, June, 1937.

© FSA/OWI Collection. Prints and Photography Division, Library of Congress. LC-USF34-009596.

everywhere, but it too was touched by poverty. Lange photographed African Americans working the fields, picking weeds and picking cotton, their long sacks hanging back behind them, their heads in large hats against a punishing sun. In Eutaw, Alabama she showed a family engaged in "hoe culture." Including monies from their young daughter's labors they still made only $50 a year. In Anniston, Alabama a white family of five hoed the fields. Only the father wore shoes.[23]

Lange identified the racism which sustained Southern poverty. In July she and Taylor visited New Orleans, where Lange took a photo of a "liberty monument" to white supremacy. The city's leaders commemorated Southerners' 1874 failed uprising against federal authorities during Reconstruction. In 1932, just four years before Lange took her photo, an additional inscription was added celebrating the national election of 1876 which, "recognized white supremacy in the south and gave us our state."[24] Lange captured the entire inscription for future generations.

Lange and Taylor sought out those who resisted these dynamics. Lange had let Stryker know she was interested in visiting the Sherwood Eddy Cooperatives in Mississippi because of the couple's interest in cooperatives. This seemed a natural assignment for her, although she acknowledged that Walker Evans might have first dibs on the project. Eddy, a New England missionary, had established the Delta Cooperative Farms as an interracial venture. He had studied under theologian Reinhold Niebuhr at the Union Theological Seminary. Eddy and Niebuhhr, liberal Christians, joined with Socialist Party and STFU members. They were supported with funds from Eddy's previous missionary work. Niebuhr called the farm, "the most significant experiment in Social Christianity now being conducted in America." The thirty farm homes had screens in the windows and doors; each one had water.[25] The cooperative established adult education classes, a store, and a credit union, and it provided medical care as well. Cooperative families made twice what a typical tenant family might earn. Stryker advised her by telegram, "Evans not covering Sherwood Eddy Cooperatives." Lange won the assignment only after Evans turned it down.[26]

Eddy's cooperative was a pioneering if unfinished experiment. It drew some families who had been mistreated by the RA/FSA and sheltered members of the STFU. Founded in 1934, the STFU attracted men and women angered by Southern political and economic injustice many were committed to interracialism. When Lange visited in 1936 the STFU was at its height with about 30,000 members. STFU members worked together, striking in 1935 and 1936 against local landowners. They publicized the conditions of continued peonage. They also faced repression; one deputy sheriff in Arkansas jailed thirteen of their members, forcing them to work his land.[27] Despite their attempted interracialism, the color line persisted at the Eddy Cooperative. Blacks and whites' homes faced one another, across the dividing line of a street. Some whites were unwilling to allow talented African Americans key responsibilities. As one white Southerner put it: "I don't believe in what these cooperative people believe in I believe in treating a colored man as fair as is reasonable to expect."[28]

Even so, when Lange first visited, the Delta Cooperative was an optimistic venture, only four months old. She depicted young African American and white children carrying melons to a community celebration. Their bright smiles challenged the rigid social order that insisted on the separation of blacks and whites. Lange also photographed the movement's leaders, and took portraits of a young, black, rank-and-file member whose overalls boasted a small STFU button. Wearing a button like this could lead to reprisals, even death. Over time, unfortunately, vigilante violence did thwart their project. Lange's photos of indigenous political activism against Southern inequality were unusual and the RA/FSA did not investigate or publicize such inequality.[29]

Stryker planned to send Lange to the Northwest in the spring or summer of 1937, but canceled her plans at the last minute as the RA/FSA was "having urgent demands from newspapers and magazines" for more "tenant pictures from the South." A week later, he insisted that she hurry; "the drive now on tenancy," he said, made it "the all-important issue."[30] Lange did not receive this letter immediately. A week and a half later, she wrote that she could not leave for almost a month. Stryker's demands to younger employees such as Lee and Rothstein could be met immediately. But for Lange, who cared for five children and who lived on another coast, it took time to organize such trips. Stryker was irked that she did not more quickly accede to his plans.

Once things were arranged, Lange buzzed with ideas for the proposed trip. She wanted the 8x10 camera, she wrote Stryker, "I mean if Walker Evans is not using it." This camera's larger plate size would allow her to illuminate the South in the greatest detail. Stryker wrote back that he was giving it to his protégée, Russell Lee. She thought the plantation myth of the song "Way Down upon the Suwanee River," could be contrasted with the realities of Southern agriculture. Her "glimpse" of the South the year before led her to believe in the publicity value of using this iconic song. Stryker concurred but with little enthusiasm. Lange also wrote of her interest in exploring the poll tax. Stryker never responded.[31]

Her second, 1937, trip had greater focus than the first. To Stryker's chagrin, Lange struggled to find "ghost towns" in the Great Plains, but she did find them along the Alabama coasts and in Florida's piney woods. There, companies had exhausted the timber supplies and then left communities in distress. In Fullerton, Louisiana, she showed a lumber town's remnants. A drugstore, sawmill, even a bank had crumbled as if hit by a tidal wave. She showed the same in Kiln, Mississippi, and Marianna, Florida, where a lumber mill was entirely dismantled. Even the railroad tracks had been pulled out.[32]

Lange and her husband Taylor found another story too: unusual flooding, the Depression, and government action were promoting mechanization. The 1927 flood had thrown nearly a quarter of a million people off the Mississippi Delta, and in 1937 another major flood in the Ohio and Mississippi Valleys caused many to flee. Flood refugees from Arkansas were heading to the Texas panhandle, where large landowners had already kicked out sharecroppers and tenants and replaced them with tractors. Machinery allowed one man to do the work of many. Lange identified the consequences, homesteads depopulated of families. She noted tenants on relief and casual day labor in place of those rooted in the land. She showed the pained face of one African American farmer near Dallas, Texas, who had worked the land for eighteen years. He'd been pushed off with sixteen other families. One of her more famous photos, taken in Childress County, Texas, shows the bites of tractors in the earth and the furrows of cultivation going up to an abandoned home. There was no place left for habitation; agriculture and domestic life were in conflict. Her letters to Stryker were full of the impact of mechanization upon Southern agriculture. Lange wrote that "highways are a part of the process of mechanization. Interstate lines of movement." Many Southerners took those highways out and never returned. As one Southerner put it: "Tractors are coming and you can't stop it." Tugwell and his successor at the FSA, Will Alexander, promoted "modern" agriculture. They saw mechanization and land consolidation as efficient and inevitable.

Lange became attentive to the growing numbers of day laborers on her second trip. Some casual laborers still lived in the countryside, but others crowded cities such as Memphis, Tennessee. These day laborers pushed themselves into the trucks

FIGURE. 7.5   Dorothea Lange, "Power farming displaces tenants from the land in the western dry cotton area," Childress County, Texas Panhandle, June 1938.

FIGURE 7.6   Dorothea Lange, "Cotton hoers loading in Memphis, Tennessee for the day's work in Arkansas," June 1937.

© FSA/OWI Collection. Prints and Photography Division, Library of Congress. LC-USF34-017302-C.

that would deliver them to the land they once claimed as home. As far as the eye could see, men, women, and children were lined up. The lines of the embankment and the telephone wires marked their numbers—an endless line of dispossessed. Lange's photos suggested ironic, painful juxtapositions. She spent much time in Macon, Georgia, where she took several shots of a boy with a cotton sac across his body; the boy's job was to pick off the boll weevil so devastating the southern crop. She took another photo of an African American wage laborer "coming home with a week of rations." Only three young children and a wife were shown, though the caption implied there were other family members. All stood barefoot. They were to eat from a package that hardly looked bigger in volume than that of the young white man with his bag of weevils. The file, as the RA/FSA called it, disclosed such information.

Lange headed far south, to the slivers of coastal Mississippi and Alabama between Louisiana and the Florida panhandle. She showed Georgia turpentine workers, North Carolina tobacco workers, and white and black sharecroppers. In Valdosta, Homerville, and Dupont, Georgia she charted turpentine production, from the "chippers" who tapped the trees by breaking the bark to extract the sap, to the overseers riding through the piney woods, to workers stilling the turpentine

FIGURE 7.7 Dorothea Lange, "Farm boy with sack full of boll weevils which he has picked off of cotton plants," Macon County, Georgia, July 1937.

© FSA/OWI Collection. Prints and Photography Division, Library of Congress. LC–USF34–017873.

FIGURE 7.8 Dorothea Lange, "Negro wage laborer and part of his family. He is coming home from the commissary with a week's rations," Macon County, Georgia, July 1937.

© FSA/OWI Collection. Prints and Photography Division, Library of Congress. LC–USF34–018040.

in small batches in wooden barrels or in large-scale processing plants. Lange noted that "this represents industrialization of the turpentine process and forecasts the decline of small processors with their stills in the woods." In focusing on historic transition, she had the RA/FSA file document how economic and political forces, including the agency itself, subsidized the termination of a way of life.[33]

Early in the trip Lange asked Styker in a letter, "Shall I emphasize white tenancy in the South?" Stryker responded succinctly, that she should "take both black and white, but place the emphasis upon the white tenants, since we know that those will receive much wider use." Southerners refused to exhibit photographs of black Americans. They complained to Styker that they'd prefer Germans or Russians. But Lange took photos of blacks and whites, typically in keeping with each group's proportion of the population. Her visual strategies for approaching each group appeared similar. In other words, she ignored Stryker's advice, refusing to negate Black Southerners' existence, instead documenting how central race was to social inequality.[34]

Retracing her steps, Lange visited Mississippi's Delta Cooperative a second time. She had been encouraged by Stryker to "emphasize the point… that one way out is not ownership, but collective effort." He told her of a "negro chap," STFU staffer Prentice Thomas, moved by Lange's sharecropping photos that the RA/FSA had lent to Howard University the previous year. Stryker thought the unionist might guide Lange, but he warned her that she could not connect the government with the STFU. Thomas, also an NAACP member, wrote Styker of a naturally beautiful countryside "marred by tumble-down shacks of sharecroppers." Worse yet were the "horrible tales of beatings, and of murders." Lange took a portrait of one victim, a young, African American boy, Clarence Weems. Weems and his family had been evicted in 1936, his father "beaten and disappeared."[35] Here Lange identified the violence, part of a "reign of terror," that resulted from the STFU's challenge to the tenancy system. Such violence was dismissed by white political officials. The governor of Arkansas, Junius Futtrell, claimed "pore white trash and shiftless [expletive for African Americans]" organized a publicity stunt around Weems' disappearance. Lange's photographs put a human face to the violence used to keep farmers from resisting.[36]

While some sharecroppers and tenants understood the economic forces that chained them, other Southerners rationalized racism and inequality. Some believed sharecroppers just didn't understand their exploitation. "They still think that they're living on a plantation but they haven't got on to the way they're cheated." One white man Lange met in 1937 gave her a thoroughgoing description of the injustices he faced, and then stated: "These [expletive for African Americans] are ignorant but they're *smart*. *They* can argue out of more." In his mind, whites could not survive the system, but somehow blacks could. Another man in the heart of Mississippi's Delta blamed sharecroppers' work ethic. "The kind of folks that won't work don't want to work, no matter where they are. We've got em here. Ride around in their automobile, sit around town, and then holler hard times." Millions of dispossessed Americans languished in the South. Still, some citizens held individuals alone responsible for their problems; they discounted the economy's social dimensions.

Lange worked hard in 1937, taking hundreds of photographs in the short span of June and July. She feared that "Cotton country's" heat "flattened" her images, so she had often woken at 4:30 am to get to the workers. Back home in Berkeley, several months later, she wrote: "I wish I could make the whole trip over again, go to the same places—knowing what I know now." But she felt she had made a "solid contribution to the files." She told Stryker her "fingertips ached, to say nothing of my head." Two weeks later she was still hard at work captioning. She wrote: "I wrote 'tenant farmer' and 'Mississippi' in my sleep."[37]

Lange returned South in 1938, with less support from the RA/FSA. Roy Stryker, citing budget cuts, had eliminated her staff position at the end of 1937. Instead, he offered to pay her three dollars a negative. His letter to her was cagey, suggesting he did not want to "exploit" her. Lange seemed to accept this situation. In May she wrote him: "Paul will always feed me, and if you will keep me in film everything will be possible." This sprightly response probably minimized her disappointment at being cut out of the program. Later in the letter she responded that "of course three dollars...is a low price for *selected* negatives." Lange could not immerse herself in environments as she had in 1937, but even so she suggested a story on "disenfranchisement in the South, as the result of the poll tax." Her enthusiasm was great—"Dynamite on this one!" She received no response.[38] Lange understood sharecroppers' powerlessness was a failure of democracy, not of individuals. She begged Stryker to meet her and Taylor when they came through Washington D.C., but their meeting was rushed, he had other engagements. The RA/FSA was struggling along. At this point even though it helped some destitute farmers, black farmers were feeling unwelcome. The *Pittsburgh Courier,* one of the nation's most popular black newspapers indicted the New Deal for establishing segregated African American colonies, and then pushing them off of land.[39] Her 1938 Southern photographs were even starker as her camera identified the structural reasons behind Southern poverty. Lange noted that apparently timeless shacks would soon be relics. Her caption for one shack, "Old Forms Remain, but they are changed at the Core," noted that the subjects had previously been sharecroppers, now they were "day laborers."[40] Lange's honesty about such dynamics may have lost her friends at the RA/FSA.

Lange's 1939 trip to the South was even shorter; much of her work focused on North Carolina tobacco production. Again she stopped at the RA/FSA offices in D.C., but she received little welcome. Stryker arranged for her to leave immediately on assignment. RA/FSA staff had come to perceive Lange as a nuisance. Unlike younger RA/FSA photographers, Lange never took a subordinate relationship to Stryker, and could openly disagree with him. He publicly praised Lange, but in private, he undermined her. He sent her to work with a social researcher from Howard Odum's Institute for Research in Social Science who brought her into rural North Carolina. The Institute's expansive research approach was akin to Taylor's work; researchers joined mapping and statistical analysis with ethnographic exploration. Despite the hastiness of the arrangements, Lange took powerful photos.

Her guide introduced her and fostered trust among her subjects toward Lange. None of her subjects had electricity or plumbing; one man kindly took twenty minutes from his day to bring the visitors water. One photo showed a young girl, perhaps six or seven, churning butter on the porch. The family economy of poor tenant farmers required child labor for survival. Novelist Richard Wright described this: "our children…help us day by day, fetching pails of water from the springs, gathering wood for cooking, sweeping the floors, minding the younger children, stirring the clothes boiling in black pots over the fires in the back yard and making butter."[41]

Stryker became increasingly insistent with her. After her trip was completed he complimented her "excellent material," but was unwilling to send her a copy of Odum's outlined study, he was saving it for other staff. He refused to send her prints of her Northwest photos until she had finished captioning the North Carolina photos. Stryker was either purposefully rude or just uncaring, as he also wrote Lange that Marion Post Wolcott was on her way down to North Carolina, and then the Delta, offhandedly informing her that while she was cut from the RA/FSA staff, new photographers were being hired. Not everyone treated Lange with such disregard. She stopped in New York City on this trip, meeting with members of the radical Photo League, which sought to document working-class life, and have workers represent themselves by teaching them how to photograph. Photo League members adulated Lange for her photographic insights and she returned their regard.[42]

Lange said little about the South in her multiple oral histories or personal or business correspondence. Ironically, just months before her death, in a lengthy KQED public television interview, she began her conversation by discussing Southern segregation; towns with their monuments to the Civil War and the boll weevil; the women and children with pellagra and bowed legs from rickets. The contours of Southern society shook her, as demonstrated by her heated anger when encountering the racism of local RA/FSA officials who cheated black sharecroppers. She sought to show America its racism. Her pointed photographs of monuments to white supremacy signal her clear appraisal of social and economic relations that devastated black Americans, and many white Southerners as well. In her first visit to Georgia, she captured a sign she encountered, "Attention Vagrants: Conviction Means Hard Labor on Gang." Poverty was a crime, to be punished with vigor. She also took photos of Jim Crow segregation. Lange's Rex Theatre for Colored People from Leland, Mississippi, proudly broadcasts the Southern caste system with the large white lettering that takes up nearly the top third of the storefront movie house. Her "Killing Time, Mississippi, 1938,"

FIGURE 7.9 Dorothea Lange, "Young Sharecropper and His First Child," Hillsdale Farm, North Carolina, July 1939.

© FSA/OWI Collection. Prints and Photography Division, Library of Congress. LC-USF34-020258-E.

identified "the board that divides service to whites and blacks." Lange's framing of her two African American subjects, a woman and man, pinions them between the plywood intended to make black citizens invisible to their white counterparts and a blurred countertop. Her subjects stare at her appraisingly, and the odd framing and vantage point implies that the viewer, who must be white, is enclosed in their own prejudices, prejudices which of course restricted their subjects.[43] But Lange was also attentive to resistance to such legalized discrimination, as seen in her investigations of the Sherwood Eddy experiment.

Publishers' hesitancy to print her photos of Southern blacks in the 1930s and 1940s provide clues to Lange's pungent critique. For example, Lange's photos dominated Archibald MacLeish's prose-poem *Land of the Free*. MacLeish was one of the nation's most prominent writers grappling with the Depression in the characteristic 1930s form, the photo-text. *Land of the Free* included the photo of the Southern planter who stoutly planted his foot on a car bumper at a grocery store, surrounded by African American laborers. And yet fulfilling Stryker's sense that African Americans were unseeable in midcentury America, MacLeish's publishers had cropped out all of the African Americans but one. The planter was represented as having "grit in [his]craw," the kind of grit that made Americans free. The publishers erased Lange's critique of Southern racism, emphasizing instead white yeoman independence.[44]

Lange's incisive commentary on the South can be found in her 1937 Greene County, Georgia photographs. In several, chimneys from old plantation houses stand, lone remnants of former grandeur. Unlike the Confederate monuments in city parks, these chimneys remind us that the war was waged over slavery, of the damages of that war, and of the South's vanquishment. The chimneys are mute evocations of a past that persists, even as it erodes. Lange also depicted the crumbling columns and foundations of grand antebellum mansions; she reminds viewers that Southern paternalism was a shell, that no social order is static. Most compelling is her shot of a former slave and his wife on the steps of "a plantation house now in decay." The man and wife sit on a simple plank staircase, weeds peek through. The front and back doors gape, open to the elements. A young white man in overalls stands aside one imposing fluted column, but he no longer commands. The couple told Lange of their subversion of a racial order—when the Yankees came around telling them they were free they had already run off with

FIGURE 7.10   Dorothea Lange, "Ex-Slave and Wife on Steps of Plantation House Now in Decay, Greene County, Georgia," July 1937.

© FSA/OWI Collection. Prints and Photography Division, Library of Congress.

the best horses and mules. This couple desperately wanted their survival; they weren't counting on Northerners to bring liberty. Lange's photos provide a powerful message about the ravages of Southern life, but also the tenacity of people to survive, and make anew the world around them.

Notes

1 Brown "Field notes," OMCA.
2 Kimberly Johnson, "Racial Orders, Congress, and the Agricultural Welfare State, 1865–1940," *Studies in American Political Development* 25 no. 2 (September 2011):156; Speech to Conference on Economic Conditions on the South July 4, 1938, at http://www.presidency.ucsb.edu/ws/?pid=15670; and Harry L. Hopkins, Works Progress Administrator, Radio Station WREC, Memphis, Tenn., CBS, August 5, 1939, available at: http://newdeal.feri.org/works/wpa06.htm.
3 Charles Johnson, Edwin Embree, and W.W. Alexander, *The Collapse of Cotton Tenancy* (Chapel Hill: University of North Carolina Press, 1935), and Embree, "Southern Farm Tenancy: The Way Out of Its Evils, *Survey Graphic,* 25 no. 3 (March 1936):149; available at, http://newdeal.feri.org/survey/36149.htm.
4 Ibid., reviewed in *Rural Sociology*, (March 1936).
5 "President's Committee on Farm Tenancy," in Dorothea Lange and Paul Taylor, *American Exodus: A Record of Human Erosion* (Paris: Editions Jean-Michel Place, 1999, reprint), 16, 19; "Tenancy: A Way Out?" *New Republic*, February 24, 1937, 61.
6 Gordon, *Lange,* 265–269; Howard Kester, *Revolt among the Sharecroppers* (New York: Covici Friedi, 1936), 50.
7 Robin Kelley, *Hammer and Hoe: Alabama Communists During the Great Depression* (Charlotte, NC: University of North Carolina Press, 1990), 43, 50, 166.
8 Natanson, *The Black Image*, 69.
9 H.L. Mitchell, *Roll the Union On: A Pictorial History of the Southern Tenant Farmers Union* (Chicago: Charles H. Kerr Publishing Co., 1987), 18, 27.
10 "Eleanor Roosevelt and Civil Rights," available at: http://www.gwu.edu/~erpapers/teachinger/lesson-plans/notes-er-and-civil-rights.cfm and Patricia Sullivan, ed. *Freedom Writer: Virginia Durr, letters from the Civil Rights Years* (Athens, GA: University of Georgia Press, 2006).
11 Jane Adams and D. Gorton, "This Land Ain't My Land: The Eviction of Sharecroppers by the Farm Security Administration," *Agricultural History*, 83 no. 3 (Summer 2009): 323–336.
12 Ira Katznelson and Quinn Melroy, "Was the South Pivotal? Situated Partisanship and Policy Coalitions during the New Deal and Fair Deal." *Journal of Politics*, 74 no. 2 (April 2012): 604–620; Steve Valocchi "The Racial Basis of Capitalism and the State, and the Impact of the New Deal on African Americans," *Social Problems*, 41 no. 3 (August 1994): 347–362; Sidney Baldwin, *Poverty and Politics: The Rise and Decline of the Farm Security Administration* (Chapel Hill, NC: University of North Carolina Press, 1968).
13 Harvard Sitikoff, *A New Deal for Blacks: The Emergence of Civil Rights as A National Issue* (New York: Oxford University Press, 1978), 58–82; Lauren Rebecca Sklaroff, *The Quest for Civil Rights in the Roosevelt Era,* (Chapel Hill: University of North Carolina Press, 2009), 15–30; and Patricia Sullivan and Armstead Robinson, eds. *New Directions in Civil Rights Studies* (Charlottesville, VA: University of Virginia Press, 1991), 81–104.
14 "The Old Folks at Home," The Center for American Music, University of Pittsburg, available at: http://www.pitt.edu/~amerimus/OldFolksatHome.html.
15 "Sowing the South Forty," *NYT*, December 13, 1936.

16 Quote from LC-USF34-017118; Richard Wright, *Twelve Million Black Voices*, (New York: Basic Books, 2002 reprint), 50; *New Republic, ibid.*

17 Embree, ibid.; and Kester, *Revolt*, 40; *American Exodus*, 14; Eleanor Roosevelt, "My Day," June 19, 1939. available at: www.gwu.edu/~erpapers/myday/displaydoc.cfm?_y=1939&_f=md055296.

18 Woman with beads, LC-USF34-017112-C; Gilbert C. Fite, "The Agricultural Trap in the South," *Agricultural History*, 60 no. 4 (Autumn 1986), 38–50; Fite, "Southern Agriculture Since the Civil War: An Overview," *Agricultural History* 53 no. 1 (January 1979) 3–21; Robert Margo, *Race and Schooling in the South, 1880–1950: An Economic History* (Chicago: University of Chicago Press, 1990), available at: http://www.nber.org/chapters/c8792.pdf.

19 Kestrel, *Revolt*, 47.

20 Wright, *Twelve Million*, 56; Dorothy Day, *America Magazine* 54 (March 7, 1936): 516–517.

21 Meltzer, *Dorothea Lange*, 146; Kelley, *Hammer*, 53; Donald Grubbs, *Cry from the Cotton: The Southern Tenants' Farmers Union and the New Deal* (Charlotte, NC: University of North Carolina Press, 1970), 130.

22 Natanson, *Black Image*, 244.

23 LC-USF34-009512-E; LC-USF34-T01-009539-C; and LC-USF34-009325-C.

24 LC-USF34-009388 and LC-USF34-009389.

25 Jerry Dallas, "The Delta and Providence Farms: A Mississippi Experiment in Cooperative Farming and Racial Cooperation, 1936–1956," *Mississippi Quarterly* 40 no. 3 (1987): 283–308; Lange to Stryker, July 4, 1936, FSA.

26 Stryker to Lange, July 1, 1936, FSA.

27 See Joe Manthorne, "The View from the Cotton: Reconsidering the Southern Tenant Farmers Union, *Agricultural History*, 84, no. 1 (Winter 2010): 20–45; Kelley, *Hammer and Hoe*; Mitchell, *Roll the Union*, 36; Grubb, *Cry of Cotton*, 134.

28 Fred Smith, "The Delta Cooperative Farm and the Death of a Vision," *Journal of Mississippi History* 71, no. 3 (September 2009): 253; Dallas, "The Delta," 294.

29 Natonson, *Black Image*, 79.

30 Stryker to Lange, April 16 and 21, 1937, FSA.

31 Lange to Stryker, May 3, 1937 and Stryker to Lange, May 10, 1937, FSA; Natanson, *Black Image*.

32 Stryker to Lange, June 9, 1937, FSA; LC-USF34- 017603-C; LC-USF34- 017750-E; LC-USF34- 017739-C.

33 LC-USF34-017647, LC-USF34-017841, LC-USF34-017845, LC-USF34-017652, LC-USF34- 017740-C.

34 Lange to Stryker, June 9, 1937, and Stryker to Lange, June 18, 1937, FSA; Natonson, 220.

35 Stryker to Lange, early 1937, and Prentice Thomas to Stryker, June 21, 1937, FSA. The badly beaten Weems fled, leaving behind a wife and eight children, Grubbs, *Cry from the Cotton*.

36 Manthorne on Thomas; Jerold Auerbach, *Labor and Liberty: The LaFollette Committee and the New Deal* (Indianapolis: Bobbs-Merrill Company, 1966), 49; Smith, "The Delta Cooperative," 244.

37 Lange to Stryker, October 20, 1937, FSA.

38 Lange to Stryker, May 1938, FSA.

39 "A 'Friend' of the Negro," *Pittsburgh Courier*, Dec. 10, 1938, in Adams and Gorton, "This Land," 33.

40 Lange, *American Exodus*.

41 Anne Whiston Spirn, *Daring to Look: Dorothea Lange's Photographs and Reports from the Field* (Chicago: University of Chicago Press, 2009), 89, 95, 115; Wright, *Twelve Million*, 62.

42 Stryker to Lange, September 7 and 25, 1939, FSA; Natanson, *Black Image,* 275, n 56; *Photo Notes* (September 1939), 3.

43 LC-DIG-fsa-8b32104;, LNG38183.2; LC-USF34-017418-E; and AS000103, New York Public Library, "Services for Negro people," of a mule vendor. KQED v.1, 1; and v. 2, 2, 8. Transcript, OMCA; Spirn, *Daring,* 95; and LC-DIG-fsa-8b32104.

44 Natanson, *Black Image,* 209, 220.

8

"MOVING ABOUT PEOPLE" AND THE GREAT PLAINS, 1935–1940

Dorothea Lange's exploration of the Great Plains region forms the backbone of how we see the economic and environmental refugees of the Dust Bowl.[1] She visited each year from 1935 to 1938, showing a land and a people unmoored. The Plains inhabitants, often called "Okies" or "Arkies" for the Oklahoma or Arkansas that they migrated from, moved "in all directions" searching for respite from their troubles. If lucky, they had a jalopy laden with a life's possessions: food, clothing, bedding, and furniture. The unlucky walked, like the Arkansas family of six that deserted their homes, ironically, due to that winter's floods, which had affected a million and a half Americans in the Mississippi River Valley. The woman pushed a wicker buggy filled with bedding. The father was fifty-five years old, old enough to have been considering retirement, but instead was pushing a large cart with the family's belongings. Their four children tramped with them. Only one had shoes. The woman had a bonnet to shade her eyes, the children none. Lange encountered them after they had crossed nearly five hundred miles to Memphis, Texas, at the heart of the Dust Bowl. They had another five hundred miles to the Rio Grande Valley, where they hoped to pick cotton. One child's overalls were torn up the sides and just below the knees. A kind of jacket hugged his shoulders, but there was nothing left of it beneath the capped sleeves. His clothing literally appeared to degrade before the camera.[2]

The road has always been associated in the American imagination with transition, optimistic change, and the possibility of re-making oneself, but not in the Depression. Mark Twain concluded his classic *Huckleberry Finn* with Huck "lighting out for the Territories," an ending considered to be at the heart of American literature and ideology. Lange photographed the road many times, stretching into the horizon, toward fields or mountain ranges. As a young woman Lange had uprooted herself and taken to the road, going west to re-imagine her life. But her photos now asserted that the road no longer led to possibility or redemption.

FIGURE 8.1 Dorothea Lange, "Flood refugee family near Memphis, Texas," May, 1937.

© FSA/OWI Collection. Prints and Photography Division, Library of Congress. LC-USF34-016911 and LC-USF34-016914.

As Oklahoma songwriter and folk singer Woody Guthrie wrote in "The Great Dust Storm," "We rattled down that highway to never come back again." One woman stands next to a billboard near El Paso, Texas. Her husband crouches beneath the shade provided by the structure. She told Lange, "Do you reckon I'd be out on the highway if I had it good at home?" Beside them on the rocky road lie their gas can, a few bottles, a frying pan and a sheet of cardboard to protect their meal from the ground.[3]

In her visits to New Mexico, Oklahoma, and Texas Lange identified the causes and processes by which these people left. A preeminent photographer of people in distress, she also photographed the earth in distress. In exploring people's relationship to the earth, she became an environmental photographer. As she wrote in a letter to Roy Stryker, her supervisor: "Erosion of soil has its counterpart in erosion of our society."[4] She documented the costs of settling the land, of subduing it without consciousness of the earth's needs.

Early in her government work, Lange captured one of the frightful "dusters" or dust storms, in Mills, New Mexico. The photo shows a menacing sky, which darkens the photo's upper right corner. The land appears pregnant, awaiting

FIGURE 8.2 Dorothea Lange, "Do you reckon I'd be out on the highway if I had it good at home?" On U.S. 80 near El Paso, Texas, June 1938.

© The Dorothea Lange Collection, the Oakland Museum of California. Gift of Paul S. Taylor.

FIGURE 8.3 Dorothea Lange, "Dust storm near Mills, New Mexico," May, 1935.

© FSA/OWI Collection. Prints and Photography Division, Library of Congress. LC-USF344-003788-ZB.

the dust's encroachment. A Kansan farmer described one of these dust storms with the black clouds that could be seen approaching for miles and that "hug the earth." The cloud blots out the landscape. "Birds fly in terror before the storm…the smaller birds fly until they are exhausted, then fall to the ground, to share the fate of the thousands of jack rabbits which perish from suffocation."[5] Air turned to dust; air needed for life, instead squelched it. Her New Mexico photographs show hulking farm machinery rusting in the dusty fields, broken dried out stalks lying dead upon the dried earth, the machinery witness to the earth's lack. Other machinery sinks into the dust, successive waves of sand covering it.

Lange was hired after the harshest years of the Dust Bowl, one of the United States' worst environmental disasters. Years of intense heat with little rain had led to drought. This drought, in combination with colliding weather patterns and uncaring farming practices, resulted in dust storms that could be so bad that they reached from the Great Plains to three hundred miles out into the Atlantic Ocean. Boats were forced to anchor. In one storm the cloud of dust, 1,800 miles wide, stretched from Nashville, Tennessee to St. Cloud, Minnesota. On May 11, 1934, twelve million tons of soil rained down on Chicago, a thousand miles from where the soil originated. The dust reached New York City, which became "veiled as if in an eclipse." People standing in the observation deck of the Empire State Building could not see Central Park, a mile in the distance. In the spring of 1935, when Lange was visiting New Mexico, a *Times* headline exclaimed "Dust Pall Hangs Over Half a Nation." A year later the nation's icons, the Lincoln Memorial,

FIGURE 8.4   Dorothea Lange, "These farm implements should never have been used for they destroyed a naturally rich grazing area." Mills, New Mexico, May 1935.

© FSA/OWI Collection. Prints and Photography Division, Library of Congress. LC-USF34-002816.

Washington Monument, and Capitol, were covered in a "clay-colored veil." Citizens "swarmed the Mall" to experience the invasion of dust.[6]

On "Black Sunday," April 15, 1935, a giant cloud near Bismarck, North Dakota, darkened the skies of Denver, Colorado, nearly 700 miles away. The storm's center moved east of that, through Dodge City, Kansas. The cloud appeared black as coal at its bottom, lightening toward its top, some 2,000 feet up. At its fastest, the storm moved sixty miles an hour, as fast as an automobile. Some winds reached 100 miles an hour; people in Kansas and Oklahoma thought a tornado had hit. The dust drove some blind, others felt suffocated by the winds and dust. Today the National Ocean and Atmospheric Administration (NOAA) calls these black blizzards "land-based tsunamis." The dust was so strong it shorted out car engines; one's hand might be invisible if placed right before one's face. An Associated Press reporter tracking Black Sunday named the suffering southern plains region, the "Dust Bowl," and the designation stuck. The Dust Bowl comprised Oklahoma, also northern New Mexico, Texas, southeast Colorado, and southwest Kansas.[7] Parts of Arkansas, Nebraska, and the northern Great Plains were also afflicted.

In 1935 Lange visited New Mexico twice, in May documenting the Dust Bowl in eastern New Mexico, and in December, tracking RA/FSA efforts to rebuild communities in its western portion. A year later, she traveled quickly through the region, but the shots she took are some of her most powerful photos, disclosing

FIGURE 8.5 Stovall Studio, "Dust clouds rolling over the prairies," Dodge City, Kansas, April 1935.

© Kansas State Historical Society.

the shocking conditions Oklahoma migrants faced. In 1937 she showed abandoned towns and people who had abandoned their dreams; men sat in dusty town centers with nothing to do and families perched along the roadside. Lange's focus in 1938 came from a photo-text she and Taylor conceived, entitled *An American Exodus: A Record of Human Erosion* (1939). They examined the suffering of American farmers in its broadest contexts, the relationship of a people to the land, of the people's relations with one another, and with international economies.

An American Exodus, a true joint venture between Taylor the economist and Lange the photographer, was one of a series of unusual documentary experiments where editors mixed photographs and text in innovative ways to elicit the Depression's tragic truths. The nation's top photographers, Walker Evans and Margaret Bourke-White contributed to this new form, as did Lange's employer, the RA/FSA.[8] *An American Exodus* explored how and why the nation's agricultural economy was pushing Americans off the land. It was the only book to examine U.S. agriculture region by region.

Lange and Taylor proposed that the Great Plains inhabitants were alienated from the land, saw it as something to profit from, instead of stewarding. The book's second section, "Midcontinent," began with a historical photograph that showed a dust-veiled panorama of settlers on horses, some 50,000 of them, galloping across the broad swath of prairie, trying to grab a land claim for themselves. European Americans did not settle the Oklahoma Territory until the late 1880s. The "Unassigned Lands" had been taken from Native Americans, most of whom had been forced there from the more fertile southeastern states in the early nineteenth century. White settlement followed the pattern set by the 1862 Homestead Act, which gave legal claim of 640 acres to anyone who lived on and improved the land. A contemporary account, written in 1889 for the well-heeled readers of *Harpers' Weekly*, provides some flavor of this settling:

> Unlike Rome, the city of Guthrie was built in a day. To be strictly accurate in the matter, it might be said that it was built in an afternoon. At twelve o'clock on Monday, April 22d, the resident population of Guthrie was nothing; before sundown it was at least ten thousand. In that time streets had been laid out, town lots staked off, and steps taken toward the formation of a municipal government. At twilight the camp-fires of ten thousand people gleamed on the grassy slopes of the Cimarron Valley, where, the night before, the coyote, the gray wolf, and the deer had roamed undisturbed. Never before in the history of the West has so large a number of people been concentrated in one place in so short a time.[9]

Of course the region was settled last because its ecology was inhospitable to traditional small farming. After being secured for the U.S. through the Louisiana Purchase, explorer Major Stephen Long called it the "Great American Desert."[10]

Lange and Taylor believed that man's inattention to the land and climate precipitated the ecological crisis of the Dust Bowl. The region had historically little rainfall, typically less than the twenty inches that cultivation required, and in the 1930s there was even less. Lange spoke with a crowd of farmers in Sallisaw, Oklahoma in August 1936. Pressed against the town's Main Street buildings, seeking a sheltering shade, they bantered amongst one another. The farmers could do nothing more, as Lange reported, "their crops" were "burn[ing] up in the fields." Were they joking, or holding on to a shred of hope when she heard them say, "Hello Bill, when's it gonna rain?" The Sallisaw farmers told Lange, "Nothing to do. These fellers," said one of them, "are goin' to stay right here till they dry up and die too." This lack of precipitation led to drought, extreme dryness of the soils. Some parts of Colorado and Kansas effectively became deserts.[11]

Lange again traveled to the region in 1936, when the U.S. experienced its most extreme heat ever. Not until 2012 did such heat again blanket a huge swath of the nation. Without air-conditioning, relief was difficult to come by. In 1934 there were sixty days when the agricultural portions of the country confronted temperatures above 100 degrees. And 1936 was even worse. Lange wrote to Stryker bemoaning the heat. She was not idly complaining; the nation had never experienced anything like it. Some 5,000 people died. The Weather Bureau in Chicago received 1,300 calls an hour. People wanted to know the temperature; they were crazed, it was so hot.[12]

But as Lange and Taylor wrote, the wind, an ever-present, buffeting force on the plains, also contributed to the Dust Bowl. Oklahoma was "the most windblown

FIGURE 8.6   Dorothea Lange, "Drought farmers line the shady side of the main street of the town while their crops burn up in the fields. 'The guvment may keep us a little I reckon.'" Sallisaw, Oklahoma, August, 1936.

© FSA/OWI Collection. Prints and Photography Division, Library of Congress. LC-USF34-T01-009669.

state in the nation," as weather systems converge there. The lower Great Plains' distinctive reddish-chestnut soil was easily depleted of its nutrients when laid bare to this wind. For millennia the soil was blanketed with buffalo and grama grasses, anchoring it to the earth. Sheepherders had understood that "the grass keeps the earth together;" but land speculators and settlers did not.[13]

Lange and Taylor maintained in *American Exodus* that the Plains inhabitants refused to steward the land. They asserted that "the roots of Oklahomans in the land are shallow;" Oklahomans had a "moving itch." The region's migrants switched between farming and industrial wage-work in oil, mining, or lumbering, in boom and bust dynamics that continue to this day. When oil or mining markets crashed, farming offered an alternative. But, if wheat prices dropped, Plains dwellers could abandon the land. Farmers often moved within the region. They would "berry" in Arkansas and pick cotton in Oklahoma or Texas, or work in the oil industry in Eastern Oklahoma, then pick cotton in Western Oklahoma.

Lange's field notes capture the despair of these people, but also their aspirations. She met one "Old time professional migratory laborer camping on the outskirts of Perryton, Texas at opening of wheat harvest." The man thrust one hand into

FIGURE 8.7   Dorothea Lange, "Old time professional migratory laborer camping on the outskirts of Perryton, Texas at opening of wheat harvest. With his wife and growing family, he has been on the road since marriage, thirteen years ago. Migrations include ranch land in Texas, cotton and wheat in Texas, cotton and timber in New Mexico, peas and potatoes in Idaho, wheat in Colorado, hops and apples in Yakima Valley, Washington, cotton in Arizona. He wants to buy a little place in Idaho," Perryton, Texas, June 1938.

© FSA/OWI Collection. Prints and Photography Division, Library of Congress. LC-USF34-018187.

his pocket, looking with chagrin at the viewer. His four children crowd around him. The daughter hides the wife, whose sprightly dress and white shoes peek out at the right corner. In effect, the daughter replaces the mother. Without a fantastic intervention, the daughter's future would be similar to her father's. He followed a path that he could not alter. "With his wife and growing family, he has been on the road since marriage, thirteen years ago," Lange wrote, migrating from Texas to Arizona and as far north as Washington's Yakima Valley to harvest apples. Lange also met farmers who had fled to the industrial North, to Chicago or Detroit, before returning to Oklahoma, and then off to California. One farmer commented to Lange, "They're goin' every direction and they don't know where they're goin'."

Plains farmers rarely practiced anti-erosion techniques, and believed they lacked the resources to do so. The "dry farming" techniques they used in this arid region had worked fine for a time, but destabilized the soils, making them vulnerable to wind erosion. Some did not fully understand the consequences of such farming techniques. Others had no reason to care. Oklahoma's tenancy rates were nearly as high as the South, at over sixty percent. Tenants never knew if they would remain on a plot of land, and as a result, many neglected the land's long-term needs.[14] Lange's fieldnotes indicate that some understood humans' impact on the land. She wrote about a Newport, Oklahoma family, "The Tragedy of One Family Soil Exhaustion in a Generation." Lange took five photos of their house. In one a dog lie, collapsed on the porch; three rickety chairs stood in for the inhabitants. Her subject told her, "There's my grandfather's house. Now my brother's camping there. Just barely existing trying to farm 30 acres. Thers' some more wore out land. I cleared that land 30 years ago."

Ironically, as some tenant farmers struggled mightily to break even, speculators envisioned large-scale agriculture for a huge profit. During WWI the Turks cut off Russia's ability to sell grain to Europe, leading to skyrocketing prices for U.S. grains. A postwar price slump was quickly followed by rising prices. Speculators made it rich off of the boom in wheat prices. Their fabulous profits promoted further mechanization and "the Great Plow Up." One Kansan, Ida Watkins, "the Wheat Queen," declared that her profits made her richer than the President of the U.S.; another, a movie mogul, bought fifty-four square miles of Texan property in three counties, and planted it all in wheat to reap the profits from then high prices. Middle-class professional men also bought up farms to squeeze profit from them. Greater mobility via the automobile and automated farm equipment, tractors and combines, made it possible for "suitcase farmers" to plant the fields and return for harvest if the futures market in grains suggested high profit. Farmers pushed hard at the earth, draining its resources. In the five years between 1925 and 1930, farmers tore up some five million acres, more than seven times the size of the state of Rhode Island. Cereal production soared three hundred percent.[15] On such delicate land, with such difficult weather, this relationship to the land had disastrous consequences.

Overproduction led to pileups, pushing prices down. So farmers left the land open to the wind. Some thirty-three million acres of vulnerable land lay naked. The "sand blows" and "black blizzards" that resulted from this mix of semi-arid land, difficult climate, and rejection of land stewardship decimated the region. Inhabitants fled. The Dust Bowl counties lost about ten percent of their population by 1940. These "tin can tourists," on the road with their jalopies when lucky, or with wheelbarrows, buggies, or wagons, were Lange's subjects.[16]

In 1937 Lange toured New Mexico and Arizona, taking only a few photos, then into Texas and Oklahoma. Stryker felt the need to coax her to take the assignment, claiming she had wanted to understand the roots of the Plains migrants arriving in California. But throughout the summer of 1937, Stryker expressed his disappointment with Lange, wondering why she was not in the locations he had expected her to be at, demanding that she stay in better touch,

FIGURE 8.8 Dorothea Lange, "On highway no. 1 of the 'OK' state near Webbers Falls, Muskogee County, Oklahoma. Seven children and eldest son's family. Father was a blacksmith in Paris, Arkansas. Son was a tenant farmer. 'We're bound for Kingfisher (Oklahoma wheat) and Lubbock (Texas cotton). We're not trying to but we'll be in California yet. We're not going back to Arkansas; believe I can better myself,'" June 1938.

© FSA/OWI Collection. Prints and Photography Division, Library of Congress. LC-USF34-T01-018191-E.

pushing her to get photos of ghost towns. Instead, Lange sent photographs of car wheels stuck in mud, reminding him of her hard-going trip. She concluded: "Oklahoma is a miserable state."[17]

Lange and Stryker often tangled over the details of her work. Before her trip in 1937, she pushed to develop a photo-story for *Life* magazine, which was making waves as a novel photo magazine. Stryker did not think much of *Life*, did not think it would succeed, but he was wrong. It became a staple of American visual culture, read in millions of American households. He permitted her, with little grace, to do up a photo story.[18]

Ultimately *Life*'s editors only used one of her photographs of an Oklahoman, but they transformed the photograph's meaning to an optimistic one. Lange's original photograph had three migrants who had landed in a government camp in California. One faces the camera head on, the other two men, a pace behind,

FIGURE 8.9 Dorothea Lange, "Ex-tenant farmer on relief grant, Imperial Valley, California," March, 1937.

© FSA/OWI Collection. Prints and Photography Division, Library of Congress. LC-USF347-016336.

have heads cast slightly downward. Their eyes fail to meet the camera eye; they look discouraged. Behind them lie others, seemingly stuck in an alienating space. *Life* cropped Lange's photo, showing only the central figure looking outward into the future, outside the frame, and also separated from the collectivity he was part of. *Life* told a story about technology's capacity to fix the Dust Bowl, and used Lange's photo to tell this story. The headline for the image, "Dust Bowl Farmer is a New Pioneer," called on the westward impetus of Manifest Destiny. *Life* lauded the drought refugee's "courageous philosophy;" the farmer had told Lange: "I figured that in a place where some people can make a good livin' I can make me a livin'." In *Life*, the Oklahoman was not someone torn from the land, getting help through RA/FSA relief, but rather a self-reliant pioneer imbued with a positive "American" approach to change. Photographs tell a story, perhaps many stories, which is why Lange and other documentarians believed corroborating text and the file itself critical to getting closer to the truth of a situation. *Life's* story suggested individual and technological triumph over the Dust Bowl, not government coming to the aid of its citizenry.[19]

That fall was when Stryker informed her that FSA budget cuts had forced him to cut her from the payroll. Only his two protégés, Arthur Rothstein and Russell

Lee, would stay on.[20] So in writing *American Exodus*, Lange was striking out on her own. In 1938 she again traveled through Texas and Oklahoma, focusing on the drought's epicenter, Dalhart, Texas. Lange seemed particularly taken with the earth itself, examining the dried-up fields, the ongoing dust storms, the hardened soil, but never forgetting the relationship between people, their social institutions, and the land.

Lange's photos from 1938 explored how the Dust Bowl affected community institutions, how people and the land are linked. One bank had shut its doors, an insolvency that followed the land's decline. Similarly, grain elevators, church-like beacons and symbols of what drew farmers to this region, stood empty and abandoned. Lange wrote to her RA/FSA supervisors that these towns' residents were superb candidates for RA/FSA support. In *An American Exodus*, Lange and Taylor explained how one community had been developed in the 1920s, when New York City speculators from the Wilson Land Corporation, sold "exceptionally choice farm land," to unsuspecting investors seeking to become small farmers. The land forced these farmers out not long after. Across Northern Texas, Lange showed homesteads standing lonely and miniscule against an all-encompassing sky, abandoned by their owners. Lange paired the photo of the grain elevator with an advertisement for the "top o' the world farm and dairy lands," showing the Wilson Land Corporation's 1925 advertising message to customers, for "peace and plenty, sunshine and contentment." Lange exposed the company's promise thirteen years later. A lone pole was stuck into the ground; the sun inscribed its

FIGURE 8.10   Dorothea Lange, "Furrowing against the wind to check the drift of sand. Dust Bowl," north of Dalhart, Texas, June, 1938.

bent shadow on the dusty earth.[21] The wire fence paralleled the horizon line, and parched furrows led back to the horizon. All bent before the sun, the wind, and the sky that pressed down.

The New Deal could not stop the Plains' wind and heat, it could not replace its soils, but it could use government power to respond to the man-made causes of the Dust Bowl. The New Deal employed multiple strategies. The RA/FSA was ill-equipped for the magnitude of an environmental devastation that was decades in the making, that crossed state borders, and that pushed hundreds of thousands of Americans onto the road. Even so, the government inaugurated a new role in its relationship to the agricultural economy. The RA/FSA coordinated with other agencies like the Civilian Conservation Corps (CCC), the Works Progress Administration (WPA) and the National Forest Service (NFS) to support farmers and reshape how the land was used. These agencies nurtured conservation practices for earth and water.

Distinct agencies established land use and watershed districts. In land districts, government officials trained farmers in proper planting techniques, including contour plowing, so that the water did not run down a hill leading to gullies, seeding with different crops, and terracing where necessary. CCC members planted thousands of trees to break the wind. In the watershed areas small dams were created so that rainwater could be conserved, and let out when needed.

The federal government began planning and oversight of soil, land, and water use to address systemic, national issues. Hugh Bennett, the "Father of Soil Conservation," had been advocating for soil conservation for over a decade, and in 1934, enjoying the government mandate, he undertook mapping the entire nation's soil with over 6,000 workers. In 1935 they focused more closely on twenty counties in the Plains. They measured erosion and evaluated land quality in 25,000 individual square miles. Bennett's national soil survey facilitated planning.[22]

The government also bought up eleven million acres of land which had been open range or over-cultivated. It set aside four million acres for National Grasslands. Twenty National Grasslands parks still exist today, stretching from Eastern North Dakota to the high deserts of Oregon, and south to Texas. The remaining seven million acres were "adjusted." Farmers, with government guidance, established new towns where the soil could better sustain them. Some experiments failed after a few years, but other towns still exist. All told, the government experimented with sixty-four towns. The RA/FSA hoped to resettle some 100,000 Americans living in submarginal lands. Limited funding allowed it to achieve only a tenth of that goal.[23]

Lange visited one of these settlements, the Bosque Farms in New Mexico, early in her work for the RA/FSA. Many of Bosque's inhabitants had come from Taos Junction, New Mexico, where land was inferior, and some had fled Oklahoma not long before that. Lange's documentation shows people's determination, but also a sense of their loss. Some of her subjects, particularly young girls, appear caught in a melancholic reverie, members of a new community that they did not yet feel part of. In "Resettled Farm Child," Lange's subject faces a fireplace, the wrought iron bed, window, and bench cant at different angles, the girl literally turns in on herself; she has nowhere to go. But other photos show men in the fields, or making adobe bricks for a local school. These men promised the rebuilding of the community. Their stance and expressions are powerful, a testament to the possibility for renewal. Similarly, a young woman stands outside a tarpaper shack holding a young boy in her arms. She holds the hand of a second, a toddler in overalls. A third young boy plays in the dirt on one side, his back against the viewer, while the woman's washing hangs from a clothesline to the far right. Her evident pride, despite the meagerness of her new abode, shines through. Bosque Falls ultimately became a settlement of forty-two homes. There were difficulties, not all could get the land they were promised, and inhabitants felt bullied by government officials. But Taylor noted that women's courage helped keep up spirits of the new residents. More recent historians have found that Mexican Americans working for the WPA and the RA/FSA migrants worked closely together, fostering unusual cross-ethnic alliances.[24]

FIGURE 8.11   Dorothea Lange, "Resettled farm child from Taos Junction to Bosque Farms project," New Mexico, December 1935.

© FSA/OWI Collection. Prints and Photography Division, Library of Congress. LC-DIG-fsa-8b27011.

The largest set of RA/FSA funds was set aside as grants and loans for struggling farmers to buy equipment, seeds, or additional land. Most RA/FSA funding went to the loan program; farmers received some $778 million dollars. Somewhere between two-thirds to three-quarters of Plains farmers received government aid. In total more than eighty percent of those grants were repaid to the government, indicating that investment in citizens could fortify family and community.

The drought was not the only problem then facing the people of the Plains as Lange and Taylor revealed. Mechanization, or "tractoring out," affected the Plains area as much as the South. Indeed, the tractor's greater efficiency and productivity contributed to the Dust Bowl by allowing the land to be turned up quickly. As in the South, the New Deal exacerbated this process. Landlords, loan companies, and a few of the most economically viable tenants took government funding awarded for crop reduction and bought tractors. They then kicked tenants off the land; they were no longer needed. Lange wrote Stryker: "Drouth refugees are really tractor refugees," pointing to the new processes that alienated farmers from the land. A week later she wrote again of her concerns. "You couldn't find a better example of exploitation in the nation than the changes in plantation life with this tidal wave of tractors." As Lange noted, "the treeless landscape is strewn with empty houses." As farms emptied, so did towns. Her photo of Caddo, Oklahoma, showed the effects of depopulation. Storefront windows gape open, there are no people in the streets, and just a lone car passes by. [25]

Lange and Taylor's *An American Exodus* compared this mechanization to the enclosure movement of the early modern period, where Britain's rich landowners seized the commons that had sustained nobility and peasants with wood for fires and fruits and wildlife for food. Lange and Taylor took a moderate stance, explaining that ultimately the enclosures were economically beneficial. But they did not shy away from the costs of mechanization, the "social disorganization and human misery" that followed. In private however, especially after she had left the RA/FSA, Lange did not mince words. In a letter to Stryker, she asked: "How can there exist an FSA in view of what is going on here in Texas?" [26]

One man described hunting two hundred square miles throughout the Texas panhandle for land. No one would rent him any; they did not need to. A landlord told Lange he would "rather have renters than tractors on my place," but when he got behind on taxes he was forced to replace his tenants with tractors. One of her most famous photographs was of a group of young, white tenant farmers, all kicked off the land, from Hardeman, Texas. Lange shared their anxieties: "Where we gonna go? How we gonna get there? What we gonna do? Who we gonna fight? If we fight, what we gotta whip?" Their confusion indicated their utter powerlessness. They did not know why they were stuck, what they could do, or who was responsible for their plight. They perceived no way out. These men were so poor they could not pay the poll tax so none of them could vote. Like black Southerners, they were disenfranchised. Contrasting two photographs that she took allows us to see her capacity to express the men's powerlessness, or their

FIGURE 8.12 Dorothea Lange, "Former Texas tenant farmers displaced by power farming," Goodlet, Hardeman County, Texas, May and July 1937.

determination. In the second image the men look like western toughs whose engaged stare indicates they will not back down. But Lange testified to their inability to alter their political circumstances.

Lange's camera represented them visually and reminded Americans of the tenant farmers' presence. She probed Americans' consciousness. Did they have a responsibility to respond to others' misery? A Lange photo from her third trip through the Dust Bowl gave a sense of how harrowing it was for citizens when only a patchwork of limited municipal or county efforts served as a safety net. The photograph testified to the need for national, coordinated governmental support. A father, his shoes worn, pulls a young girl in a wagon. She sits atop bedding and clothing. Following some twenty feet behind is the mother and three other children, including one who pushes a baby carriage. The group had walked from southeast Oklahoma toward its center, over one hundred miles. The family had lost its farm when the father caught pneumonia. He was not fit enough to work on

FIGURE 8.13 Dorothea Lange, "Family walking on highway, five children. Started from Idabel, Oklahoma. Bound for Krebs, Pittsburg County, Oklahoma. In 1936 the father farmed on thirds and fourths at Eagleton, McCurtain County, Oklahoma. Was taken sick with pneumonia and lost farm. Unable to get work on Work Projects Administration and refused county relief in county of fifteen years residence because of temporary residence in another county after his illness," June 1938.

a WPA project, and country relief rejected him. He had lived in the county for a decade, but because he had become sick in another county he was ineligible for aid.

In 1938 Lange photographed Nettie Featherstone, a mother of three living in a two-room shack. She described feeding her children black-eyed peas day after day—that was all that stood between her family and starvation. The family had left their Oklahoma home for California, but only made it to the Texas panhandle. A farmer let her family stay in the shack if they picked his cotton. In *An American Exodus*, Lange and Taylor placed her photograph next to a windmill. Her lanky form, clothed only in the simplest torn cotton sack shift dress, emphasizes the brutality of her situation. Her thin arms hold up her forehead and neck, a support, a comfort. On the facing page, a broken-down windmill, its blades missing, is anchored to the earth by taut rope. Featherstone, like the mill, is poised against elemental earth and sky, both subjects broken by their unceasing travail.

Lange is known as a photographer of the Dust Bowl diaspora, really a massive movement of people from Missouri and Arkansas through the Great Plains and Southwest, moving ever westward, from drought, flooding, and mechanization. Later in her life, she disputed her public identification with the Dust Bowl itself, claiming she had only spent a few days in the region, but that was not so.[27] But

FIGURE 8.14   Dorothea Lange, "Wife of a migratory laborer with three children, Nettie Featherston," near Childress, Texas, June 1938.

© FSA/OWI Collection. Prints and Photography Division, Library of Congress. LC-DIG-fsa-8b32434.

unlike the South that pulled at her, or her home of California, the Plains never grabbed her heart. Even so, her images testify to the pain of its residents.

"Okie" culture, as with southern cultural representations, circulated in 1930s media. Lange and Taylor's *An American Exodus* included a photo of a thin farmer in a light chambray shirt, his belt pulling his pants tight on his thin frame. Lange's caption, "I'm goin' where the climate fits my clothes," invoked a popular folk song, sometimes called "Lonesome Road Blues," or "Goin' Down the Road Feelin' Bad." The song's lyrics, which were recorded early in the twentieth century, and were produced during the 1920s and 1930s by well-known artists such as Bill Monroe and Woody Guthrie (and more recently, by the Grateful Dead), were a cry of despair. The singer lamented his poor diet, badly fitting clothes, time spent in jail, and being pushed down the road, all the while singing, "I ain't gonna be treated this a-way."[28] Lange's photos indicate a sense of identification with a people under pressure, partly caused by their own actions, and partly inflicted by a poverty they were desperate to flee.

Another Woody Guthrie song was popular in the 1930s, written in reproach to Irving Berlin's "God Bless America." Guthrie wondered, instead, was "This Land Made for You and Me?" He walked "the ribbon of highway," but observed the "no trespassing" signs, the relief offices, and the hungry. Lange's photos, like Guthrie's song, followed a people, asking them, asking with them, was it theirs?

Notes

1 Lange to Roy Stryker, June 6, 1937, FSA.
2 "Flood of 1937," *Encyclopedia of Arkansas,* http://www.encyclopediaofarkansas.net/encyclopedia/entry-detail.aspx?entryID=4878.
3 Annette Kolodny, *The Land Before Her: Fantasy and Experience of the American Frontiers, 1630–1860* (Chapel Hill, NC: University of North Carolina Press, 1984) explores "the road" and the pastoral as gendered experiences. "Dust Storm Disaster," available at: http://www.woodyguthrie.org/Lyrics/Dust_Storm_Disaster.htm.
4 Lange to Stryker, Spring 1937, FSA.
5 Lawrence Svobida diary, in Sarah Richardson, "Kansas: The Land Blew Away," *American History* 50 no. 4 (October 2015): 58–61.
6 "Dust Bowl," *Gale Encyclopedia of U.S. Economic History* (1999), available at: http://www.encyclopedia.com/doc/1G2-3406400265.html; *Washington Post*, March 22, 1935; Timothy Egan, *The Worst Hard Time: The Untold Story of Those Who Survived the Great American Dust Bowl* (New York: Mariner Books, 2006).
7 Geoff Cunfer, "The Southern Great Plains Wind Erosion Maps of 1934–1935," *Agricultural History* 85 no. 4 (Fall 2011): 540.
8 See Archibald MacLeish, *Land of the Free* (New York: Harcourt and Brace, 1938), Walker Evans and James Agee, *Let Us Now Praise Famous Men* (Boston: Houghton Mifflin, 1941); Margaret Bouke-White and Taylor Caldwell, *You Have Seen Their Faces* (New York: Modern Age Books, 1937); and Richard Wright, *Twelve Million Black Voices* (New York: Viking Books, 1941).
9 William Willard Howard, "The Rush to Oklahoma," *Harper's Weekly* 33 (May 18, 1889): 391–394.
10 Egan, *Worst Hard Time,* 19; Richard Dillon, "Stephen Long's Great American Desert," *Proceedings of the American Philosophical Society* 111 no. 2 (April 14, 1967): 93–108.

11 LC-DIG-fsa-8b29739; Climatologists define as desert any area that receives less than ten inches of rain in a year. "Drought in the Dustbowl Years," National Drought Mitigation Center: http://drought.unl.edu/DroughtBasics/DustBowl/DroughtintheDustBowlYears.aspx; and Clayton Koppes, "Dusty Volumes: Environmental Disaster and Economic Collapse in the 1930s, *Reviews in American History* 8 no. 4 (December 1980): 535–540.

12 Phillip J. Hutchison, "Journalism and the Perfect Heat Wave: Assessing the Reportage of North America's Worst Heat Wave, July-August 1936," *Journalism Quarterly*, 25 no. 1 (Winter 2008).

13 Harry McDean, "Dust Bowl Historiography," *Great Plains Quarterly* 1 no. 1 (Spring 1986): 117–126; Koppes, quoting Donald Worster, *Dust Bowl: Southern Plains in the 1930s* (New York: Oxford University Press, 1979), 78.

14 McDean, "Dust Bowl," 117; Richard Hornbeck and Pinar Keskin, "The Evolving Impact of the Ogallala Aquifer: Agricultural Adaptation to Groundwater and Climate," *NBER Working Papers*, (November 2011): 1–40.

15 Donald Foster, "The Dirty Thirties: A Study in Agricultural Capitalism," *Great Plains Quarterly* 6 (Spring 1986): 107–116; Handbook of Texas Online, Donald Worster, "Dust Bowl," http://www.tshaonline.org/handbook/online/articles/ydd01; Donald Worster, *Under Western Skies: Nature and History in the American West* (New York: Oxford University Press, 1992), 99–100.

16 Worster, *Under Western Skies*, 100.

17 Stryker to Lange, April 16, 1937 and June 11, 1937; Lange to Stryker, June 1937, FSA.

18 Lange to Stryker, March 17 and 19, 1937; Stryker to Lange, March 23, 1937, FSA.

19 Roland Barthes calls the photograph "polysemous;" the photo can have many meanings. "The Rhetoric of the Image," *Image, Music, Text* (Chicago: Hill and Wang, 1971). "U.S. Dust Bowl," *Life*, June 21, 1937, available at: https://books.google.com/books?id=1UQEAAAAMBAJ&printsec=frontcover&source=gbs_ge_summary_r&cad=0#v=onepage&q&f=false.

20 Stryker to Lange, September 30, 1937, FSA.

21 Grainery in Everett, Texas, LC-USF34-018291. Captions to this photograph "Furrowing against the wind to check the drift of sand. Dust Bowl, north of Dalhart, Texas," June 1938, indicate that Lange took the photograph to promote FSA anti-erosion practices. However, for *American Exodus*, she took advantage of the aesthetic harshness of the landscape to make a different point about land speculation and capital extraction from the soil. LC-USF34- 018240-C.

22 Douglas Helms, "Conserving the Plains: The Soil Conservation Service in the Great Plains," *Agricultural History*, 64 no. 2 (Spring 1990): 58–73.

23 Richard Melzer, "New Deal Success or 'Noble Failure'? Bosque Farms Early Years as a Federal Resettlement Project," *New Mexico Historical Review* 85 no. 1 (January 2010): 1–37.

24 LC-DIG-fsa-8b27011; and LC-USF34-001642 and LC-USF34-002770; Melzer, "New Deal Success," 19-22.

25 LC-USF34- 018258-C; Drouth was a common term in the 1930s; Lange to Stryker, June 23, 1937, FSA.

26 Lange to Stryker, June 22, 1938; FSA.

27 KQED tape of Lange, 1964, tape 1, 13, OMCA.

28 Patrick Huber, "Ghost Singers, City Billies and Pseudo Hillbillies: Freelance New York Recording Artists and the Creation of Old Time Music, 1924-1932" unpublished paper, February 2010, available at: http://scholarworks.gsu.edu/cgi/viewcontent.cgi?article=1008&context=popular_music.

9

"IN THE DITCHES AT THE END OF BEAUTY"

California in the Depression, 1935–1940

As Dorothea Lange photographed California agriculture, Charlie Chaplin, as the internationally known Tramp, fought for the "little man" in his Depression-era classic, *Modern Times*. The twentieth-century comedian and moviemaker's dream sequence of California showcased the Golden State's earthly abundance. The Tramp kicked up his heels in a suburban, Spanish stucco ranch home. He reached out the dining room window for oranges; from the kitchen he placed a pitcher on the ground and whistled for a cow, which milked itself as he munched on the grapes that crowded through the doorframe. In *Modern Times*, industrial life ground down working people; the Tramp literally travels through the gears of the machine. But in Chaplin's California, the sun always shined and the earth bestowed its fruits for human consumption. The state and its growers had promoted a similar vision of California as the nation's garden. By the 1880s, California's premier industry was agriculture. And California boasted grand and "wild" nature that Lange's friends, Edward Weston and Ansel Adams, magnificently photographed. Nearby, the Pacific Ocean crashed on bluffs north and south of Lange's Berkeley home, the redwoods marched up the coast, and the Sierra Nevada mountain range cradled crystalline lakes like Tahoe.

Before working for the RA/FSA, Lange would have experienced California much as the Tramp had. She traveled with her first husband, Maynard Dixon, into the mountains, she reveled with photographer friends on the Monterey coast, and she camped with her children near Tahoe.[1] But in the mid-1930s she explored California's other side, where the soil's richness benefited the few, and where farmworkers eked out the barest of existences. Agricultural work was back-breaking, wages were minimal, living conditions vile. In the valleys, alluvial plains, and coastal areas where migrants worked, landowners, often with the help of local police and vigilantes, enforced this order by guns. The Depression exacerbated these conditions. As the only photographer who was not based in the RA/FSA's Washington D.C. offices, Lange had primary responsibility for capturing California. Nearly a third of her output of 4,000 photos were of that state.

Lange was a relentless observer of the interconnections between California's agricultural system and its workers' exploitation. In *American Exodus,* California was the "Last West," in Lange and her husband Paul Taylor's words; where the "distressed, dislodged, determined Americans" hit "hard against the waters of the Pacific." Lange's photographs invited Americans to reconsider the Promised Land's premise, the American Dream of individual mobility and potential in a land of plenty. Simultaneously, Lange explored how workers collectively fought their economic distress through unionization and citizen-supported government relief.

California growers purveyed images of the mythic independent yeoman, who toiled his plot and formed the basis of Jeffersonian democracy. Yet California agriculture's structure was "industrialized." As Lange and Taylor wrote in *American Exodus,* "41% of the large-scale dairy farms, 53% of the large-scale poultry farms, 60% of the large scale truck farms and 60% of the large scale fruit forms of the U.S. were located in California." Workers toiled in "open-air farm factories," Taylor said. Carey McWilliams, the most famous student of California agriculture, an activist lawyer and journalist who fought racism, and who railed against migrant labor's exploitation, called them "factories in the fields."[2]

As in other industrialized sectors, growers sought to keep wages low by amassing a large labor pool to work their farms. The "harvest gypsies," "fruit tramps," "bindlestiffs," today called migrant farm labor, planted or harvested, then moved on to another crop, another county, another region. A farm or ranch that sustained twenty workers year-round needed a hundred times that number during harvest, typically just for a week or two. Growers first drew from the mass of single miners who had arrived with the Gold Rush. These itinerants returned to San Francisco each fall, and rooming houses and cheap hotels lodged tens of thousands of such men. By recruiting many more workers than needed, growers could pay fewer wages. Industry spokesmen clarified their mandate, arguing landowners were "sharing too much of his dollar with labor… We are not husbandman. We are not farmers. We are producing a product to sell."[3] Desperate workers often accepted less.

Agricultural workers experienced this process differently than the owners. Marie De L. Welch's poem, "The Nomad Harvesters," prefaced McWilliams's *Factories in the Field* (1939), and it describes the "land of nomad harvesters" who "till no ground, take no rest, are homed nowhere." These migrants picked lettuce "in the flats by the sea," cherries "in the amber valleys," and grapes in the "low blue hills," but always "Rest nowhere, share in no harvest," while they "camp in the ditches at the edge of beauty." Lange captured these migrants' travails, workers and their families who produced the food that fed a nation, but who lacked roots, and could barely feed their families.

California's history and settlement patterns led to its unique agricultural system. Under Spanish colonial rule, priests settled "Alta California," establishing missions from San Diego to Sonoma. Missions brought cattle-herding and wheat to California. After Mexican independence in 1821, Mexico wrested control of California from the Catholic Church, creating large *ranchos* and conferring land rights upon elite colonists. With the Mexican American War, the U.S. won control of California. Unlike states settled under the Homestead Act's one hundred and sixty-acre plots, California's huge plots facilitated unequal social relations. This pattern persisted with the resale of land granted to the railroads, furthering speculation and land monopoly. Farming expanded, and as mines were exhausted two decades after the Gold Rush, farmworkers outnumbered miners.[4]

California was a farmer's mecca. Its unique geography contributed to a temperate climate, making growing feasible for two-thirds of the year, and in some regions yearround. Lange's first husband's family had moved from the South with other "Alabama settlers" in the early 1870s, when cowboys herded sheep and cattle. Maynard Dixon's art often featured the flats of the San Joaquin Valley and its marvelous, never-ending sky. Fertile soil and huge swaths of level, treeless land made grain farming inevitable. Plots in that region were so big that a combine harvester might roll across one row of crops and not return until the next day.[5]

Growing conditions fed grower consolidation. In some regions water was scant. Land "reclamation" through large-scale irrigation readied land for farming. Reclamation impelled cooperation, centralization, and monopoly. Major corporations headquartered in San Francisco often took control through investment. And particular crops drew farmers together. Fruits and vegetables, labor-intensive crops, required skill to nurture, and "fruit culture," as it was called, engendered cooperation. By 1920 sixty growers' cooperatives organized the harvesting, processing, shipping, and marketing of half of all California's crops.[6]

California's varied climate and geography facilitated growing different crops: hops for beer, grapes, nuts, citrus, all other kinds of vegetables and fruits, and cotton. The San Joaquin Valley's fruit farms only required forty to eighty acres, but the Imperial Valley's cotton plots were larger at 500–1,000 acres. Citrus growing extended out sixty miles from Los Angeles, fueling the metropolis' expansion. Peas and asparagus were grown north of Santa Barbara, raisins produced near Fresno. By 1900, California dominated world production of apricots, almonds, olives, and lemons, along with prunes, plums, and raisins; Sicily, Bosnia, and Spain lost their transatlantic markets. With the transnational railroad and refrigerated rail cars, California fruits and vegetables became a mainstay in American diets.[7] And after WWI, California became the nation's second-greatest producer of cotton.

California did not just grow crops; it offered a vision of the good life and marketed food in new ways. Growers and the state promoted citrus, raisins, and nuts as necessary for health. Previously, starch, breads, and meats dominated diets. Americans had been leery of vegetables and fruits, which they thought carried cholera and other germs. To make products enticing, California growers first individually wrapped citrus fruits. Orange and grape crate labels depicted the state as a verdant garden cosseted by the Pacific and inland mountain ranges. Raisin bunches were also individually wrapped, before growers realized boxing was easier. Growers associations developed branding campaigns, such as SunMaid Raisins, or Sunkist oranges. Diamond Brand and Blue Diamond have marketed nuts for over a century. [8]

Lange observed the care put into growing crops—each one had a distinct work process. California had pioneered labor-saving mechanization, but farm work still required intense human attention and labor. An early photo of Salinas Valley workers suggests the workers' travails. The Filipino American laborers lumber toward Lange's camera. Bent at the waist, their hands reach down to the ground to cut the lettuce. The earth is dry and cracked in the furrows; the lettuce leaves furl out. A sea of lettuce surrounds them. Imagine twelve or more hours bent in this stance. If anything, industrialization increased agricultural labor's monotony and misery. Clearing potato fields required in Lange's words, "endurance but no special skill." Her photos from Shafter, California showed potato harvesters carrying

FIGURE 9.1 Dorothea Lange, "Filipinos cutting lettuce, Salinsas, California," June 1935.

"a sack which is suspended from their waist," which hung between their knees. Workers spent the day straddled across the row, placing the potatoes in a sack until it was ready for sorting and grading. One of the migrants derided mechanization as one further step in his degradation. "They're fixin' to free all us fellows—free us for what?... They're aimin' at keepin' fellows such as me right down on our knees—aimin' at making slaves of us. We've got no more chance than a one-legged man in a foot race."⁹

"Truck farming," the cultivation of small fruits and vegetables for market, required even more intensive labor. Peppers were grown as seedlings in a greenhouse, and workers then transplanted them into the fields. Lange showed one man carrying his wooden box full of seedlings, nestling them into the ground, and then covering them with "sticks, palm leaves and paper for protection against wind and cold." Mexican American men weeded and "capped" cantaloupe, covering them with a "wire wicket" and waxed paper to warm them in the cold desert nights.

FIGURE 9.2 Dorothea Lange, "Mexican gang of migratory laborers under a Japanese field boss. These men are thinning and weeding cantaloupe plants. Wages thirty cents an hour. These young plants are 'capped' with wax paper spread over a wire wicket to protect against cold and to accelerate growth," Imperial Valley, California, March 1937.

FIGURE 9.3   Dorothea Lange, "Off for the Melon Fields (Mexican Labor)," Imperial Valley, California, June, 1935.

© FSA/OWI Collection. Prints and Photography Division, Library of Congress. LC-USF34-001620.

Lange could celebrate workers' labors. She caught Mexican American migrants heading off to work on top of a flatbed truck. The men face the camera; one doffs his hat, another holds himself elegantly like a dancer, while yet another shines a gleaming smile. These men, languid and casual and so comfortable in their bodies, could be extras in a Hollywood film. Lange showed a Mexican American grandmother, who traveled each year from Arizona to California, whose entire body engaged in the act of pulling tomatoes from the earth. Later, this same dignified, ageless woman walked through the fields, looking like so many harvesters depicted nobly by painters for hundreds of years, a woman outside of time.

Economic exigency, however, left most workers desperate. Lange encountered one carrot puller and his family who described "sleeping in the rows" so that they could work the next morning. They feared being replaced. Many had no resources to leave. One elderly man perched on the side of the field. When the first pea crop froze, he had to wait weeks more for the second crop to mature. Relief provided funds for an inadequate diet, but not enough for shelter.

FIGURE 9.4   Dorothea Lange, "Mexican grandmother who migrates with large family each year from Glendale, Arizona, following crops thru California and return. Here shown harvesting tomatoes," Santa Clara Valley, California, November 1938.

© FSA/OWI Collection. Prints and Photography Division, Library of Congress. LC–USF34–018576.

Lange investigated California's uniquely heterogeneous workforce, a "large, landless and mobile proletariat," that began with the white itinerants of the 1850s, and moved through multiple ethnic groups, before circling back to white migrants in the Depression. Growers recruited, hired, and paid workers different wages based on gender, race, and ethnicity. Some sixty percent of California farmworkers were waged labor, like workers in steel, textiles, and the auto industry. These workers who "worked in… orchards of peaches and prunes," and "slept on the ground in the light of the moon," mostly, in Woody Guthrie's words, came "with the dust and were gone with the wind."[10]

Lange portrayed a remnant of California's earliest labor force, underemployed, out of luck, single men. Her 1935 "Fifteen Years Following the Fruit" showed a middle-aged man who squinted at the camera. Eyes and mouth pressed together, the farmworker resisted the photographer, but his bowed shoulders communicated vulnerability. These fruit tramps had been largely discarded by growers by the twentieth century. "Bindlestiffs" were known by for blankets they slung

FIGURE 9.5 Dorothea Lange, "More than twenty-five years a bindle-stiff. Walks from the mines to the lumber camps to the farms. The type that formed the backbone of the Industrial Workers of the World (IWW) in California before the war. Subject of Carleton Parker's 'Studies on IWW,'" Napa Valley, California, December 1938.

© FSA/OWI Collection. Prints and Photography Division, Library of Congress. LC–USF34-018795.

diagonally over their backs, marks of their itinerancy. Their turnover was some-times as high as two or three hundred percent, which frustrated growers.

Landowners were explicit about switching to immigrant labor, and segmenting labor by gender and race to give themselves the upper hand. With the exception of California-born Mexicans, Chinese immigrant men were the first ethnic workers. The 1854 *California Farmer* favorably compared Chinese American workers to Southern enslaved. The Chinese were "to be to California what the African has been to the South. This is the decree of the Almighty, and man cannot stop it." Contractors, often themselves Chinese American, channeled laborers from major cities such as Sacramento and San Francisco. White Californians forced Chinese Americans into specific quarters, neighborhoods, and businesses, but ultimately vigilantism, such as the 1877 burning down of a Chinese American lodging home by the "Order of Caucasians," and the 1882 federal Chinese Exclusion Act dra-matically cut Chinese immigrant workers in the fields. Lange's 1936 "Old time Chinaman of the type that originally followed the crops" testified to their history in California's fields.[11]

Growers exploited other ethnic groups for cheap labor as poverty in Asia propelled many to the U.S. Japanese American workers dominated by the nineteenth century's end; growers prized them for their agricultural knowledge. They too met racism and xenophobia, though Japan successfully advocated for its citizens' welfare. Japanese Americans leased land as tenants, and soon became managers and owners. Their marketing cooperatives and mutual benefit associations helped them win contracts. They dominated markets in strawberries, asparagus, potatoes, among other crops. Japanese Americans controlled half or more of the irrigated acreage in San Joaquin, Colusa, Placer, and Sacramento counties. Lange photographed few Japanese Americans picking crops in the fields; she was more apt to show Filipino and Mexican American laborers working in ranches owned or managed by Japanese Americans.[12] "Hindustanees," mostly married Sikh men from the Punjab, also arrived on the Pacific coast from 1907-1915. Hundreds, even thousands immigrated until the 1917 Immigration Act, or "Asiatic Barred Zone Act," added the first literacy test for immigrants, denying entry to nearly all Asians. South Asians worked the fertile San Joaquin Valley raisin fields, the Imperial Valley cotton fields, and the Sacramento-area rice fields.

Growers next recruited Filipinos, almost exclusively single young men, as a new, low-wage labor source. The Johnson-Reed Act of 1924 further restricted immigration, but Filipinos could work as U.S. nationals, without citizenship, until 1934. Even so, California extended anti-miscegenation laws to Filipino Americans; the young men could not mix with white women. Riots occurred in Tulare, Watsonville, Stockton, and Imperial, which included the killing of one Filipino American laborer and the bombing of a local taxi-dance hall, where Filipino American men had dared to pay white women for ten cents a dance. The writer and activist Carlos Bulosan described police shaking down Filipino migrants. Lange showed Filipino Americans dotting the hillside near Pismo Beach as they worked in peas, crating lettuce in the Imperial Valley, and cutting cauliflower and thinning beets in mid-coastal California.

Her captioning and pictures tended to emphasize that they worked in gang labor, unable to commence their day until the leader told them to, moving along the rows in unison.[13] Her earlier 1935 shot of Filipino American workers made viewers aware of the men's physicality, the burden on their bodies as they use the *cortado* to cut the lettuce (see Figure 9.1). But in her image, "Filipino Boys Thinning Lettuce," the men strung out in rows appear to be part of some larger mechanism that controls their labor, much like corporate photography tended to represent workers as part of an industrial setup organized by managers.

Lange also photographed the Mexican Americans and Mexican nationals who increasingly worked the crops after World War I. The Mexican population "quadrupled" from 1910-1930, making them three-quarters of the farm labor force by the later date. Some came from as far south as Michoacan, some 1,500 miles to the U.S. border, and often traveled north, "following the fruit" over the season, another five hundred plus miles into California. They were helped by organizations like the Agricultural Labor Bureau of San Joaquin Valley, which was

FIGURE 9.6 Dorothea Lange, "Filipino boys thinning lettuce," Salinas Valley, April 1939.

© FSA/OWI Collection. Prints and Photography Division, Library of Congress. LC-USF34-019432-E.

"financed by several county farm bureaus, chambers of commerce, and marketing cooperatives." These groups threatened deportation if workers organized themselves for better pay or work conditions.[14]

Mexican American labor had no ladder up. Unlike Japanese Americans, Mexican Americans only owned six farms a generation after their arrival. But like Asian immigrants before them, Mexican Americans faced residential and labor segregation. Lange showed their makeshift homes in dusty, unpaved *colonias*, or neighborhoods. Mexican Americans also encountered blunt racism, signs in the windows of restaurants, billiard parlors and the like, reading "White trade only," or in Spanish, "We only serve the white race," or "Americans." Like Southern textile workers or tenant farmers, these immigrants tended to work in a family unit—they had no choice. Growers claimed to like Mexican American labor because "they will undertake work that white labor will not or can not perform." They toiled "under excessive heat, dust, isolation," and were amenable to "temporary jobs" and gang labor.[15] Guidebooks maintained Mexican Americans' needs were few: "so long as he earns enough one day to enable him to be idle the next, he is content." Rationalizing Mexican Americans' extraordinary poverty, a poverty created by growers' low wages, they claimed Mexican Americans had "no disposition to acquire land and make permanent settlement." One grower told Taylor, "the Mexicans are a happy people, happier than we are; they don't want responsibility, they want just to float along, sing songs, smoke cigarettes."[16]

The Depression gave *Anglos* (whites) rationale to deport Mexicans. Before Lange worked for the RA/FSA, California had already kicked Mexican Americans off of relief rolls. And the state's 1931 Alien Labor Act prohibited them from working on public works project. The federal government tightened the border, and began deportations in 1931. Unions such as the AFL pushed for deportation, despite growers' desire for a surplus labor pool. Somewhere between 300,000 to two million Mexicans were "repatriated," particularly in the Depression's early years.[17]

Lange also showed the human costs to the many children who worked the fields. When Chinese Americans were forced out of the fields in the late 1880s, growers believed "deserving white boys" could replace "coolies," and they thought they could pay ostensibly more productive white youth less. They were wrong. Institutions serving these boys quickly learned that wages were no compensation for such backbreaking labor. Mostly children worked because they had to. Their parents needed their wages for basic needs, even though they themselves worked incessantly. A writer for *Collier's* described "the babies—seven year olds who crawl along, ten hours a day, for nine months and more a year." One young migrant farmer remembers pulling a sixty-pound bag of potatoes that he had harvested when he was nine years old.[18] Migrant children were often exempt from California's child labor laws as growers only had to prove that the child struggled educationally or was disabled, something camp conditions caused.

Lange's photo of Imperial Valley carrot pickers, "A Labor Market Where None Are Refused," shows a woman crouched at a furrow, behind her, her husband stares into the distance.[19] Her two children, appearing barely three years old, stand nearby, looking at the photographer. Some children work, like the group of Mexican American children who tie the tops of carrots together. Lange showed a young bob-haired blond girl, who looks no more than five years old, who rubs the sleep from her eyes. She wears a coat against the desert morning cold, but her bare legs are a reminder of her vulnerability. Behind her trails a cotton sack; its length is several times her height.

The New Deal's 1938 Fair Labor Standards Act (FSLA) abolished most child labor. But agriculture remained exempt. Southern Democrats and growers wanted to make sure that workers stayed on the farm, so to speak. This problem persists. Today, somewhere between 300,000 and half a million children, some as young as seven, go into the fields to pull the fruits and vegetables that we enjoy on our tables.[20]

Altering the calculus of Depression-era migrancy was a new group, or "Okies" as they were derogatorily called. Lange believed that she noticed the "first wave"

FIGURE 9.7 Dorothea Lange, "Children of migratory Mexican field workers. The older one helps tie carrots in the fields," Coachella Valley, California, February, 1937.

© FSA/OWI Collection. Prints and Photography Division, Library of Congress. LC-DIG-fsa-8b31867.

of drought refugees coming over the border on a weekend in April 1935, before they became a "deluge." At least a quarter of a million arrived between 1935 and 1938, though some observers think twice that many came. They followed migrants from Texas, Oklahoma, Missouri, and Arkansas who had come in the previous decade. The Plains people lived in settlements called "Little Oklahomas" in Los Angeles and on the outskirts of towns in the San Joaquin Valley, where they displaced Mexican American workers. One subject told Lange, they were "burned out, blowed out, eat out," from drought, dust storms, and insect plagues; they were also "tractor'd out."

Both Taylor and popular author John Steinbeck believed the Plains refugees' entrance into the labor market heralded a new day for workers: "Farm labor in California will be white labor, it will be American labor, and it will insist on a standard of living much higher than that which was accorded to the foreign, "cheap labor.'" But those on the bottom, even white workers, were intended to stay there. Like other white farmworkers, "Okies" were given first dibs on "ladder crops," things such as hops, cotton, or citrus that did not require stoop labor. One Agricultural Labor Bureau manager proffered this racist rationale: "They

FIGURE 9.8   Dorothea Lange, "Young cotton picker, Kern County migrant camp," California, November 1936.

© FSA/OWI Collection. Prints and Photography Division, Library of Congress. LC-USF34-009884-E.

[Okies] can squat and sort, but they cannot squat and walk like a Mexican; hence they are not good in asparagus." Ultimately, Plains migrants took any work they could find.[21]

Many believed that Okies lacked a culture of resistance, that those from the Plains were more individualistic and suspicious toward collective action. A poem in the *Weed Patch Cultivator*, a newspaper put together by the migrants expressed this complacency: "Don't be what you ain't/Jes' be what you is… If you're just a tail/Don't try to wag the dog./If you're just a little pebble/Don't try to be the beach." The Okies' plight entered the nation's consciousness in ways that Mexican Americans and Asian Americans had not. Some maintain that Lange and Taylor moved from depicting Mexican American migrants to the Okies as they better pulled at the nation's heartstrings. White citizens were more apt to respond to white Americans' plight, than that of the Filipino Americans or Mexican Americans. Certainly, this seemed true when Steinbeck's *The Grapes of Wrath* went through ten printings between March and November, and the novel was quickly turned into an Oscar-winning film.[22]

But within California, Okies became a despised class. When work petered out in the winter, they had no savings to tide them over. This disconcerted locals, who were used to workers, in the words of a Kern County health official, "miraculously appearing" and then "silently slipping away" when they were no longer needed. In the mid-1930s, six California counties increased their populations by half; Kern County's population nearly doubled. Because growers externalized costs to local governments, counties were forced to pay more for sanitation, health, and education. And hysteria over the "indigent influx" led police to establish an unconstitutional "bum blockade" for several weeks in 1936. Los Angeles's Police Chief sent officers to the border of Arizona, on Route 66, where many of the migrants crossed into the state, and some eight hundred miles north, to the Oregon border. One Central Valley theater required that "Negroes and Okies" sit in the balcony. One physician called them "shiftless trash who live like hogs," and another doctor thought of them as "a different race." The *LA Times* fulminated against Okies as criminals engaged in "sordid depraved acts," and demanded that RA/FSA camps be closed. A California Republican state senator argued "let them starve," and localities passed laws prohibiting Okies from receiving relief. Residency of one year was required, soon amended to three years. Intoned the California Citizens Association's secretary: "California jobs should go to Californians and not to the horde of empty bellies from the Southwest." In some counties, they were not allowed to register to vote even after they had established permanent residence. The conditions faced by the Plains people had been faced by many before them, but the extraordinary contempt with which migrant labor was treated had been largely invisible when it occurred to non-white migrants.[23]

Lange, of course, documented the horrific social conditions that migrant workers faced. Children's education was largely bypassed, families needed their wages, or sometimes they could not afford clothing to attend school. Investigators found one thirteen-year-old girl who had only overalls that others laughed at, her seven-year-old sister had no underwear, only diapers. Steinbeck found children with "gunny sacks" around their distended bellies. Local educators saw migrant children as a drain on the system, and they looked the other way when youth were taken from classes. One school district reported that a fifth of migrant children over six had never attended school at all. Parent Teacher Association members blamed migrant children for their children's illnesses, and thought they spread "bad moral conditions" too. Migrants' impoverishment let to poor diets and health: oatmeal mush, dandelion greens, and boiled potatoes, or fried cornmeal might be all families could afford or scavenge. Nutritional deficiencies led to illness and even malnutrition. As Taylor and Lange wrote, nearly a quarter of the migrants were ill, and a quarter of those could not better their diets for recovery.[24] More than a tenth of the children in one study of cotton pickers had rickets. Milk, eggs, or orange juice, all plentiful in California, would have prevented this illness. Migrants also lacked basic health services. Californians thought hospitals were for residents, not workers. As Steinbeck wrote: "The counties seem terrified that they might be required to give some aid to the labor they require for their harvests."

FIGURE 9.9   Dorothea Lange, "Children of Oklahoma drought refugees on highway near Bakersfield, California. Family of six; no shelter, no food, no money and almost no gasoline. The child has bone tuberculosis." June 1935.

© FSA/OWI Collection. Prints and Photography Division, Library of Congress. LC-USF343-003802-ZE.

Housing for California's agricultural workers was woefully inadequate. Large growers tended to provide barracks-style shelter, sometimes lifted above the ground, or a platform with a tent above it. Workers were forced to live in this company housing if they wanted a job. This was another profit stream for the company owners, who charged migrants unreasonable rates. Smaller farms provided even less, perhaps a spit of land on which to pitch a tent. In labor contractors' camps, workers might be lucky to get a platform and a tent, or a place to park their truck. John Steinbeck's tour of workers' housing found "one-room shacks usually about 10 by 12 feet, have no rug, no water, no bed... Water must be carried from a faucet at the end of the street. Also at the head of the street there will be either a dug toilet or a toilet with a septic to serve 100-to-150 people." He described "typical ranches" with a single bath house for 400 people. Water scarcity in the camps meant that people bathed then drank from the ditch irrigation water. They knew they would sicken, but had little option.[25]

Finally, there were the squatters' camps, places of unbelievable squalor for those without work, or for those forced from camps closed by county health officials. People just parked their car along the road. Steinbeck noted that "from a distance" the squatter camps looked like city dumps; often they were found on the dumps' margins. "Homes" would be made out of "a litter of dirty rags and scrap iron, of houses built of weeds, of flattened cans or of paper" that would "slop down into a brown pulpy mush" with the first rain. Sanitation was nonexistent. Children might squat where they were to defecate—spreading hookworm among others.[26] One squatter who had been kicked out of a San Joaquin Valley camp closed for lack of running water told Lange: "They chase them out of one camp because they say it wasn't sanitary—there's no running water—so people live out here in the brush like a den o' dogs or pigs." For migrants, there was no relaxation, no shelter, no destination. In a photo Lange took along California Route 99, a Union Pacific billboard's base supports a ragged tarp shielding three families from the elements. Their stove and rocking chair lie beneath a blistering sun just below the billboard advertisement of a soft pillow cushioning a young man's head. The advertisement reads, "Travel while you sleep"; the image and text dwarfs the migrants' meager domestic arrangements. One of Lange's photo subjects lamented: "People has got to stop somewhere. Even a bird has got a nest."[27]

Workers often fought back against their exploitation, and Lange dignified their struggles with her photographs when she could. White "bindlestiffs" had just walked off the job, and each ethnic group in turn had either walked out of the fields or worked collectively to resist their exploitation. Buoyed by New Deal support of labor and motivated by Depression-era wage cuts reaching forty percent, workers fought back. In 1930 Imperial Valley pickers had struck in an unusual coalition of Filipino, Mexican, Sikh, Chinese, Japanese, and African American field hands, joined by radical remnants of the Industrial Workers of the World and the Communist Party. Their walk-out involved over 5,000 workers.[28] In 1933 a multi-racial group of cotton pickers, some 18,000 of them, struck in an area more than a hundred miles long. Taylor claimed, "it was the largest strike by agricultural laborers in the nation's history, before or since." In 1934 Filipino American and Mexican American labor struck together, exhibiting a high degree of labor consciousness. Previously, owners hired ethnic Mexicans as scabs when Filipino Americans struck, but this time the Filipino Labor Union coordinated with the Mexican Labor Union. Growers responded with violence, getting Filipino Americans falsely arrested, burning their camps, and forcing out five hundred migrants by gunpoint from the Pajaro Valley. But struggle ultimately won workers a pay raise and concessions such as lunch breaks and a maximum 48-hour work-week. In 1934 there were some thirty strikes involving over 47,000 workers in peas, peaches, pears, cherries, and finally in cotton. In cotton, more than ten thousand workers came out from six different counties. Again strikers were met with violence. Three strikers, including one woman, were killed in Pixley when vigilante ranchers shot point blank into a crowd.[29]

In 1938 Lange could follow workers' activism. She focused on several thousand cotton workers who struck under the United Cannery, Agricultural, Packing and Allied Workers of America (UCAPAWA) of the Congress of Industrial Organizations (CIO). The CIO believed multi-racial, multi-ethnic organizing was critical to union victory. Lange was keen to capture their efforts. Kern County, where Lange photographed, had a higher proportion of small farmers and remnants of "labor, populist and socialist movements," along with strength in the Communist Party. The UCAPAWA and local labor federations lobbied county and federal authorities to provide relief to strikers. Growers and the anti-union Alliance for Farmers wanted to starve workers out. The union and its supporters also worked with RA/FSA camp managers, who tried to soften the strike's effects on workers. In October she wrote her supervisor, Roy Stryker, asking for better credentials to ensure her safety. "When you do need [a letter of introduction], you sure do need one." She had tried to photograph "a mass of pickets," but was almost run over by a "cop [who] galloped up to me on a very large horse." Ultimately, vigilante patrols made it impossible for her to reach the strike line.[30]

Instead, Lange's photos showed how workers built solidarity in their community. She documented local business and farm support for strikers. Small farmers were themselves vulnerable to the large growers. One Kern County tenant farmer told Lange: "The big fellows have got us all with a ring in our nose. You take the small farmer like me—we can't come out. There's no difference hardly between me and my pickers—only I've got a place to stay out of the rain." She

FIGURE 9.10   Dorothea Lange, "Gas station," Kern County, California, November 1938.

© FSA/OWI Collection. Prints and Photography Division, Library of Congress. LC–USF34–018401–E.

displayed small business owners' disaffection with large-scale growers in her well-known photo of a gas station, whose owner had attached a sign advising "This is your country, don't let the big men take it from you." Lange also depicted those working in alliance with the strikers, such as the Steinbeck Committee to Aid Agricultural Organization, and the International Labor Defense, a Communist group that had provided support to the Scottsboro Boys and distributed needed clothing and shoes to the strikers.[31] Particularly strong were her four portraits of a strike leader who had been a Dust Bowl migrant. In the most striking he stands in front of a barn with a poster of the soon victorious gubernatorial candidate, Culbert Olson, a politician Lange and Taylor trusted would fight for migrants. Lange's subject was a "leader of the "Flying Squadron," which picketed corporate farm fields by moving strikers from place to place via automobile caravans. Lange wrote, "He drove the first car." The man looks determined, his cap tucked onto his head at a sprightly angle; he conveys labor's strength. Her placement of the

FIGURE 9.11 Dorothea Lange, "He came from an Oklahoma farm in April, 1938. Became a migratory farm worker in California, joined the United Agricultural Packing and Allied Workers of America (Congress of Industrial Organization-CIO) at the beginning of the cotton strike of October, 1938 and became the leader of the 'Flying Squadron' which attempted to picket the large fields of corporation farms by automobile caravans. He drove the first car." Kern County, California, November 1938.

© FSA/OWI Collection. Prints and Photography Division, Library of Congress. LC-USF34-018616-C.

union leader next to Olson suggests the need, not just for elected leaders' support, but support from the people, to address inequality. Lange expanded the circle of unionization's benefits by depicting a young girl, "under nourished," who Lange explained had joined her parents for a strike meeting. This image suggested union struggle was not only about workers but also their families and communities.

The 1938 strike failed after two weeks. There were just far too many impoverished migrants who would accept any wage for survival. Lange wrote to Stryker about how dispiriting the result was. She had caught "the tail end of a long, heart-breaking strike, unsuccessful, no field activities except with strike breakers where it was too dangerous to go." She described the "half empty" RA/FSA camps and the "hostility" toward her and the RA/FSA, because growers thought the RA/FSA supported the strike. During the Depression era, California agriculture suffered some "140 strikes, which involved over 127,000 workers."[32] Lange insisted on using her camera to testify to workers' struggles to better the conditions of their lives.

FIGURE 9.12   Dorothea Lange, "Undernourished cotton picker's child listening to speeches of organizer at strike meeting to raise wages from seventy-five cents to ninety cents a hundred pounds. Strike unsuccessful," Kern County, California, November 1938.

© FSA/OWI Collection. Prints and Photography Division, Library of Congress. LC-DIG-fsa-8b32810.

The strike, like many, had failed because of growers' political potency. At the local, county, and state level, the nexus between business interests, politicians, police, county sheriffs, and other community leaders such as news publishers, the American Legion, school boards, PTAs, and even local ministry was tight, reaching back to the nineteenth century. Local police suppression, for example, had overwhelmed strikers, particularly when over 100 picketers were jailed in a mass arrest. Growers' control was sometimes codified into law. Criminal syndicalism legislation, often vaguely worded laws prohibiting labor organizing by linking it with sabotage and violence, passed early in the century, and allowed prosecutors to charge strike leaders with breaking the law. Growers could threaten workers with deportation, or have people thrown into jail without booking them, or make sure their bail was too high for release. Workers who didn't comply might have night riders beat them, or be blacklisted, or be thrown out of company housing, or have their water turned off to force them out. Vigilantes paraded, sometimes thousands strong, in shows of force. One WPA writer described growers' willingness to use extralegal violence to sustain control over labor, noting that the California sun, which had brightly reflected the "sparkle" of workers' union buttons, had been "replaced by the glint of rifle barrels." He described the repression, where there was "scarcely a valley in the state that has not echoed to the crackle of rifle fire, or whose fresh air has not been tainted with the acrid fumes of tear gas."[33]

The press typically propagandized against the strikers, taking growers' side. One community paper complained about Mexicans who were able to work the Valley "through our suffarnace, (sic)," and paid ads fomented against "Communists," and agitators, "the viper that is at our door." Papers derided "professional sobbers;" labor activists were "criminals." Major metropolitan dailies' one-sided reports typically ignored grower and vigilante violence.[34]

California's rural valleys were not quite fiefdoms, but neither did they appear like American democracy; workers' civil liberties were not protected by the state. When *The Grapes of Wrath* came out, its exhibition was banned in some communities. Others burned the book given Steinbeck's bleak portrayal of California's agricultural capitalism. The Associated Farmers, California's primary anti-union group, maligned Taylor and Lange as communists. Federal agents even showed up in Taylor's Berkeley office; he found them riffling through his papers. Carey McWilliams called this "farm fascism."[35]

Lange used photography to demonstrate the positive impacts of government care for citizens, another form of collective support. She showed RA/FSA clients who established new cooperative farms with government loans. In February 1936 she visited the El Monte settlement near Los Angeles, taking many photographs of the small settlement of one hundred homes, where residents' rent went toward home ownership.

Each home came with an acre of land. Lange represented a lovely and loved community, with highly idealized shots of a community; in many shots

FIGURE 9.13   Dorothea Lange, "Children at the El Monte subsistence homesteads,"
California, February 1936.

© FSA/OWI Collection. Prints and Photography Division, Library of Congress. LC-USF34-001677-C.

tree branches frame the view much as in early landscape paintings. Residents
worked outside the community at blue- and white-collar jobs; gardens just
outside their doors supplemented their income. Men and women plowed and
hoed crops in Lange's photographs. Children gleefully ran through El Monte's
streets, making them look much like postwar suburban subdivisions, havens
from modern life.[36]

Her study of Kern County demonstrated the range of government aid the
RA/FSA provided. The Arvin Camp in Kern County housed unemployed
migrants, many new to California. Nationally there were some fifty-three
camps, twelve in California.[37] Arvin was an RA/FSA experiment in providing
migrants the most basic of necessities. She and Taylor had been some of these
camps strongest advocates. Lange explored people's living situations in slice-
of-life photographs. There was a community barbershop, and also a nursery.
Those struggling with health problems, like the young tubercular mother who
had no previous recourse, received RA/FSA-funded medical services. Women
crowded the communal sinks in the "women's laundry" on the exterior of the
newly constructed camp building, their backs curved over their efforts. Lange's

many panoramic shots of the migrant camp were unusual for a photographer known for her probing portraits. Her photograph of Arvin's playground displayed the camp's perimeter, set on a dusty square of land. Lange stood far from the children playing on swings, pushing a tetherball, or just horsing around. Their bodies at play, poised to push the ball or mount a swing, broke the stark environment's monotony. Her bird's-eye view of their play suggested a society in miniature that liberated the children from the tight confines of jalopy, tent, or worse, work in the fields.[38]

Lange's more familiar close-ups arrested; they showed migrants building their community with care. In one, an elderly woman with a weather-beaten face and wisps of hair escaping her bun gathers two tow-headed young boys close to her ample front. Her gentle clasping of her grandchildren signals love; they are two of twenty-two. In another photo, three lanky young men hang out under the eaves of Arvin's community center. They sport the slight scowls of adolescence. One cuts the hair of a young boy sitting on a barrel atop a chair. The man brushes the boy's neck; here too, Lange exhibits everyday nurturance. Photos of the first aid center and nursery show young mothers and a dozen toddlers overflowing out of their entryways. This image forces viewers to consider what had brought the children there, what conditions they had contended with, and what would become of them.[39] Lange's Kern County RA/FSA migrant camp photos emphasize community members, playing, grooming, and caring for one another, not individuals facing indifference. In contrast to those lost on the road, or stuck in ditchwater camps, residents recreated home. She showed the Mothers Club meetings organized to purchase kerosene collectively to bring prices down; residents sought control over their lives. One man remembered the Arvin camp from his childhood, and its director, Tom Collins, which *The Grapes of Wrath* immortalized. The man's family had made their way from Oklahoma once his mom had died, their crops withered from lack of water, and their father could no longer trap skunk skins to make a living. He described passing through the Tehachapi Mountains and finding the wonder of a California valley filled with oranges, grapes, and alfalfa. At Collins' camp, they enjoyed dances, pie suppers, organized sport, and organized religion.[40]

Lange's photos also featured RA/FSA public health initiatives, which pioneered health care strategies we take for granted today, such as preventative health care, primary care physicians who direct patients to more specialized care, and the use of physicians' assistants, nutritionists, and social workers. The RA/FSA's Mothers Health Clubs provided pre- and post-natal care.[41] These programs served nearly a million people. Lange's photos documented fathers and mothers bringing their children in for well-baby visits. Others brought their elderly parents, who still worked the fields. These elders were broken. In many of the photos, the nurses minister to the sick, garbed in their gleaming white uniforms and snappy white high heels, in contrast to the barefoot mothers with their

FIGURE 9.14 Dorothea Lange, "Young migrant mother with six week old baby born in a hospital with aid of Farm Security Administration (FSA). She lives in a labor contractor's camp near Westley, California. 'I try to keep him eatin' and sleepin' regular like I got him out of the hospital,'" April 1939.

© FSA/OWI Collection. Prints and Photography Division, Library of Congress. LC-USF34-019486-E.

barefoot babies in their tattered, grimy clothing. A young mother from Stanislaus County told Lange, "I try to keep him eatin' and sleepin' regular like I got him out of the hospital." The woman was all dressed up in a ruffled dress and shoes and socks, her baby also in bright white clothing and knitted booties. But Lange also included in the shot the headboards of a crib, just sitting on the dirt floor, the bed leg stuck in a coffee can tin to keep pests away.[42] But it was the mother's commitment that mattered. Like many of Lange's subjects, and like many of the camp residents, their inner strength might get them through, if other citizens' support was available.

While employed at the RA/FSA, and then briefly for the Bureau of Agricultural Economics (BAE), Lange championed the positive effects that government could have upon U.S. citizens. In her photographs of government-sponsored migrant camps, grant-supported coops, and health care initiatives, she detailed how the government's reinvention, its commitment to ensuring

Americans' freedom from want, could make a positive difference in citizens' lives. As Roosevelt argued in his 1941 State of the Union address, sometimes referred to as the Four Freedoms speech:

> The basic things expected by our people of their political and economic systems are simple. They are: Equality of opportunity for youth and for others. Jobs for those who can work. Security for those who need it. The ending of special privilege for the few. The preservation of civil liberties for all. The enjoyment of the fruits of scientific progress in a wider and constantly rising standard of living.

FDR's New Deal had dramatically broken from a nation-state unwilling and structurally unable to ensure its citizens' security, to one that pushed for equal opportunity, and promoted a basic standard of living for many. Lange helped to build the nation's new welfare state by showing other Americans how very necessary such care and security was. She publicized how it could be achieved, and nowhere more so than in California.

But Lange insisted on reminding Americans of California's underside, despite New Deal efforts. She increasingly represented California's agriculture's industrial nature. Her photographs of sugar beet harvesting by the major San Francisco corporation, Spreckels, had its beet processing factory spanning the horizontal line; the factory weighed down upon the earth.[43] Another shot that Lange took in the Salinas Valley showed the crop rows and furrows marked by tractor tires. Lange stood far above the fields, which seemed to reach into the sky. The photograph disoriented because of Lange's unusual vantage and the uneven horizon line. Lange pushed viewers to see California's "large scale, commercial agriculture" as something alien, less connected to human life. And her captioning reminded viewers of agricultural monopoly, that a single county and a handful of growers accounted for nearly half the lettuce consumed in the U.S.

She reminded viewers of the labor segmentation growers used to limit solidarity among workers, the "large, landless and mobile proletarian," putting Mexican and Filipino Americans in the fields, while white women packed the food. These agricultural workers remained exempt from many of the New Deal's labor protections as California growers, like Southern Democrats, resisted their provision. Not only was child labor exempt, but agricultural workers received no Social Security, no Unemployment Insurance, no minimum wage, nor any limits on their hours. Taylor believed that California had never answered for itself a question posed as early as 1874, when it first experimented with exploiting foreign labor. "What sort of rural society did Californians want for themselves, family farmers, or vast plantations worked by a rural helotry?"[44]

Lange's 1940 photo for the Bureau of Agricultural Economics, "Between Weedpatch and Lamont, Kern County, California. Children living in camp" posed

FIGURE 9.15 Dorothea Lange, "Large scale, commercial agriculture. This single California county (Monterey) shipped 20,096 car lots of lettuce in 1934, or 45 percent of all car lot shipments in the United States. In the same year 73.8 percent of all United States car lot shipments were made from Monterey County, Imperial Valley, California (7,797 car lots) and Maricopa County, Arizona (4,697). Production of lettuce is largely in the hands of a comparatively small number of grower-shippers, many of whom operate in two or all three of these Counties. Labor is principally Mexican and Filipino in the fields, and white American in the packing sheds. Many workers follow the harvests from one valley to the other, since plantings are staggered to maintain a fairly even flow of lettuce to the Eastern market throughout the year," Salinas Valley, California, February 1939.

© FSA/OWI Collection. Prints and Photography Division, Library of Congress. LC-USF34-018899.

a similar question. Lange's framing of two young girls looking out at the world and at the viewers is so tightly framed it practically squeezes the subjects. Doors are intended to be walked through, windows to be seen in and out of. Yet these young girls, of about eight and five years old, barely have space to peek through the broken door. Their home, unseen, seemed more a jail than a place of comfort. Viewers cannot engage with them as the girls were largely out of view, paralleling their impoverished circumstances, which cut them off from a full life. The Great Depression pushed the nation to reinvent itself in the 1930s. But that transformation was never complete, even in the nation's garden, even today.

FIGURE 9.16   Dorothea Lange, "Between Weedpatch and Lamont," Kern County, California, April 1940.

© Bureau of Agricultural Economics, National Archives. 83-G-41456.

Notes

1 Sturtevant interview, UCB.
2 "Industrial Relations and Labor Conditions," *Monthly Labor Review* (March 1929): 59; Carey McWilliams, *Factories in the Field* (Boston: Little, Brown and Co., 1939).
3 Lange and Taylor, *American Exodus*, 147.
4 "Spanish Colonization and Californios, 1769–1800s," available at: http://www.calisphere.universityofcalifornia.edu/calcultures/ethnic_groups/subtopic3a.html; and "USDA Census of Agriculture Historical Archive," 1910s, available at: http://usda.mannlib.cornell.edu/usda/AgCensusImages/1910/06/01/1833/41033898v6ch2.pdf.
5 Alan Olmstead and Paul Rhode, "The Evolution of California Agriculture, 1850–2000," in Jerry Siebert, *California Agriculture: Dimensions and Issues* (University of California Giannini Foundation of Agricultural Economics, 2003), available at: http://s.giannini.ucop.edu/uploads/giannini_public/4e/a8/4ea8b9cc-df88-4146-b1ae-e5467736e104/escholarship_uc_item_9145n8m1.pdf; and David Zuckerman, "Seeds of Change: The Beginnings of California Agriculture," at http://www.ebparks.org/Assets/files/Seeds_of_Change_06-01-09.pdf; Hagerty, *Maynard Dixon*, 80, 86.
6 Kevin Starr, *Inventing the Dream: California Through the Progressive Era* (New York: Oxford University Press, 1986), 161.
7 David Vaught, *Cultivating California, Growers, Specialty Crops, and Labor, 1875–1920* (Baltimore, MD: Johns Hopkins Press, 1999) offers a careful study of agricultural labor and the roots of California's corporate agriculture; Starr, *Inventing the Dream,* 134–135.

8 Edward Pessen, *Jacksonian America: Society, Personality, and Politics* (Champaign, IL: University of Illinois Press, 1985 edition); K. Annabelle Smith, "Why the Tomato Was Feared in Europe for More than Two Hundred Years" (June 2013), available at: http://www.smithsonianmag.com/arts-culture/why-the-tomato-was-feared-in-europe-for-more-than-200-years-863735/?no-ist= ; and Nina Teicholz, "How Americans Got Red Meat Wrong," *The Atlantic* (June 2014), available at: http://www.theatlantic.com/health/archive/2014/06/how-americans-used-to-eat/371895/; Gary Kurutz, "California in Color," *California State Library Foundation Bulletin*, no. 99, (2011): available at: http://www.cslfdn.org/pdf/Bulletin99.pdf; John Ott, "Westward Contraction: Maynard Dixon Paints the Great Depression," in Marian Wardle and Sarah Boehme, *Branding the American West* (Norman, OK: University of Oklahoma Press, 2016); Starr, *Inventing,* 143.

9 "Near Shafter California," May 1937, LC-USF34-016533-E, *American Exodus,* 114.

10 Elizaneth Sine, "Grassroots Multiculturalism, Imperial Valley Farm Labor and the Making of Popular Front California from Below," *Pacific Historical Review* 85 no. 2 (2016): 227–254. Guthrie lyrics from "Pastures of Plenty."

11 Paul Taylor, "California Farming: A Review" *Agricultural History*, 42 no. 1 (January 1968), 49–54; Rajani Kanta Das *Hindustani Workers on the Pacific Coast* (Berlin: Walter de Gruyter, 1923); LC-USF34-009929.

12 Raymond Barry, "The Parade of Races in California Agriculture," Federal Writers Project, Oakland, California, 1938, available at: http://content.cdlib.org/view?docId=hb88700929;NAAN=13030&doc.view=frames&chunk.id=div00122&toc.depth=1&toc.id=div00122&brand=calisphere; and USDA agricultural statistics, available at: http://usda.mannlib.cornell.edu/usda/AgCensusImages/1920/Farm_Statistics_By_Race_Nativity_Sex.pdf, 294, 310; and http://usda.mannlib.cornell.edu/usda/AgCensusImages/1930/02/03/1828/03337983v2p3ch7.pdf, 518.

13 Alex Fabros, "When Hilario Met Sally: The Fight Against Miscegenation Laws," *Filipinas Magazine (February 1995)*, available at: http://www.positivelyfilipino.com/magazine/when-hilario-met-sally-the-fight-against-anti-miscegenation-laws; Carlos Bulosan, *America is in the Heart: A Personal History* (New York: Harcourt Brace and Company, 1946), 157.

14 Vaught, *Cultivating California,* 186.

15 Paul Taylor, *Survey Graphic*, January 1933; Paul DiMaggion and Patricia Fernandez-Kelley, *Art in the Lives of Immigrant Communities in the United States* (New Brunswick, NJ: Rutgers University Press, 2010); "Labor and Social Conditions of Mexicans in California," *Monthly Labor Review* (January 1931), 83; Alan Watt, *Farm Workers and the Churches: The Movement in California and Texas* (College Station, TX: Texas A & M University Press, 2010), 25.

16 Stephanie Lewthwaite, "Race, Paternalism, and "California Pastoral": Rural Rehabilitation and Mexican Labor in Greater Los Angeles," *Agriculture History*, 81 no. 1 (Winter 2007); and Zaragoza Vargas, *Crucible of Struggle: A History of Mexican Americans from Colonial Times to the Present* (New York: Oxford University Press, 2011).

17 Francisco Balderamma and Raymond Rodriguez, *Decade of Betrayal: Mexican Repatriation in the 1930s* (Albuquerque, NM: University of New Mexico Press, 2006), 67–82 and 149–151.

18 *Collier's* quote from 1922, in Barry; "Child Labor in California," Ted Landphair, "Weedpatch Dust Bowl Memories," Voice of America (2011) available at: http://blogs.voanews.com/tedlandphairsamerica/2011/08/24/weedpatch-dust-bowl-memories/.

19 LNG35066.1.

20 Reid Maki, *Children in the Fields: America's Hidden Child Labor Problem in The World of Child Labor: An Historical and Regional Survey*, Hugh Hindman, ed. (New York: Routledge, 2009).

21 James Gregory, *American Exodus: The Dust Bowl Migration and Okie Culture in California* (New York: Oxford University Press, 1991), 89, 66; John Steinbeck, *Harvest Gypsies,* (Berkeley, CA: Heyday Books, 2002), *xi*; Michael Grey, "Dustbowl, Disease and the New Deal: The Farm Security Administration Migrant Health Programs, 1935–1947," *Journal of the History of Medicine,* 48 (January 1993): 3–39; and James Hamilton "Common Forms for Uncommon Actions," *American Journalism,* 16 no. 1 (1999): 79–103.

22 Hamilton, "Common Forms," 91.

23 Gregory, *American Exodus,* 80, 95–98; Steinbeck, *Harvest Gypsies,* xii.

24 Federal Writers Project, Oakland, California, "Child Labor in California Agriculture, 1938 at http://content.cdlib.org/view?docId=hb88700929;NAAN=13030&doc. view=frames&chunk.id=div00001&toc.depth=1&toc.id=&brand=calisphere; Steinbeck, *Harvest Gypsies,* 48.

25 Steinbeck, *Harvest Gypsies,* 34.

26 *Ibid.,* 30.

27 "Billboard along U.S. 99 behind which three destitute families of migrants are camped." Kern County, California, November 1938, LC-USF34-018619-C; Lange and Taylor, *American Exodus,* 141.

28 Barry, "Oriental and Mexican Labor Unions and Strikes in California," available at: http://content.cdlib.org/view?docId=hb88700929;NAAN=13030&doc. view=frames&chunk.id=div00092&toc.depth=1&toc.id=div00092&brand=calisphere&query=undercut; Sine, "Grassroots Multiculturalism"; Howard Dewitt, "the Filipino Labor Union: The Salinas Strike of 1934," *Amerasia,* 5 no. 2 (1978).

29 Dewitt, "Filipino Labor," 6, 11, 15; Anne Loftis' *Witness to the Struggle: Imagining the 1930s California Labor Movement* (Reno, NV: University of Nevada Press, 1998), 10, 12, 27.

30 Hamilton, "Common Forms;" Lange to Stryker, October 13, 1938, FSA.

31 Lange's caption, LC-USF34-018379-E; Devra Weber, *Dark Sweat, White Gold: California Farm Workers, Cotton, and the New Deal* (Berkeley, CA: University of California Press 1994), 153–161.

32 Lange to Stryker, November 7, 1938, FSA; Weber, *Dark Sweat;* Sine, "Grassroots," 7.

33 Paul Taylor, "Documentary History of the Strike of the Cotton Pickers in California," in *On the Ground in the Thirties* (Layton, UT: Gibbs Smith, 1983), 73–92; Steinbeck, *Harvest Gypsies,* 37; Barry, "The Parade of Races," 1.

34 Taylor, "Documentary History," 168; Gregory, *American Exodus,* 95; Loftis, *Witness,* 23, 29.

35 Taylor interview; McWilliams, *Factories,* 230.

36 LC-USF34-001676; LC-USF34-001675; LC-USF34-T01-001712.

37 Hamilton "Common Forms."

38 LC-USF33-015328-M1; LC-USF34-009899-E; LC-USF34-T01-001890-C; LC-USF33-015326-M1.

39 LC-USF34-009899-E; LC-USF33- 015327-M2.

40 LC-USF33-015327; LC-USF34-018532-E; Landphair, "Weedpatch Dust Bowl."

41 Grey, "Dustbowl Disease."

42 LC-USF34-019495-E.

43 LC-USF34-019386-C.

44 Starr, *Inventing the Dream,* 174.

10

"WOMAN CAN CHANGE BETTER'N A MAN"

Women in the Great Depression, 1929–1940

In her files, Lange kept a Shakespeare quotation that idealized women's traditional caretaking role. "Good grows with her; in her days every man shall eat in safety, under his own vine, what he plants, and sing the merry songs of peace to all his neighbors." In this quotation, the world spools out from women; they engender life and peace. Toward her life's end, Lange meditated upon women's lives. She organized an exhibition and book, *Dorothea Lange Looks at the American Country Woman*, about the "women of the American Soil." She celebrated rural women, "not our well-advertised women of beauty and fashion," but rather "*themselves* a very great American style." She concluded the book with a portrait of Arkansas's Mom Conroy, who raised twelve children, half of whom had died, and not one of whom had prospered. Lange's women were survivors; the majority appeared to be over sixty years old. Lange linked these women's perseverance to community, religion, and life, through gardening, food preparation, and child rearing, processes of recreation and reproduction. For Lange, women were taproot to the nation.[1]

Lange's camera dignified women's labor, but *American Country Women*, as many Lange photographs, held up the maternal figure as an ideal, aligned with the larger culture's embrace of motherly caring during the Depression and afterward. Lange's art furthered that ideology, even as such ideas constricted her life. The Depression crystallized contradictions in women's lives, even exaggerating them, as the economic crisis altered women's demographics: their marriages, fertility and work patterns. Lange herself experienced these contradictions as a worker and mother.

Economic traumas shaped Lange's intimate life, as with many Americans. Marriage rates "fell drastically" in this era, and the age at which women married rose. State-sanctioned love was unaffordable. Unlike Lange and Dixon who divorced, many couples could not afford legal fees, so desertion rates rose. Women had fewer children as well; fertility fell precipitously. One quarter of women never had children during the Depression. Lange likely used contraception as she and Dixon had only two children, and she and Taylor had none. Birth control usage soared in the 1930s, with a six-fold increase in clinics. Abortion was also common, across class, religious and racial lines. Families changed structures in other ways. Many doubled or tripled up to try to get by and other families took in boarders. Some families boarded their children as Lange and Dixon had done. The number of children crowded into institutions like family homes and orphanages increased by half in the Depression.[2]

Lange contended with twentieth-century womanhood's demands and suffered from the whipsaw for women, of whether they could "have it all," work and career, decades before this was articulated, in the 1980s. Yet Lange never advocated feminism, even though she came of age as the first wave of feminism won women the vote and women increasingly worked. She accepted a gender binary that placed domestic and emotional demands on women, and established the home as their sphere of influence. Even as Lange's photographs documented the costs of these gendered burdens, they enshrined these labors as women's.

Lange rarely discussed the difficulties of being a professional woman in America's midcentury and navigating what sociologist Arlie Hochschild today calls the "second shift" of unpaid domestic labor. As we saw in Chapter Three, Lange believed she could not prioritize her photography as the modernist photographer Paul Strand had. Instead, her job as a wife was to keep things "smooth and happy," the emotional and domestic labors assumed to be woman's work. Lange's second husband embraced her professional commitments and promoted her career, but Lange retained responsibility for domestic labors as Taylor's 1970 oral history with Susan Reiss betrays.

Taylor: After we were married… there were family situations to face. There were the children of two families… it was not altogether easy.

Riess: I am thinking of… the difference between the situation of the two of you on the road as a team, and then when you come home, it is not a team any more because one member of the team…

Taylor: … has to do the cooking.

Riess: … is harnessed to the house…

Taylor: … not a liberated woman. [laughter]

By 1970 feminism had again politicized domestic labor. Aware of the inequalities of having one partner be solely responsible for this labor, Taylor minimized her work. She "wasn't free as a bird," but he rationalized this by complimenting her "unbelievable" and "marvelous" handling of personal relationships.[3] But Taylor may have been rewriting the consequences of his inattention. Motherhood challenged Lange; she was in equal measure devoted and stern and controlling. This was how she had been raised by her grandmother; her mother she thought too soft. Lange used emotional pressure to get the children to behave. The eldest, Daniel, ran away and had trouble with the law, her son John believed her distant, and a permanent rupture transpired with Taylor's daughter Kathy, whose hostility festered as it had with Consie, Maynard Dixon's daughter. The anger could explode. Daniel remembers even the quiet Taylor knocking him down after Daniel verbally attacked his mother. But the children's clamor generally did not discomfort Taylor, who could nap, work, or retire to his nearby office. Lange built a world-famous artistic reputation while retaining responsibility for the home and childrearing.

Gender shaped Lange's most crucial photographic subject. She made visible the invisible, women's poverty. Writer Meridel LeSueur described women's hidden poverty in a style she called "reportage," fictional accounts so close to the truth that they paralleled journalistic accounts and documentary photographs. In "Women on the Breadlines," LeSueur wrote:

> It is one of the great mysteries of the city where women go when they are out of work and hungry. There are not many women in the bread line. There are no flop houses for women as there are for men, where a bed can be had for a quarter or less. You don't see women lying on the floor at the mission in the free flops. They obviously don't sleep in the jungle or under newspapers in the park.

One is reminded of Lange's many photos of breadlines, of "White Angel Breadline," or her photos showing men sleeping on sidewalks and in parks like bundles of rags spit out by the economy. Her men ranged against buildings, and squatted in fields and street corners with nowhere to go. Her "Line Up at Social Security in Early Days of the Program, 1937" showed a crowd of men from above, illuminated by the shafts of light. Dozens of men and not a single woman.[4]

But Lange did picture the Depression's other victims, women and children, white, black, and Latino and she communicated women's particular distress. In her 1934, "A Sign of the Times, Mended Stockings, Stenographer," a woman's feet are placed on a dusty, wooden floor. Her leather, braided, Mary Jane pumps grab attention. Though fashionable and snappy, they, like the floor, were dingy and scuffed. The woman's stockings were mended straight up the shin of each leg, but they run in either direction of the repairs. Despite her best efforts, the Depression marked this woman's self-presentation. As LeSueur wrote:

> A woman will shut herself up in a room until it is taken away from her, and eat a cracker a day and be as quiet as a mouse so there are no social statistics concerning her… a woman will do this unless she has dependents, will go for weeks verging on starvation, crawling in some hole, going through the streets ashamed, sitting in libraries, parks, going for days without speaking to a living soul like some exiled beast, keeping the runs mended in her stockings, shut up in terror in her own misery.[5]

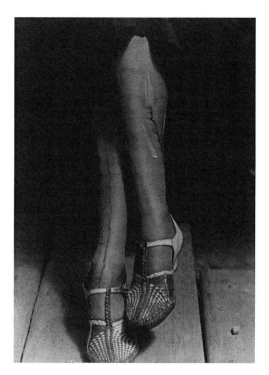

FIGURE 10.1   Dorothea Lange, "A sign of the times—Depression—mended stockings—
stenographer," circa 1934.

© The Dorothea Lange Collection, the Oakland Museum of California. Gift of Paul S. Taylor.

In LeSueur's view, women could make no demands of their families or of the
state. Lange's photo, in a few feet of a woman's legs, articulates the gendering
of poverty, the misery that was uniquely female, the stockings that could not
be mended.

Lange's portraits of women did not objectify them as in popular culture; they
are a people weighted down, yet persisting. Nettie Featherston, the gaunt, angu-
lar Texan who Lange quoted as saying, "If You Die, You're Dead, That's All," or
her "Ex-slave with a Long Memory" show women flayed by circumstances, and
yet they stood tall. Lange's 1937 shot of the latter, an Alabaman who clutched a
stick with both hands, and stared out pitilessly at the fields around her, was living
monument to African Americans' trauma and a nation's disgrace. She was a sur-
vivor; the woman appeared ethereal yet rooted. Lange's "Damaged child" offered
a youth so coruscated by circumstances her eyes burn right into the viewer, even
today. Similarly, Lange's photographs of farmer Chris Adolph's daughter, pinned
against a barbed wire fence, as her mother looks on, seemingly powerless to alter
her or her daughter's life circumstances, haunts. But other photographs show bur-
dened women, attentive, pensive, considering. "Ruby from Tennessee" depicted

FIGURE 10.2   Dorothea Lange, "Ex-slave with a long memory," Alabama, 1937.

© The Miriam and Ira D. Wallach Collection of Art, Prints and Photographs, New York Public Library, NYPL 1615148.

the daughter of a coal miner who had come to Sacramento, California's outskirts with her parents and five siblings. Ruby's family had traveled much of the state, picking grapes, walnuts, and timbering, before returning to Tennessee, and then back to the Golden State where they worked in canning. Lange took several portraits of Ruby. In some she looks abject, as if her circumstances are too much. But in another, she gazed directly at the viewer, as if to inquire, "Why am I here; why are we here?" Her gaze challenges. Though unhappy, she was not a victim.

Lange's women worked the fields, bought provisions at company stores, attended church services, hung laundry, nursed the sick, displayed their home canning, canned in industrial sheds, and cooked Sunday supper in a dugout base-ment home. Her women kept RA/FSA loan accounts and said grace over sup-per. Barefoot Southern women, black and white, sat on their porches. But Lange often captured women on the road with no home at all. Some were forced to pull water for washing out of muddy ditches, others cooked by the side of the road, their lone protection the giant billboards of consumer culture flanking the roads. She showed women washing dishes in the backs of cars, and behind govern-ment organized migrant camps. Lange's photography is so powerful because its representation of female and familial poverty strikes at the heart of the American

FIGURE 10.3 Dorothea Lange, "Child living in Oklahoma City shacktown," or "Damaged child," August, 1936.

© FSA/OWI Collection. Prints and Photography Division, Library of Congress. LC-DIG-fsa-8b38490.

Dream that suggested Americans could always remake themselves. With little food, cleanliness, or shelter, that re-creation was near impossible.[6]

And then there were the women who appeared unfazed by the Depression's ravages. A woman in an elegant white dress carefully held her daughter's hand as they crossed a ditch on broken planks. One mother and family living in a carrot pickers' camp swept her dirt floor of refuse, leaving behind the dirt and dust. Women wore their best smiles and best clothes; some had no other option. One mother in a sprightly dress, scuffed white shoes and black hat sat on her lone luggage; her child crouched next to her as another, barefoot, suckled at her breast. Her husband stood, sharp white shoes facing the road, while his shirt billowed behind him. They looked young and restless and cool, like Bonnie and Clyde with kids, youngsters on the road. But this couple had lost their car on the way westward.[7]

Many Lange subjects suckled their children before the camera eye. Breastfeeding was the most common way of providing nourishment to babies, unless women were so malnourished that their milk ran out. These women broke the boundaries of the private sphere as the economic crisis tossed people willy-nilly. In one popular Lange photo, "Drought refugees from Oklahoma camping by the roadside.

FIGURE 10.4   Dorothea Lange, "One of Chris Adolph's younger children," Yakima, Washington, August 1939.

© FSA/OWI Collection. Prints and Photography Division, Library of Congress. LC-DIG-fsa-8b34383.

They hope to work in the cotton fields," Lange showed the harsh California light crowding into the frame, evoking the relentless heat. The young woman's thin breast pokes out at her child, who also looks at us. Her stony expression was at odds with her act of feeding the child, or was it? Mothering in these circumstances required an indomitable will. Women were to belong at home, in nineteenth-century ideology, but as Lange's photos showed, women's vulnerability, their very bodies, entered public view in the Depression.[8]

One Lange photo more than any other promoted the maternalist ideal. "Migrant Mother," considered "the most reproduced image in the world" has become the symbol of the Depression for many Americans.[9] The photograph showed a woman, holding tightly to her baby as two young, bob-haired daughters averted their faces and rested their heads on the mother's shoulders." Its Library of Congress caption is: "Destitute pea pickers in California. Mother of seven children. Age thirty-two. Nipomo, California." Lange took seven photographs of her in March 1936. In the most acclaimed, the mother gazed off into an unknowable, perhaps unendurable future, the hand at her chin a gesture of self-support. Lange claimed her photo of Florence Owens Thompson, "had a life of its own," making

FIGURE 10.5   Dorothea Lange, "Drought refugees, Ruby from Arkansas," 1935.

© FSA/OWI Collection. Prints and Photography Division, Library of Congress. LNG35201.1.

it "her picture, not mine." Roy Stryker, said "Migrant Mother was "*the* picture of Farm Security." He wrote, "she has all the suffering of mankind in her but all of the perseverance too." "Migrant Mother" demonstrated Lange's ability to visually calculate the Depression's personal and social costs.

Lange described taking "Migrant Mother." Late on a cold, rainy winter afternoon, Lange was driving home to Berkeley. She had been alone for a month, on the road, working. As she passed through Nipomo on the coast, she "barely saw a crude sign with pointing arrow which flashed by me at the side of the road, saying PEA-PICKERS CAMP." Her family beckoned and her cameras were already packed, so she continued for another twenty miles. Still the sign nagged at her. She decided she must see what was there, so she turned around. Lange found the mother and her children huddling under a filthy canvas held up by several poles. They lacked even a tent. The lone furniture was a bent-hickory rocking chair and a suitcase as their table. The mother sat on a cardboard box. There was no picking and the family had stalled in the camp. They subsisted on peas gleaned from the fields and birds they killed. Lange recollected:

> I do not remember how I explained my presence or my camera to her, but I do remember she asked me no questions. I made five [actually seven]

FIGURE 10.6 Dorothea Lange, "Example of self-resettlement in California. Oklahoma farm family on highway between Blythe and Indio. Forced by the drought of 1936 to abandon their farm, they set out with their children to drive to California. Picking cotton in Arizona for a day or two at a time gave them enough for food and gas to continue. On this day, they were within a day's travel of their destination, Bakersfield, California. Their car had broken down en route and was abandoned," August 1936.

© FSA/OWI Collection. Prints and Photography Division, Library of Congress. LC-DIG-fsa-8b38486.

exposures, working closer and closer from the same direction. I did not ask her name or her history. She told me her age, that she was thirty-two... There she sat in that lean-to tent with her children huddled around her, and seemed to know that my pictures might help her, and so she helped me. There was a sort of equality about it.[10]

Because the photograph resonated with the American public, we know much more about Thompson today than Lange learned in 1936. Born Florence Leona Christie in an Oklahoma teepee in 1903, Thompson was part Cherokee or Choctaw. At seventeen, Thompson married and moved to California. The young couple might have picked peaches, or worked in saw mills, or picked cotton. Such murkiness matches the realities of those confronting job insecurity. Her husband died in 1931 from tuberculosis or Valley Fever. The family, mother and six children, had to burn everything he touched. Thompson's affair with a local

FIGURE 10.7 Dorothea Lange, "Drought refugees from Oklahoma camping by the roadside. They hope to work in the cotton fields. The official at the border (California-Arizona) inspection service said that on this day, August 17, 1936, twenty-three car loads and truck loads of migrant families out of the drought counties of Oklahoma and Arkansas had passed through that station entering California up to 3 o'clock in the afternoon," August 1936.

© FSA/OWI Collection. Prints and Photography Division, Library of Congress. LC-DIG-fsa8b38480.

businessman and resulting pregnancy led the family to return to Oklahoma. But soon they came back, to California and to migrancy. When Lange encountered them, Thompson had a new husband and seven children. Thompson arranged for fieldwork, each day from sunup until sundown, and cooked the children's meals afterward. She out-picked most men, picking four to five hundred pounds of cotton each day, even though she weighed less than a hundred pounds. The children had no toys, only sticks, dirt clods, and rocks. They were repeatedly pulled out of school as they moved, one daughter some fifty times before eighth grade. Thompson's identity became known in 1978 when a California reporter sought her out. They had felt shamed by the photo, considering it "a bit of a curse." But many Americans wrote to the family of how powerfully the image had touched them. Increasingly, they felt pride. On Thompson's tombstone, the family inscribed "Migrant Mother—A Legend of the Strength of American Motherhood."[11]

FIGURE 10.8   Dorothea Lange, "Destitute Pea Pickers, Mother of Seven Children," Nipomo, California, or "Migrant Mother," 1936.

© FSA/OWI Collection. Prints and Photography Division, Library of Congress. LC-USF34-T01-009058-C.

In its time the photograph's effect was near immediate. Its publication in the *San Francisco News* led to channeling some $20,000 in food and aid for the camp. The *News's* editor applauded the "Nipomo Agricultural Workers" story and Lange's "exceptional photography," writing her that they made a "splendid argument for the Federal Resettlement Administration camps." Taylor credited the photograph with consolidating California support for establishing camps for new migrant labor.[12] *Survey Graphic* published "Migrant Mother" in September with the caption "Draggin'-Around People" and the *Mid-Week Pictorial,* a national photomagazine printed the photograph, asking readers to, "Look into Her Eyes."[13] "Migrant Mother" also appeared in *U.S. Camera,* and in their sponsored exhibition of 1936's best photographs, which toured the U.S. and Europe.[14] "Migrant Mother" was beginning to attain iconicity.

"Migrant Mother" has become widely recognized, redrawn and redeployed for many purposes: political, aesthetic, and even commercial. She sported the cover of the Venezuelan women's magazine *Bohemia* for Mother's Day, and was repurposed for a 1972 Black Panther newsletter, drawn as a modern black mother with an Afro, holding tight to her children. She has appeared on the cover of a country album, and on a U.S postage stamp. Postmodernists have appropriated her image, remaking her as celebrity Paris Hilton or a Star Wars Clone Trooper. British woodcarvers have whittled her image, and "Migrant Mother" inspired Marisa Silver's 2013 novel, *Mary Coin*.[15] Eighty years after Lange took the photograph, it still provokes.

The photo became iconic for many reasons: its evocation of the Western tradition of Madonna and child as seen in painting and sculpture such as Michelangelo's Pietà; its universal exploration of "human heartbreak," read in the mother's apprehensive expression; and its embodiment of the tensions between distress and resilience that marked Americans' ambiguous relationship to the Depression. The mother is careworn, her children vulnerable. But the mother appears unyielding, and the children find comfort in her. Viewers also find comfort in her stoicism. Her placement in the two-dimensional photograph thrusts her forward, toward us. We cannot look away. Even Roy Stryker, who knew Lange's work so well later said: "I still get that picture out and look at it… So many times I've asked myself what is she thinking?" Viewers want to understand what the family experienced.[16]

"Migrant Mother" was only one of Lange's many images that promoted the concept of maternalism to great effect. In her 1940 photograph of a migrant laborer in Arizona for the Bureau of Agricultural Economics, she showed an African American woman who looked probingly and joyously at her child, who lay in her arms in restful sleep. The mother's embrace cushioned her from outside social burdens; the baby was protected. In another photograph of a homeless mother of seven who was walking from Phoenix to San Diego, the mother seemed dazed. Though dressed in a glamorous fur-collared coat, her anguish was evident, yet she clutched her child. They each drew support from one another.[17]

Lange's photographs celebrated motherhood, even as the Depression upended traditions with more women joining the job market over the 1930s. As a New York City working girl and then sole proprietor of a portrait studio, Lange had typified revolutionary shifts in gender roles and labor. Single women characterized women's move to waged work from 1870 to 1920, after which married women led the charge.[18] Consequently, when Lange married in 1920, she participated in another historic economic shift. But working women were still irregular. Twenty percent of women over ten years old worked in 1920, and one quarter in 1940. In contrast, eighty percent of men worked. Most women worked in domestic service or manufacturing. Only one in eight of employed women were professionals, primarily school teachers, music teachers, and nurses. As a working wife and a professional photographer, Lange was highly atypical.[19]

Lange struggled as a worker. She had established a thriving portrait business, but government assignments required integrating herself within a larger bureaucracy, which Lange found trying. RA/FSA administrators seemed to distrust a woman. Roy Stryker, Lange's boss, had a hectoring tone with many of his employees, but Lange's requests seemed to particularly anger him. A 1952 interview with Lange, Russell Lee, Arthur Rothstein, and Stryker was telling. Lange pushed at the men

FIGURE 10.9 Dorothea Lange, "Migrant cotton picker and her baby," near Buckeye,
Maricopa County, Arizona, November 1940.

© Bureau of Agricultural Economics, National Archives. 522540.

to consider the documentary legacy; she sought something tangible. They instead
relaxed and discussed the RA/FSA photography project, deprecating her desire
for something more. Miss Lange, as she was referred to in the transcript, could
never be one of the boys.[20]

The Depression provoked shifts in women's employment patterns. Light
industry, such as electronics, clothing, or food processing, that employed higher
levels of women, recovered more quickly than a male-dominated industry like
steel. Employers also kept women on because their labor costs were lower; they
paid women less. More married women found jobs; their numbers increased by
fifty percent in the 1930s. And one-third of all working married women were
their family's sole breadwinners. But racism shaped these labor patterns, further
injuring black women workers. As more white women worked, they pushed
black women out of factory jobs or out of the job market entirely. Black wom-
en's employment dropped five percent in the 1930s. They were crowded further into fields they already dominated: domestic service and agriculture, where
more than eighty percent worked. Black women's wages were twenty-three
cents to a man's dollar, not even half of what white women earned. Unemployed
black and Latina women had difficulty accessing New Deal services if they

could not work; county officials often rejected them for immediate relief they were eligible for.[21]

Perversely, as women entered the labor market for survival, Americans disparaged their paid work and embraced the gendered binary prioritizing married men's work. George Gallup, whose opinion polls were new in the mid-1930s, argued that eighty-two percent of Americans (and seventy-nine percent of women) thought married women should not work. Only opposition to "sin and hay fever" was as high. Censure came in many forms: shaming women for taking jobs from men, legislating against women working, and reasserting that women's maternal role was her most important social role. Magazines published articles entitled, "You Can Have my Job: A Feminist Rediscovers Her Home," or "The New Woman Goes Home." "Working Wives and Others' Bread" appeared in *Literary Digest*, its glib title implying the illegitimacy of women's work. Women took "others' bread;" they had no rights to wages or the fruits of their labor. Even women's advocates shamed women. The President of Barnard College told graduates they should have the "courage to refuse to work for gain." Frances Perkins, then New York State's Industrial Commissioner, who became the first woman to hold a U.S. cabinet position as Secretary of Labor, chided college women whose desire for "pin money" took jobs from men or working women. One New York Assemblyman called working wives "undeserving parasites."[22]

Legislators tried to protect male breadwinners, affecting Lange. FDR's Federal Economy Act of 1932 prohibited two married people from working for the federal government. Speaking before the National Women's Party, Civil Service Commissioner Jesse Dell argued "this strange freak of legislation is merely a reaction against the employment of women on the part of men who… still cannot push aside their biased opinions."[23] Other household members, fathers and sons or brothers and sisters, were never prohibited from holding federal jobs. The law reflected prejudices against married women working, as did state and local laws. Just as the ardent feminist, Henrietta Rodham, who had taught at Lange's high school had been fired for not reporting her marriage in the 1910s, many school districts continued to fire mothers well into the 1960s. In the Depression, twenty-six states pushed legislation barring married women from employment. Local school boards were the worst. Seventy-seven percent of school boards would not hire a married woman, and half of the school boards fired women upon marriage. Companies did too. Milton Hershey of the Hershey Chocolate Company fired married women, so workers hid their marriages. And United Auto Worker (UAW) union contracts in the 1930s required that married women be laid off first. Before their marriage, Lange and Taylor wrote each other letters, strategizing in advance about how to work around such limitations. Because Taylor worked for the Social Security Administration, and she worked with the RA/FSA they dodged the federal rule.[24]

Lange deferred to women's traditional role in the "private" sphere as mother and nurturer. Her beliefs, embodied in photographs, paralleled the art of other

Depression-era cultural producers. The 1930s saw a pivot away from the edu-
cated, political, bohemian, or working New Woman, or the sexually-free Jazz
Age flapper. Instead, proletarian fiction, Hollywood movies, and contemporary
art extolled a selfless, nurturing mother who provided stability, as did New Deal
art, particularly government-funded murals, and the RA/FSA photographs.
Hollywood certainly showcased working girls, some foul-mouthed and brazen,
others spunky. But Hollywood also purveyed maternalism, particularly in the
Oscar-winning *The Grapes of Wrath*, adapted from John Steinbeck's novel. Ma
Joad, the story's emotional heart, is distraught at the family's expulsion from
Oklahoma, but kept her family together. Her strength and wisdom sustained
them. Ma Joad fed her family, even mustering enough of a meal to feed the starv-
ing children at the crowded, dismal migrant camp where the Joads landed. Ma
Joad's words ring out in the film's conclusion: "A woman can change better'n a
man… With a woman, it's all in one flow like a stream… That's what makes us
tough… We're the people that live. They can't wipe us out. They can't lick us.
And we'll go on forever… 'cause… we're the people." Ma Joad mixed a call for
the people's survival, with the gendered notion that women are closer to life
due to their biology. Her words articulate Depression-era culture's celebration of
traditional womanhood, tied to maternity, even as women's economic role channeled them in new directions.[25]

"The People" was a populist theme of the 1930s, along with the Forgotten
Man, the Common Man, the Little Guy, and the heroic laborer, almost always a
male figure. The people became a universal symbol for the nation as it resisted
economic tragedy. Public art extolled the workingman and farmers' strength, their
bulging muscles directed toward production even as the economy had crashed.
The female counterpart was the mother who rejected mass consumer culture's
glamorous or sexualized role for women. Murals commissioned by the Treasury
Section of the U.S. government, often for U.S. Post Offices, showed women as
mothers engaged in childrearing, homemaking, or agricultural labors, rarely far

FIGURE 10.10 Harry Sternberg, "The family, industry, and agriculture," Ambler,
Pennsylvania Post Office, 1939.

© U.S. Treasury Department, Section of Painting and Sculpture.

from their home. In one example, "The Family, Industry, and Agriculture" painted by Harry Sternberg for the Ambler, Pennsylvania Post Office, a couple is located in the mural's center, their farm home behind them.[26] They sit on a picnic blanket, a diapered baby in front of them. The mural is equally divided between industry, read as male, and the farm, read as female, tied to the family and the land.

Just as Lange's photographs idealized traditional family roles, the women reformers who helped construct the welfare state built one based on traditional understandings of family and gendered labor. Women's role as moral center and nurturer had been the wedge that allowed women to initiate reform movements in the nineteenth century and later enter the political sphere. Women reformers, black and white, had built careers by caring for others through settlement homes, factory inspection and regulations, union label drives, anti-sweatshop campaigns, and other civic and labor activism. In caring for others, they incrementally built the foundations of the welfare state.

But the federal policies they helped craft in the Depression promoted backward-looking ideals of independent families headed by men (typically white) who did waged work outside the home while women did unpaid emotional and domestic labor inside the home. Reformers imagined women as dependents relying upon a male breadwinner, not economic actors in their own right, or workers who might have dependents. The U.S.'s distinctive welfare system ultimately institutionalized sexism and racism into welfare programs, ensuring that many citizens could not access them, or could only access inferior "needs based" programs such as Temporary Assistance for Needy Families versus entitlements such as Social Security.

Entitlement programs were designed to maintain recipients' "dignity" they were "insurance" programs for those who paid in. Legislators and reformers rationalized the exclusion of women, Latinos, and African Americans by claiming they could not collect from these groups. As Alice Kessler Harris identifies, "These exclusions omitted more than three-quarters of all female wage earners from coverage and about 87 percent of African American women workers," in agricultural and educational institutions, nonprofits, retail, and office work. Women who worked in agriculture, sometimes from daybreak until sunset, or for long days inside someone else's home, were never eligible for unemployment or disability. They were not covered by the Fair Labor Standards Act, which set maximum hours and minimum wages. Nor were they covered by Social Security, which raised millions of white workers out of poverty.[27]

And legislators gave women less. With Social Security, experts testified to policy makers that women just did not need as much as men. Women, legislators believed, could cook, or care for their children's children. In the words of one administrator, she could "adjust herself to a lower budget as… she is used to doing her own housework whereas the single man has to go out to a restaurant." Another said, "the grandmother helps in the raising of the children and helps in home affairs, whereas the aged grandfather is the man who sits on the front porch and can't help much in the home."[28] U.S. welfare programs, disability insurance, unemployment insurance, or Social Security, so miserly in comparison to those of other industrialized nations, imagined a male head of household, whose security must be bolstered. In most developed nations, all citizens had the right to security, men and women.

Lange's photographs must be understood in light of how the Depression reconfigured women's social roles, even as Lange contributed to that reconfiguration. Lange discussed the burden of gender roles, the conflict between her craft and women's labors in her oral history. "I would disappoint my family very much if I devoted myself to photography… My husband… would understand it, but he wouldn't know how to adjust to it, really." Lange did not think herself "ruthless" enough to demand an artist's uninterrupted time. Then she went further, linking her difficulties to a social condition faced by many twentieth-century women.

> I'm not focusing entirely on myself, I'm speaking of the difference between the role of the woman as artist and the man. There is a sharp difference, a gulf… There are not very many first-class woman producers, not many. That is producers of outside things… [Women] produce in other ways… I would like to have one year…just one, when I would not have to take into account anything but my own inner demands.

These are nearly the last words Lange said to her interviewer. She changed the direction of the conversation, ending with, "Today is the first day of autumn. Have you felt it? The summer ended this afternoon at two o'clock. All of a sudden. The air got still, a different smell, a kind of funny, brooding quiet… Can you feel it? And the cracks in my garden are wide." Lange moved from marking women's exclusion from greatness due to their domestic and emotional labors to insisting on her ties to nature, her ability to intuit autumn's entrance. This oblique conclusion, a seeming non-sequitur, "the cracks in my garden are wide" suggests the distance between her caring relationship to the living world and her ability, as a woman, to fully participate in that relationship. As a working woman, she could never care enough, and as an artist, womanhood's demands threatened her very existence.

Notes

1 Lange papers, v. 6, OMCA.
2 On birth rates, National Center for Health Statistics, Vital Statistics, "Table 1-1. Live Births, Birth Rates, and Fertility Rates, by Race: United States, 1909–2000" http://www.cdc.gov/nchs/data/statab/t001x01.pdf; *Historical Statistics,* 64; On children: Dennis Bryson, "Family and Home, Impact of the Great Depression on." *Encyclopedia of the Great Depression*, edited by Robert S. McElvaine, vol. 1 (New York: Macmillan Reference, 2004), 310–315.
3 Taylor interview, 149–152.
4 Meridel Le Seuer, "Women on the Breadline," in *Ripening* (New York: Feminist Press, 1993); LC-USF346-BN-018312, LC-USF34-T01-016147, LC-USF34-016153.

5 *Ibid.*

6 LC-USF34-001619-C; LC-USZ62-50521; LC-USF34- 009995-C.

7 LC-DIG-fsa-8b38487; LC-USF34-021000-E; LC-DIG-fsa-8b33359.

8 Jan Goggans's *California on the Breadlines* informs this chapter. LC-DIG-fsa-8b38480; LC-USF34-T01-009666-E; LC-DIG-fsa-8b38481.

9 See Martha Rosler, "Some notes, in, around, and afterthoughts on documentary photography" from Richard Bolton, ed. *Contents of Meaning: Critical Histories of Photography* (Cambridge: MIT Press); Karen Ohrn, *Dorothea Lange and the Documentary Tradition,* footnote 32 page 329 in Goggans, see Bibliography; Stryker, *Proud Land,* 19.

10 Dorothea Lange, "The Assignment I'll Never Forget," *Popular Photography* (February 1960).

11 "Iconic Dust Bowl Women Florence Owens Thompson Lived in Oroville," (November 2011), at http://www.chicoer.com/20121116/iconic-dust-bowl-woman-florence-owens-thompson-lived-in-oroville/1;Interview with Katherine McIntosh and Norma Rydlewski, by Blackside, Inc., March 9, 1992, for *The Great Depression.* Washington University Libraries, Film and Media Archive, Henry Hampton Collection, Available at: http://digital.wustl.edu/cgi/t/text/text-idx?c=gds;cc=gds;rgn=main;view=text;idno=mci00031.00607.019; Ben Phelan, "The Story of Migrant Mother," available at: http://www.pbs.org/wgbh/roadshow/stories/articles/2014/4/14/migrant-mother-dorothea-lange/; "NBC interview," available at: http://www.today.com/id/51067427/ns/today-books/#.WCenQfkrKUn; Bill Ganzel, *Dust Bowl Descent* includes Thompson audio interview available at: http://www.livinghistoryfarm.org/farminginthe30s/water_06.html); http://www.dailymail.co.uk/news/article-2290879/I-lost-hope-Startling-interview-unearthed-woman-iconic-Great-Depression-image-talking-just-years-death-1983.html#ixzz4PdqsByMM; Geoffrey Dunn, "Photographic License," *Metro: Santa Clara Valley's Weekly Newspaper,* vol. 10 (January 19–25, 1995): 20–24.

12 *San Francisco News* March 10, 1936; clippings, vol. 5, OMCA; Paul Taylor, "Migrant Mother, 1936," *The American West,* 71 no. 3 (1970): 41–45.

13 LC-DIG-ppsca-12901; LC-USZ62-117092; LC-USF34-016105-C.

14 Erika Zerwes, "The Mother from Estremadura and the Idea of a Photographic Icon," *Roots/Routes: Research on Visual Cultures,* available at: http://www.roots-routes.org/?p=13999.

15 Vicki Goldberg, *The Power of Photography: How Photographs Changed Our Lives* (New York: Abbeville Press, 1993), 141;"I never lost hope…," available at: http://www.dailymail.co.uk/news/article-2290879/I-lost-hope-Startling-interview-unearthed-woman-iconic-Great-Depression-image-talking-just-years-death-1983.html; See Sandro Miller on Malkovich, available at: http://www.telegraph.co.uk/photography/what-to-see/john-malkovich-recreates-iconic-photos-by-warhol-bailey-leibovit/migrant-mother-1936-by-dorothea-lange/; John Kroll woodcut, available at: http://www.flickriver.com/photos/tags/migrantmother/interesting/.

16 Stryker and Wood, *Proud Land,* 19.

17 LC-DIG-fsa-8b33233.

18 Claudia Goldin, "The Work and Wages of Single Women, 1870 to 1920," available at: https://dash.harvard.edu/bitstream/handle/1/2643864/Golding_WorkWages.pdf?sequence=2 I.

19 "Working Women in the 1930s," *American Decades,* edited by Judith S. Baughman, et al., vol. 4: 1930–1939, Gale, 2001. *U.S. History in Context,* available at: link.galegroup.com/apps/doc/CX3468301237/UHIC?u=sand55832&xid =4a83ab53. Accessed April 3, 2017; Agnes Peterson, "What the Wage-Earning Woman Contributes to Family Support," *The Annals of the American Academy of Political and Social Science,* 143 Special Edition, "Women in the Modern World" (May 1929): 74–93; and Rebecca Onion, "Vintage Infographics: Where Women Worked in 1920," *Slate,* March 11, 2013,

available at: http://www.slate.com/blogs/the_vault/2013/03/11/women_workers_infographics_show_women_s_employment_in_1920.html.

20 Interview with Roy Stryker at John Vachon's Apartment, 1952, OMCA.

21 Jacqueline Jones, *Labor of Love, Labor of Sorrow: Black Women, Work, and the Family, from Slavery to the Present* (New York: Basic Books, 2009) and Kessler Harris's *Out to Work: A History of Wager Earning Women in the United States* (New York: Oxford University Press, 1982).

22 "New Woman Goes Home," *Scribner's,* February 1937; Agnes Rogers Hyde, "Women Walking on Their Hind Legs, *Harpers* (1931); *Literary Digest,* May 15, 1937; Martha Patterson, *The American New Woman Revisited: A Reader, 1894-1930*; Poppy Cannon, "Pin Money Slaves," *The Forum* (August 1930): 98–103.

23 David Dismore, "Founding Feminists: September 25, 1932," available at: https://feminist.org/blog/index.php/2013/09/25/founding-feminists-september-25-1932/.

24 Carol Quirke, *Eyes on Labor: News Photography and America's Working Class* (New York: Oxford University Press, 2012), 121; Paul Taylor Correspondence, Banc MSS 84/38 c, v. 89, *UCB*; Dorothy Sue Cobble, *The Other Women's Movement: Workplace Justice and Social Rights in Modern America* (Princeton, NJ: Princeton University Press, 2004), 73–75.

25 *The Grapes of Wrath,* Directed by John Ford (Los Angeles: Twentieth Century Fox, 940).

26 Harry Sternberg, "Family, Industry and Agriculture, 1939" in the Living New Deal, available at: https://livingnewdeal.org/projects/post-office-mural-ambler-pa/; Barbara Melosh, *Engendering Culture: Manhood and Womanhood in New Deal Public Art and Theater* (Washington, DC: Smithsonian Institution Press, 1991).

27 http://www.nber.org/bah/summer04/w10466.html; http://www.cbpp.org/research/social-security/social-security-keeps-22-million-americans-out-of-poverty-a-state-by-state.

28 Alice Kessler-Harris, "In the Nation's Image: The Gendered Limits of Social Citizenship in the Depression Era," *Journal of American History*, 86 No. 3 (December 1999): 1251–1262.

11

"THIS IS WHAT WE DID, HOW DID IT HAPPEN, HOW COULD WE?"

Democracy Under Assault, 1940–1945

In 1940, after Lange had left the RA/FSA and she and Taylor published their photo-text, *An American Exodus*, the two bought a dark redwood shingled home in the Berkeley Hills. An oak tree in the new home became Lange's reference point. Its roots reached deep into the soil; its powerful, twisted branches reached out toward their bedroom window. She took many photos of the tree over time; a darkroom assistant later said: "She felt very much part of that tree…she thought the tree understood her." The oak's simplicity and strength mirrored her values. Lange found and furnished the home, making it a work of art. Many windows kept their home bright, and a living room fireplace warmed visitors.

Decorating her home brought Lange joy. She placed driftwood and rocks culled from walks on the Pacific in the garden, and she planted so there were always flowers. The home's exterior was rustic; inside was clean-lined. Lange was ruthless in her austerity; one friend described her "Shaker-like orderliness." She did surround herself with beautiful objects from her voyages and photographic trips. These objects of everyday life were often made by local craftsmen. Their elegant utility spoke to her: bowls, jars, trays, textiles, baskets. Friends never knew what they would encounter when they visited as Lange shifted her decor. Theirs was a lively home, with Lange's sons, and a shifting mixture of Taylor's children. Darkroom assistants dropped by as Lange mentored their careers, and Lange and Taylor frequently entertained. Lange loved to cook from scratch, and guests loved the pleasing atmosphere she created for their meals.[1]

Lange also built herself a studio on the property, close to the house. From the outside, it looked ordinary, a fourteen by twenty-two-foot wood box with windows. Her eldest son Daniel claimed it kept his mother away from "the domestic interruptions which so often conspire to heckle professional ladies clean out of their professions," which acknowledged her work, rather dismissively. Lange's space met her exacting needs. She had windows on two sides, bathing the open studio in light. Photo historian and curator Beaumont Newhall recalled that Lange's studio, like her home, had a board with a constantly changing "show" of famous quotations and a mix of her photos and other evocative images. Newhall said Lange called her studio her "plant." This word suggests multiple relations to her craft. Like a factory plant, her studio was where she produced her work. But her studio was also a place of generation, like a plant that grew under the sun. And like the oak tree she identified with, her self was planted in her studio. Her work was her passion.[2]

As her relationship to the RA/FSA was severed, and other government commissions wound down with the Depression's end, Lange sought new sponsors. She applied for a prestigious Guggenheim grant, one of the most highly sought awards among American artists and academics. In 1941 Lange became the first woman photographer to win the grant; there would not be another for nearly two decades. Lange's grant proposal stated she wanted to photograph "selected rural American communities," exploring their change and continuity and study "the relation of man to the earth and man to man," maintaining her social and environmental interests. Lange planned to focus on religious cooperatives: the Hutterites of South Dakota, the Amanas in Iowa, and the better-known Mormons. Two of the groups, the Hutterites and the Amana Society, shared her German heritage and had strong pacifist roots. As the world moved toward war with Hitler's annexations and invasions in Europe, these peaceful communities, ground in cooperation and the land must have appealed. They expressed humankind's capacity to renew and cherish, not destroy or plunder.[3]

Things did not go as planned. "Depleted" from years of work, and feeling "pushed" by her husband, Lange became disenchanted. The Amana Society's mass-consumer electric refrigerators and washing machines led her to believe they had relinquished their mission. The Hutterites she found "rigid." Despite Lange's assessment, some photos retain much power. Atmospheric photos show Amana farmers in a haze of light settling a nimbus of hay under the clean-lined barn beams. Her photo of a Hutterite Bible offered simple shapes, and the Bible's bright pages in contrast to a door's mysterious darkness evoked a private, contemplative space. Lange sought tranquility and answers in backward-looking, regionally specific cooperative efforts. But the lure of modern life and pressing social turmoil called to Lange more.[4]

And personal troubles pulled her from her project. She, Taylor, and her first husband Maynard Dixon struggled with Dan, who was sixteen. From early adolescence, he ran away. He also stole, taking Lange's top-of-the-line Rollei camera. Lange's troubles with her brother Martin were also severe. Martin had maintained close if tension-laden relations with Lange. He went to sea in the Merchant Marine, traveling the world, but landed near Lange on the West Coast. He worked construction on the Boulder Dam and in the timber industry, but never settled on one job. Martin delighted all around him as he was a great raconteur, drawing on the wealth of his experience, spinning out tales over drinks. In 1941 he was working for California's unemployment bureau, which he and three co-workers defrauded. They were caught. Lange supported her brother as he was jailed for six months and then put on probation for a decade. Lange called this a "serious catastrophe," and she "deserted" her studio for months. World War II altered her plans more significantly.

"Yesterday, on December 7, 1941, a date which will live in infamy, the United States of America was suddenly and deliberately attacked by the naval and air forces of the Empire of Japan." FDR's entrance to the House Chamber of the Capitol was greeted with thunderous applause; across the nation, citizens turned on their radios to hear his address. Americans drew together in the face of their collective shock at Pearl Harbor's trauma, where Japan's air attack killed over two thousand U.S. citizens. Within an hour of Roosevelt's speech, Congress declared war on Japan. War was already raging in Europe. Once Hitler had invaded Poland on September 1, 1939, Great Britain declared war. Appeasing Hitler had failed. The Axis powers, Germany and Italy, in alliance with Japan, declared war on the U.S. The U.S. responded in kind, enmeshing the nation in a global conflict carried out on multiple fronts. It is difficult to comprehend the magnitude of this war, where Nazis killed twelve million in industrially organized death camps and by primitive forms of violence simply because they were Jewish, Gypsy, homosexual, or disabled; where the U.S. dropped two atomic bombs that immediately killed over 100,000, and many more times that in the aftermath; where the world lost over fifty million people in less than a decade. World War II is often remembered as "the Good War," where U.S. citizenry knew its fight was just, but at the time it often seemed as if humanity was staring into an abyss.

Many photographers made their names covering these events. Robert Capa's shots of the June 6, 1944 D-Day landing on Omaha Beach have been immortalized, most recently in Hollywood's *Saving Private Ryan*. AP's Joe Rosenthal showed Marines and Navy soldiers plunging the U.S. flag into a slight rise in his iconic "Raising the Flag at Iwo Jima." *Life* photographer Margaret Bourke-White triumphed against military brass who did not want a woman to cover combat, and documented aerial bombing missions; her photographs of the Buchenwald concentration camp still sear. Lange never left the U.S.; nonetheless, she witnessed how war shapes society by charting the constriction of civil liberties with the mass incarceration of Japanese Americans. She also explored the growth of the West Coast defense industry.

Lange's record of the internment offers an inside look at how war curtails commitments to democracy. Under the perceived pressures of war, leaders have often trod on cherished civil liberties with citizens' acquiescence. Abraham Lincoln suspended the constitutional right of *habeas corpus* during the Civil War; local, state and federal authorities jailed nearly a thousand pacifists and socialists for publicly opposing World War I with U.S. Supreme Court approval; and after September 11, 2001, the U.S. government jailed foreign nationals in Guantanamo claiming they had neither the protection of the U.S. Constitution nor the Geneva Convention. The forced internment of tens of thousands of Japanese Americans during World War II, the vast majority of whom were American-born citizens, was a grave abrogation of the nation's democratic creed. The U.S. detained limited numbers of German and Italian ethnics, but within two days of Pearl Harbor, the U.S. jailed some 1,200 Japanese American leaders who had been placed under surveillance. And on February 19, 1942, two months after Pearl Harbor, FDR signed Executive Order 9066, which allowed the military to exclude "all persons" from a fifty-mile distance from the Pacific Ocean and into Arizona. The government called the centers that it forced Japanese Americans into "assembly centers" and "relocation centers." FDR referred to them as "concentration camps."[5]

Of the 130,000 Japanese Americans who lived on the mainland, some 90,000 resided in California, though they comprised less than two percent of the population.[6] Agriculture was the primary employment for *issei* and their children, the U.S.-born *nisei*. Japanese American knowledge of labor-intensive growing led to their control of markets for fruits and vegetables. Those eating strawberries, tomatoes, celery, or snap peas were likely eating fruit and vegetables farmed by Japanese American hands. They controlled ten percent of California's agriculture by 1920, and in 1941, a third of "commercial truck crops" or farmed vegetables and fruits. Lange had photographed these farmers as "field bosses" over Mexican

FIGURE 11.1   Dorothea Lange, "Japanese mother and daughter," near Guadaloupe, California, March 1937.

© FSA/OWI Collection. Prints and Photography Division, Library of Congress. LC-USF34-016129-C.

American migrant laborers and in Madonna and child-style familial portraits in the fields for the RA/FSA.[7]

Issei and *nisei* were subject to gross discrimination. The ironically named "Gentlemen's Agreement" (1907–8) that restricted Japanese immigration was provoked by white San Franciscans' attempt to segregate Japanese American students from white school children. President Theodore Roosevelt intervened and stopped the segregation, while limiting Japanese immigration. *De facto* discrimination kept Japanese Americans from many jobs. In professions such as medicine, they could only serve their own ethnicity, and exclusion from unions restricted their access to better-paid industrial jobs. Japanese American farm hands were often paid significantly less than white farmers, and they were forced to pay more to rent land. As with African Americans and Mexican Americans, their access to public space and accommodations such as swimming pools or theaters was restricted. One man who tried to get his hair cut at a barbershop described being "drove out…of the place…as if…a cat or dog." Japanese Americans could not buy homes due to restrictive covenants. One family that purchased a home in a white neighborhood was met by protests led not by hooligans but by university professors holding placards against the "Yellow Peril."[8]

De jure discrimination kept Japanese immigrants, like the Chinese before them, from ever becoming naturalized citizens. The Naturalization Act of 1790 restricted U.S. citizenship to "free white persons…of good character." The Fourteenth Amendment and the Naturalization Act of 1870 extended citizenship to former slaves or those of African descent, a redress to their historic exclusion. But white prejudice against Asians led first to the 1875 Page Act, ostensibly intended to protect Chinese women from prostitution, but used to tightly restrict Chinese women's ability to immigrate, and then to the Chinese Exclusion Act of 1882, the first legislation that singled out an ethnic group as impermissible in the body politic.[9] Other Asian immigrants also lacked citizenship protections and security. Takao Ozawa challenged the law's application to Japanese immigrants, but in 1922 the Supreme Court upheld his permanent alien status. The Gentleman's Agreement did allow Japanese women to immigrate to stabilize family life. Many of these women came over as "picture brides" in arranged marriages. Women's labor sustained Japanese American agricultural success. But this immigrant attainment led to further legal restrictions. California passed laws limiting Japanese Americans from buying or leasing land. Laws could be bent or evaded, but from 1909 until the 1930s, no Japanese-born could own farmland; they could only work other people's farms.[10]

Racism and discrimination saturated the West long before war hysteria solidified the move to Japanese American incarceration. As one Los Angeles Chamber of Commerce leader stated in 1921, "It is not a question of whether the Jap is assimilable or not…we do not want to assimilate him." In Hawaii, where Japanese Americans were a third of the population, leaders in government, media, and the armed services insisted on restraint. West Coast leaders, however, fomented panic.

The head of the Western Defense Command, General John DeWitt, called for their "mass removal."[11] A *Los Angeles Times* editorialist compared Japanese Americans to "vipers," loyal to their land of family origin.[12] Media portrayals dehumanized the Japanese as "yellow," "nips," and "japs;" these were the kinder terms. Farmers' organizations openly demanded that "the brown man" be kicked out, so the white man could take over their fields and businesses. The American Legion rallied its members in support of "concentration camps" and a poll of western governors had nine stating: "No Japanese wanted—except in concentration camps." Such hysteria took a toll. In January of 1942 most Americans did not believe Japanese Americans should be restricted, but by March, over ninety percent of Americans thought this policy warranted.[13]

Flouting the Constitution by this major dissolution of civil rights appeared to weigh lightly upon Roosevelt, even though nothing this complex had ever been attempted. U.S. Attorney General Francis Biddle argued against the internment, but FDR favored his Secretary of War's direction and citing "military necessity," he signed Executive Order 9066. The Senate unanimously passed legislation making Japanese American presence in militarily restricted areas unlawful, hence political leadership agreed upon this policy.

General DeWitt of the Western Command controlled the detentions, done on an *ad hoc* basis over time. Though the word internment has often been used to describe these camps, there is much debate about this term, even among Japanese Americans confined within the camps. In legal terms, internment implies aliens who are detained by the U.S. Department of Justice as individuals. But most Japanese Americans were citizens, making this a mass incarceration. Some scholars, like Roosevelt, use the term concentration camps. Other scholars reject the term, believing it evokes German extermination camps where three million were put to death.[14]

The War Department commissioned Lange to document the "largest, single forced migration in American history." Possibly, officials sought to demonstrate their good intentions. More likely, bureaucratic imperatives shaped authority's decision. Since the 1870s Department of Interior western land surveys photographed by Timothy O'Sullivan, William Henry Jackson, and other photographers, the government has used the camera to aid in documentation and categorization. New Deal technocrats intensified photography's use, as did agencies propagandizing for social programs, such as Lange's RA/FSA.[15]

Lange began not long after the order came out. Panic already stalked the Japanese community, as those detained immediately after the war began could not communicate with their families. Officials provided little explanation. One twelve-year-old boy remembers walking his father to the streetcar one morning. The father was detained and transferred to multiple camps in Oklahoma, Louisiana and North Dakota, without the family ever learning his whereabouts. The father died; his son never again saw him. Authorities gave Japanese Americans conflicting information. In Los Angeles, residents of Terminal Island were told they had a month to leave; ten days later, as they packed, they received a directive ordering them to "vacate their homes within two days." General DeWitt next moved to the Washington State's Bainbridge Island. Japanese American farmers had a mere six days to pack everything and dispose of their business affairs. Families were told they could bring nothing more than "bedding, linens, toiletries, extra clothing and dining utensils and plates." Families sold their possessions, businesses, and land at cut rates. Many lost everything and could not recover their livelihoods once they were freed. Children were torn from their schools. Some wrote to their teachers, trying to maintain a close connection to the outside world; others, mere months from graduation, were denied their high-school diplomas.[16]

Lange worked feverishly from March through May, taking a mere three days off as she worked twelve- and fourteen-hour days, attempting to track this tragedy. Lange visited the many towns around San Francisco where Japanese Americans farmed, towns on the bay such as Mountain View, and the hot, inland

FIGURE 11.2 Dorothea Lange, "Family in front of farmhouse, Mountain View, California. Members of the Shibuya family are pictured at their home before evacuation. The father and the mother were born in Japan and came to this country in 1904. At that time the father had $60 in cash and a basket of clothes. He later built a prosperous business of raising select varieties of chrysanthemums which he shipped to Eastern markets under his own trade name. Six children in the family were born in the United States," April 1942.

© War Relocation Authority no. A–60 National Archives. 536037.

valley towns outside of Sacramento and Stockton. Lange showed the prosperous, such as the Shibuya family, who'd arrived in the U.S. with sixty dollars in their pockets and built a flower empire by conveying gorgeous chrysanthemums to the East Coast. Their four eldest had gone to college. When they posed on their lawn in front of their graceful home, they looked more like a televised postwar family from *Father Knows Best* than a family facing evacuation and incarceration.[17] Lange also showed Japanese American field hands enjoying a barbecue before they were forced off the land. One man, his back to the camera, sat on a crate in his empty farmyard, dejectedly smoking a cigarette. Lange's photo of an outdoor clothes line, with gingham and floral-print kimonos waving in the breeze, suggested the Japanese Americans soon to be erased from the fields and from public consciousness. Lange heard one white American parent respond to their child, who asked where they had gone: "They were Japanese... They just disappeared."

Lange perceived the Japanese Americans as ethnically different, but she insisted on their citizenship, highlighting their allegiance to their nation and the cold-hearted racism underpinning the internment. Before she received her government contract, she had taken a photo of a fruit stand owned by a University of

FIGURE 11.3 Dorothea Lange, "Wash day 48 hours before evacuation of persons of Japanese ancestry," San Lorenzo, Santa Clara County, May 1942.

© War Relocation Authority no. C-193, RG 210, National Archives. 1372774.

California graduate. Racial prejudice had ghettoized Japanese Americans like him into small-business ownership. Across much of Wanto and Company's storefront the owner had put in bold letters: "I AM AN AMERICAN." But Lange's photo showed a realtor's sign: the property had already been sold. Lange photographed racist signage: signs saying "We Don't Want JAPS" strung on telephone poles, and bespectacled white American retailers standing behind their cash registers adorned with anti-Japanese notices. She also depicted the evacuation orders. As she later said; "All these proclamations, all over town, on the telephone poles— big proclamations telling the people where to go." Lange visited schools where Japanese American students intermingled with students of other backgrounds, and showed students pledging allegiance to the flag. In one photo, young boys of every nationality and race stood, hands on hearts as one boy held the flag; in another, young girls of all backgrounds pledged. The children were at the age

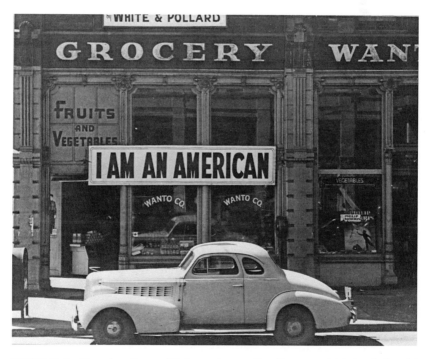

FIGURE 11.4 Dorothea Lange, "A large sign reading 'I am an American' placed in the window of a store, at 401–403 Eighth and Franklin streets, on December 8, the day after Pearl Harbor. The store was closed following orders to persons of Japanese descent to evacuate from certain West Coast areas. The owner, a University of California graduate, will be housed with hundreds of evacuees in War Relocation Authority centers for the duration of the war, Oakland, California," March 1942.

where their front teeth were missing; their broad gleeful smiles showed their human vulnerability.[18]

Lange described witnessing the "process of the processing," the bureaucracy by which tens of thousands of people were forcibly moved, over hundreds of miles, in a few months. She documented the interminable waiting, the "baffled, bewildered people" learning about plans for their evacuation, as fellow Japanese Americans inoculated them, as they met with social workers who directed plans to dispose of their property, and as they waited for transport to a local "assembly center." She described "oceans of desks, with oceans of people with their papers." In her photos, elderly people sat on chairs inside offices and outside their homes. One elderly woman who was missing her teeth sat atop her luggage as her family members wrote to relatives living in Texas. Some looked at the camera appraisingly, others were dazed, their bodies near broken by decades of agricultural labor. In one photo, a young, beautifully coiffed woman in a fetching swing coat looked anxiously down the block. In another context, she could be awaiting her boyfriend. Around many of the photos there was an aura of solemnity and dejection. Once processed, young and old alike would be ticketed, all equalized before the bureaucracy. Like the many photographs Lange took of duffel bags, giant boxes,

FIGURE 11.5 Dorothea Lange, "The Mochida children, tagged like baggage, awaiting evacuation," Hayward, California, May 8, 1942.

© War Relocation Authority, National Archives. 210-G-C155.

sacks, and suitcases, the government, with public support, had reduced individuals to things to be cataloged and moved.

Lange followed the migrants to their first way station, the temporary assembly centers organized by the Wartime Civil Control Administration located just outside major population centers. Lange visited several, in Sacramento, Stockton, and Turlock. In San Bruno, at Tanforan, she caught the long lines of people as they entered. Lange was not allowed to photograph the armed guards who stood on either side, nor the barbed wire encircling the camp. Lange showed peoples' bags as they were inspected; she could not show the men being strip searched. Tanforan had been a racetrack; people were housed in the horse stalls heavy with the acrid odors of urine and manure. Other assembly centers included fairgrounds and stockyards. One photo showed families who had had their belongings flung near muddy ruts on the grasses outside their barracks' doors. Lange noted: "Unfortunately, there have been heavy rains." Some people could not sleep as the odor was so bad; inadequate sewerage contributed to the stench. The camps had little privacy, with their communal bathrooms. Families had two single rooms that were not fully closed off from the rest of the barracks. One room had no

FIGURE 11.6   Dorothea Lange, "Near view of horse-stall, left from the days when what is now Tanforan Assembly center was the famous Tanforan Race Track. Most of these stalls have been converted into family living quarters for Japanese," San Bruno, California, June 1942.

windows; each room was barely bigger than a bed. Single men slept in barracks of three to four hundred. Japanese Americans had no control over their schedules; they were forced to eat meals at pre-established times.[19]

Some, feeling trapped, fell into lassitude. Entertainment consisted of watching other evacuees arrive. Others played basketball, established libraries or nursery schools, or dug gardens. Lange was lucky; she never had to document "Hell's Acre," outside Fresno, where the temperature was recorded at "120 degrees in the shade." Helen Harano Christ remembers walking to the fence with its armed guards walking back and forth, and hearing a snake in the undergrowth. It could slither out. She thought, "that garter snake has a lot more freedom than I do."[20]

The government believed these assembly or "reception centers" were inadequate to the task of containing Japanese Americans, so the military, under the War Relocation Authority, established ten permanent camps in inhabitable spots across Arkansas, Colorado, Arizona, Wyoming, Utah, Idaho, and California. Lange went to Manzanar in California, where she covered the camp's initial settling.

FIGURE 11.7 Dorothea Lange, "Third grade students working on their arithmetic, Manzanar Relocation Center," Manzanar, California, July 1942.

Manzanar is in high, cold desert, nothing but snow peaked mountains, sky, sage brush, cactus, and scrubby trees. Lange remembered "the meanest dust storms there and not a blade of grass;" the interned recalled dust so thick that they could not breathe. Lange described cruel spring winds, and "when those people arrived they couldn't keep the tarpaper on the shacks," the gusts blew them down. Manzanar's location provided natural barriers circumscribing the lives of the internees, but armed guards were still stationed in guard towers, and the barracks were surrounded by five lengths of barbed wire.

Manzanar detained ten thousand, nearly ninety percent from Los Angeles. The government allotted these urban dwellers a twenty by twenty-foot room, with a stove for each family. They were given army cots and blankets. The barracks had no running water. Lange captured school-children struggling to do math lessons; the authorities had provided no tables for these children. As in the temporary assembly centers, eating was done communally, and children and parents were often split up, kept from sharing meals. Bathing and latrines were also communal. In *Citizen 13660*, art student and internee Miné Okubo drew an illustration expressing women's sense of compromised dignity. Her illustration has a line of five women in open stalls. Women hide behind wooden doors they had pulled to cover the stalls, or curtains they had pinned up.

FIGURE 11.8   Miné Okubo, "Community Toilets," from illustrated memoir, *Citizen 13660*.

© The Japanese American National Museum.

Lange photographed the internees attempting to maintain everyday life; they wanted to survive. Some established gardens, or produced rough-hewn furniture out of the crates and boards strewn about. They held talent shows and art and English classes. The U.S. government established local camp councils among the internees. These however provoked great conflict, even riots. Some believed "self-government" under the government's control constituted an acceptance of their internment. Others, particularly women and *issei*, valued their first vote. Internees also worked. Manzanar was constructed with their "volunteer" labor. The evacuees also raised food for the complex, made camouflage netting for tanks, and even policed the camp.

Photographing the internment devastated Lange. An assistant remembers her "in some sort of paroxysm of fear…she had gotten so consumed" by "the erosion of civil liberties." And when she was done, her photos were "impounded" by the federal government. Lange could not see her negatives until years later. She told a later interviewer, the government did not want a "public record." The government did allow publication of her photographs in the *Survey Graphic*, and Caleb Foote, a pacifist and leader for the Fellowship for Reconciliation, an interdenominational social justice group, produced a pamphlet entitled "Outcasts!: the Story of America's Treatment of Her Japanese Minority" that featured Lange photographs. But not until after her death were Lange's internment photos widely viewed, as Americans grappling with the Vietnam War and newly politicized Japanese Americans demanded to know more of their families' histories. Their activism led the federal government to offer a formal apology and symbolic monetary compensation to the former internees in 1988.[21]

Other photographers took pictures at Manzanar, but as one critic said, the Japanese American internees appeared as if they "were on an extended holiday or at a company picnic."[22] Lange conveyed her concern about the internment to her friend Ansel Adams, pushing him to go to Manzanar. She wrote; "Now is the time, not six months or a year from now, because the situation is constantly shifting and I fear the intolerance and prejudice is constantly growing. We have a disease, this Jap-baiting hatred. You have a job on your hands to do to make a dent in it—but I don't know a more challenging nor more important one." Adams went, as did *San Francisco Chronicle* press photographer Clem Albers. Both photographers sought to valorize the Japanese Americans, but they minimized their containment. Commercial photographer Toyo Miyatake, an internee, smuggled a camera in. Over time, as camp rules loosened, Miyatake was made the camp photographer. Some Miyatake photos indicted the incarceration. In one three young boys held onto the barbed wire fence. But many of his photos were prosaic, akin to his studio photographs. Lange's best work was infused with her sense of injustice. Not long before her death, she stated: "This is what we did. How did it happen? How could we?" Her questions echo today.[23]

Despite her frustration at the U.S. government, Lange continued freelancing for it until 1945. She photographed for foreign-language publications aimed at promoting U.S. styled democracy for those liberated from the Axis powers. As "feature picture editor" under the Office of War Information (OWI) Lange depicted, in her words, "minorities," Yugoslav Americans, Spanish Americans and Italian Americans; she also took photos of college life, and of the nascent U.N. Lange also photographed *braceros* or Mexican citizens allowed into the U.S. solely to harvest crops. Her earlier RA/FSA work featured Mexican American agricultural laborers, but many had been deported without due process in the Depression. With war the nation needed agricultural workers. The *bracero* program did not offer Mexican workers citizenship, just temporary contracts for seasonal work. Conditions were horrible for laborers, who were often locked up at night in camps, only allowed out for work. Lange had documented migrants' exploitation, yet the October 1943 *Survey Graphic* story her photos were attached to ignored the difficulties these migrants faced. Lange understood her work was manipulated but she did not reject its purpose. "The harder and the more deeply you believe in anything, the more in a sense you're a propagandist. Conviction, propaganda, faith. I don't know, I never have been able to come to the conclusion that that's a bad word." She, like many Americans, believed World War II just; her photos could help the war effort.

Lange examined another aspect of, in her words, the "war booming world… the vast upheavals of people, and the radical and profound changes" affecting Bay area society. The West saw explosive economic and demographic growth with the new defense industries. Fifteen million moved during World War II, with two million landing in California.[24] Shipping, the aerospace industry, and military bases drew Americans to the "promised land." After a decade of staggering unemployment, employers could not find enough workers. Women and ethnic groups previously denied good employment found better jobs and better pay. A newly powerful labor movement provided workers additional protections.

Lange adapted herself to fewer government commissions by reaching out to mainstream publications. *Fortune*, magazine to that era's corporate elite, hired Lange and Ansel Adams to explore nearby Richmond, California, called by one historian America's "quintessential war boom town." In five years its population nearly quadrupled, from 23,000 in 1940 to 90,000. Richmond boasted Kaiser, the nation's biggest shipbuilding plant, which employed over 90,000 workers. Many defense workers were new to the area. African Americans had been few prior to the war, but by 1947 their numbers had increased by an astonishing 5,000 percent, becoming fourteen percent of the population. White migrants from Oklahoma, Arkansas, Texas, and Louisiana also streamed in, along with Filipino, Mexican, and Chinese American industrial laborers. Many workers were women, the "Rosie the Riveter" so emblematic of this era's social change.

Higher wages and new jobs created opportunity but dislocation. Cities could not house all the people seeking work. The more fortunate shared rooms or lived in trailer camps, each unit packed closely next to the other. People lived out of buses, camped in the tents that they had traveled in from the Great Plains, or slept beside their cars, with tarps stretched out from the door for protection. Some worked the night shift so they could sleep on the grass by day when it was warmer.[25] With population growth the school population sextupled. Classrooms were packed with nearly seventy students per classroom.

Lange followed these concentrations of people in their communities and at their worksites. She got into "the flow of things," according to her assistants. One said; "Lange hobbled around quietly, made herself part of the crowd." Another thought; "She had a peculiar facility for just melting away and for not seeming to be photographing at the same time that she was sticking a camera in somebody's face."[26] Lange expressed Richmond's growth, what the city manager called an "avalanche," with her image of hard-hatted men, young and old, mustachioed immigrants in spectacles, cap, and cardigan, goggled African American in overalls and women of all races and ethnicities leaving work. Some smile, others gaze downward as they trod by. There was a confidence about this endless flood of people who moved forward in collective determination.

Lange did not shy away from difficulties. Lange took one noted photograph of a couple arguing, which showed, "husband and wife, uprooted...wandering a thousand miles from home...and driven apart by the pressures of long and conflicting hours." She depicted their strain: "It's the space between them

FIGURE 11.9 Dorothea Lange, "Shift change, 3:30, coming out of Yard 3, Kaiser Shipyards," circa 1942.

© The Dorothea Lange Collection, the Oakland Museum of California. Gift of Paul S. Taylor.

FIGURE 11.10   Dorothea Lange, "Shipyard worker and family in trailer camp," 1943.
© The Dorothea Lange Collection, the Oakland Museum of California. Gift of Paul S. Taylor.

that counts." But generally Lange's photos were upbeat. She captured gleeful women, industrial workers, as they doffed their hard hats, some holding hands as they headed in or out of work.[27] Others showed capable women, staring implacably at the camera eye. Lange's wartime subjects are largely in motion, passing by on streets, walking out of stores, looking into windows, smiling or gazing at someone just out of the photo frame. Lange thought the new migrants were relinquishing what was valuable in their pasts for a barren consumerism, and she titled many photos she took "Consumer Relations." The photos are deeply ambiguous. The people carrying groceries home in brown paper bags, or peering into display windows, or passing by on streets are disconnected from one another, often caught in their own private reveries. And yet the subjects are energized and often resolute. As titles like "Race Relations" indicate, the war industries had set in motion new dynamics in race and gender relations giving women and African Americans' new economic power. The African American woman shipbuilder on a Richmond Street, California street exemplified profound social transitions. She would no longer "serve," her intense stance and gaze declare.

As one of her last governmental projects, the State Department asked Lange to photograph a conference on the founding of the United Nations (U.N.) in

FIGURE 11.11 Dorothea Lange, "New California and race relations, McDonald Street, Richmond, California," circa 1943.

© The Dorothea Lange Collection, the Oakland Museum of California. Gift of Paul S. Taylor.

spring 1945. The idea of a world congress that would transcend narrow national interests, a democracy of democracies, appealed to her. The U.N. became politically viable given U.S. cooperation with allies during the war, and the growing sense that the welfare of the U.S. was enmeshed with the welfare of other nations. But authorities limited her access, making it impossible for her to capture anything of interest. Months of this frustration gnawed at her. In a final indignity, she learned that her negatives for her wartime work had mostly been lost as the OWI closed its doors.

The U.N. project was Lange's last one for many years—the strains she faced were too much and she collapsed. Doctors were unsure what troubled her, believing at first the illness was psychosomatic. She could barely eat, and suffered intense stomach pains. Her weight had dropped two years before, in 1943, to a mere eighty-seven pounds. She had multiple surgeries, and she nearly died from a hemorrhage. Acid constricted her esophagus and made it hard to eat. She remained slight the rest of her life, as she could only swallow small amounts of food.

In her physical distress, a William Saroyan tale, "The Warm Quiet Valley of Home," buoyed Lange. She must always have felt much ambiguity about home as tensions swirled around her family life. And to be an artist, she herself left the home she lovingly nurtured. Though her second husband believed in her ability to weave people together, she struggled with her children and step-children, who were often angry at her. For a decade, her life's work had been photographically testifying to the tearing apart of homes that came with Depression and war. Saroyan's words must have comforted: "This was my valley where I had been born. This earth and sky was home. This temperature was. My cousin was. The way he talked was." Lange had no other choice, she just had to be.

Notes

1 Page and Gardiner interview, OMCA.
2 Milton Meltzer, *Dorothea Lange: A Photographer's Life* (New York: Farrar, Straus and Giroux, 1978), 233.
3 Lange papers, v. 5, OMCA.
4 "Hutterite Bible," 1940. LNG41041.4.
5 Linda Gordon and Gary Okihiro, *Impounded: Dorothea Lange and the Censored Images of Japanese American Internment* (New York: W.W. Norton, 2006); Roger Daniels, "Incarcerating Japanese Americans," *OAH Magazine of History* 16 no. 3 (Spring 2002): 19–23; Robert Higgs, "Landless by Law: Japanese Immigrants in California Agriculture to 1941," *The Journal of Economic History* 38 no. 1, (March 1978): 205–225.
6 Ronald Takaki, *A Different Mirror: A History of Multicultural America* (Boston, MA: Back Bay Books, 2008.)
7 Takaki, *Different Mirror,* 268-9; Higgs, "Landless," 206; LC-USF34-016168-C, LC-DIG-fsa-; LC-USF34-016129-C, LC-USZ62-129071.
8 *Ibid.* Higgs, "Landless," 208; Takaki, *Mirror,* 271.
9 Sucheng Chan, *Entry Denied: Exclusion and the Chinese Community, 1882–1943* (Philadelphia: Temple University Press, 1991).
10 Higgs, "Landless," 207, 221; Takaki, *Mirror,* 380; Gordon and Okihiro, *Impounded,* 16.
11 Dr. George P. Clements, Los Angeles Chamber of Commerce, U.S. Congress, House of Representatives, Committee on Immigration and Naturalization, Japanese Immigration: Hearings, 66th Cong., 2d sess., (1921), 404, 873–876, 1008; Higgs, "Landless," 47; Okihiro, *Impounded,* 48.
12 W.H. Anderson, "The Question of Japanese Americans," *Los Angeles Times,* February 1942.
13 *San Francisco News,* March 2, 1942; Caleb Foote's *Outcast* at http://www.american-suburbx.com/2012/06/caleb-foote-dorothea-lange-outcasts-the-story-of-americas-treatment-of-her-japanese-american-minority-1943.html; Gordon and Okihiro, *Impounded,* 22, 62.
14 Takaki *Different Mirror,* 381; Daniels, "Incarcerating Japanese," 20; Okihiro, 59, 52–3, 64–5; Frank Hays, "The National Park Service: Groveling Sycophant or Social Conscience: Telling the Story of Mountains, Valley, and Barbed Wire at Manzanar National Historic Site," *The Public Historian,* 25, no. 4 (Fall 2003): 73–80; Roger Daniels, "Dorothea Lange and the War Relocation Authority: Photographing Japanese Americans," in Elizabeth Partridge, *Dorothea Lange: A Visual Life* (Washington, DC: Smithsonian Institution Press, 1994).
15 Paul Taylor, "Our Stakes in the Japanese Exodus," *Survey Graphic* 39 no. 9 (September 1942); Carl Fleischauer and Beverly Brannan, eds., *New Deal Photography, 1935–1943* (Berkeley, CA: University of California Press, 1988).

16 Okihiro, *Impounded,* 54, 60, 65; and Nancy Matsumoto, "Documenting Manzanar," available at: http://www.discovernikkei.org/en/journal/2011/6/27/documenting-manzanar-1/

17 Daniels, "Dorothea Lange," 52; Lange's photographs are now available online through the National Archive, Record Group 210: https://catalog.archives.gov/search?q=*:*&f.ancestorNaIds=536000&sort=titleSort%20asc; many were also placed at UCB. See "Mountain View, A Pre-Evacuation Barbecue," at http://ark.cdlib.org/ark:/13030/ft0x0n99g6. Many photos are available in Gordon and Okihiro's *Impounded.*

18 "Flag of allegiance pledge at Raphael Weill Public School," and "Evidence of evacuation is seen in the Japanese quarter two days prior of evacuation of residents of Japanese ancestry from this city," Sacramento, California May 11, 1942, vol. 62, Section G, WRA no. C-566, *UCB.*

19 Gordon and Okihiro, *Impounded,* 145.

20 Ibid., 68; Mine Okubo, *Citizen 13660* (Seattle, WA: University of Washington Press, 2014), 78; Helen Harano Crist interview, 2008, *Densho Encyclopedia,* available at: http://encyclopedia.densho.org/sources/en-denshovh-chelen-01-0016-1/.

21 Gardner interview; Foote, "Outcast;" Daniels, "Dorothea Lange," 49.

22 Daniels, "Dorothea Lange."

23 Jean Houston, *Farewell to Manzanar* (New York: Ember Press, 2012), 187; Anne Hammond, *Ansel Adams at Manzanar* (Honolulu, HI: Honolulu Academy of Arts, 2006); *Matsumoto, Documenting Manzanar; Gerald Robinson,* Elusive Truth: Four Photographers at Manzanar *(Carl Mautz, 2002); Robert Nakamura, dir. Toyo Miyatake: Infinite Shades of Gray/Moving Memories* (DVD), 2002.

24 "Social Changes During the War," *Digital History,* available at: http://www.digitalhistory.uh.edu/disp_textbook.cfm?smtID=2&psid=3493; Charles Dorn, "I Had All Kinds of Kids in My Classes and It Was Fine": Public Schooling in Richmond, California during World War II, *History of Education Quarterly* 45 no. 4 (Winter 2005): 538–564; Shirley Ann Wilson Moore, *To Place Our Deeds: The African American Community in Richmond, California, 1910–1963* (Berkeley, CA: University of California Press, 2000); Gretchen Lemke-Santangelo, *Abiding Courage: African-American Migrant Women and the East Bay Community* (Chapel Hill, NC: University of North Carolina Press, 1995); Roger W. Lotchin, *Fortress California: 1910–1961* (New York: Oxford University Press, 1992), 15; Gerald Nash, *The American West Transformed: The Impact of the Second World War* (Lincoln, NE: University of Nebraska Press, 1985), 69, 16; Lange papers, vol. 13, "An Avalanche Hits Richmond," OMCA.

25 Carl Nolte, "World War II Created Industrial, Cultural Revolution in Bay Area," available at: http://www.sfgate.com/bayarea/article/World-War-II-created-industrial-cultural-2503378.php and "Richmond Shipyards," available at: http://www.calisphere.universityofcalifornia.edu/themed_collections/subtopic5d.html; Dorn, "All Kinds of Kids," 543.

26 Page and Gardner interview.

27 "Shipyard at End of Shift, Yard One," Richmond, California, September 1943. LNG42083.3.

CONCLUSION

"The Last Ditch:" Dorothea Lange and the Persistence of Vision, 1945–1965

"Use the camera as though tomorrow you'd be stricken blind," Dorothea Lange once stated, and she lived her life this way.[1] After her collapses at World War II's end, she could not photograph for five years. Chronic illness remained. But from 1950 until her death in 1965, though debilitated by pain, weakness, and exhaustion, she remained indomitable; her passion for photography never waned. Lange anchored cameras unobtrusively throughout her home; during seaside rests she walked with her camera slung over her neck. Sometimes she could not get out of bed, sometimes she could only cook or sew or garden, at times depression deadened her ardor. But she almost always wanted to photograph and advance new projects. Lange remained concerned with social disequilibrium. She advocated for photography as a medium of social documentation and an aesthetic for insight and social change. Her ambitions remained high for herself, and for her fellow photographers.

Lange enjoyed her status as a nationally recognized documentary photographer. She led discussion at the 1951 Aspen Institute, which still brings prominent thinkers and policymakers together to foster dialogue. She and top photographers such as her friend, Ansel Adams, Laura Gilpin, who studied with Clarence White in the late teens when Lange did, and Berenice Abbott, along with museum directors, curators, and photo editors sought a more precise meaning of the documentary years after they made the aesthetic so popular. She also became a founding editor of *Aperture*, which remains one of the nation's top photography magazines. In its second issue, with her son, Daniel Dixon, she co-authored an essay, "Photographing the Familiar." Conscious of how Cold War technological knowledge had led to the possibility of human annihilation with the atom bomb, they promoted creativity as an antidote. Much as when a visitor told Lange and her first husband Maynard Dixon that "photography was going to save the world,"

Lange argued for the medium's power to change consciousnesses. In a world that seemed out of control, the photographer had a unique ability to "endow the machine" with "humanity and passion."[2]

Though Lange had often criticized the "success boys," famous photographers working for the glossy photographic weeklies who had expense account budgets to burn and paid researchers, writers, and editors at their call, she now put her hat in the ring. The plum, *Life Magazine,* founded by Henry Luce in 1936, had twenty million readers each week. *Life* portrayed a nation enjoying consumer affluence, largely untroubled by social dislocation, not a perspective typical for Lange. One 1954 photo-essay, "Three Mormon Towns," done in collaboration with Ansel Adams and her son, Daniel Dixon, for whom she sought emotional and financial support, explored the miraculous way Mormons had squeezed life from their harsh environment.[3] And she and Dixon visited Ireland, exploring the lives of Irish peasants in County Clare who lived outside the whirl of twentieth-century consumerism. Lange's images are gorgeous and melancholic, the soft misty countryside, the wet fields, the glowering skies, and the people, often too poor to buy their own land, with many men thus condemned to a solitary life. As MOMA curator John Szarkowski said: "He felt the damp wind blowing out of one."[4]

Lange retained an interest in people and their relationship to the land, and she used her camera to observe California's overdevelopment. In an important investigation predating the contemporary environmental movement, photographer Pirkle Jones joined Lange in the late 1950s to document the flooding of the Berryessa Valley for a reservoir for California's water needs. The two witnessed the "killing" of the Valley; farm equipment and homes were sold and taken apart for valuables, electric wires pulled down, everything was "leveled to the ground." Lange wrote of a centuries' old tree, brutalized and twisted, that she photographed: "The big oaks were torn out, cattle had rested in their shade for generations, on old maps and deeds they had served as landmarks." She showed the denuded landscape on fire, and her "Terrified Horse," showed the animal galloping across a bulldozer-scarred field, a stranger in its home. Lange's story was a cautionary one, of the weight of populations and economic advances on the environment. As Minor White wrote in introducing the photo-essay in *Aperture:* "Bulldozers are only slightly slower than atomic bombs...the nature of destruction is not altered by calling it the price of progress."

Lange received increasing attention from museums, particularly the Museum of Modern Art (MOMA), photography's greatest champion, which pushed to see photography as an art form. She appeared in two group shows, in 1949 and 1952.[5] Lange also contributed greatly to the 1955 "Family of Man" show, one of the world's largest and most discussed photo shows. Modernist photographer Edward Steichen curated this blockbuster show of two hundred photographers from sixty-eight countries who produced a "sweeping panorama of...the universality of basic human emotions." More than a quarter of a million people saw the show in New York City, breaking all records. Eventually, more than four million would see it as the show toured nearly forty other nations. The exhibition catalog sat on the best seller list for nearly all of 1955. Nearly half a million people bought it that year, and sixty years later *The Family of Man* remains in print.[6] The show insisted on humankind's commonalities by focusing on everyday life and mankind's life-course: birth, adolescence, love, marriage, childbirth, and death.[7] Criticized for oversimplifying, universalizing human experience, and ignoring major issues such as colonialism, racism, and militarization, the exhibition testified to the public's interest in documentary photography, if in sanitized form. Lange helped Steichen find photographers, and she promoted the involvement of West Coast photographers.

Lange's photography formed the backbone to another Steichen exhibition in 1962, "The Bitter Years." Nearly half of the two hundred images were by Lange.[8] Dozens of photographers worked for the RA/FSA, but Lange's work remained the most probing. Steichen wanted to remind Americans of the Depression, just a generation before, of the "American epic" of those "uprooted from the soil." In the 1960s, the U.S. experienced historic levels of affluence but pockets of poverty seemed impervious to government action. Policymakers and citizens were concerned. The famous broadcaster, Edward Murrow's television documentary, "Harvest of Shame," (1960) touched on Appalachian poverty, and Michael Harrington's influential *The Other America* (1962) argued that more than a quarter of Americans still lived in poverty. Lyndon Johnson made the "War on Poverty" a priority in 1964, introducing or expanding social insurance programs such as Medicare, Medicaid, Food Stamps, and Social Security. Johnson's use of a war metaphor was unwise, as poverty was not eradicated: however, it was cut in half, to just over ten percent, an effective government campaign.

Lange's Depression-era photos reminded Americans of the government's capacity to address abject poverty. But her documentation also pointed to public attitudes that restricted the provision of welfare to American citizens. One Lange print of a Missouri family that had landed in California suggested how racism shaped the contours of the U.S. welfare state. The woman told Lange, "just scrappin' along; we're not tramps; we hold ourselves to be white folks. We was forced out; we couldn't stay there." The War on Poverty helped black and white Americans, but welfare came to be perceived by many as something that only black Americans took advantage of. Lange captured the racial calculus that led some whites to feel that they were superior to African Americans and therefore reject governmental aid that cared for Americans of all colors.[9]

Lange confronted new physical and intellectual challenges when Paul Taylor's expertise in land redistribution was called on to address global concerns. Major foundations, the U.N., and the State Department, including the U.S. Agency for International Development (AID), funded Taylor's research. Taylor thought land redistribution could lead to substantial social reform. Lange traveled with Taylor, despite her ill health. Her doctor's unsympathetic advice: "What's the difference whether you die here or there?" Their world travels provided an education and a new scope for her photography.

Their first trip in 1958 was to Asia. Lange enjoyed hospitality as the wife of a U.S. aide, delightful embassy dinners with fine champagnes and wines and travel with chauffeurs. Yet the disjuncture between these occasions and the poverty they were investigating was a "bombardment," leaving her feeling lost. She photographed the fine dinners, and also local markets, transportation, or farmers planting. She thought Asian peasants better understood land stewardship, so she investigated village life, particularly in Korea and Vietnam. She couldn't connect with her subjects as in the U.S., however. The Balinese "simply flowed around her," as if she weren't there, making it easy to photograph. But in other countries, such as Korea, people pressed around her, trying to stroke the hair of the woman with the camera, making it difficult to get shots. She later said she could not "grasp and record" the "vast pageant" before her. When Lange photographed poverty in the U.S., it was with an aim to address it. Her record of Asia had no political purpose, and she was skeptical of U.S. intentions in the region, further complicating her work. Other trips followed. In 1960 Taylor and Lange went to Ecuador and Venezuela, commissioned by the U.N. Their final trip abroad, was to Egypt, in 1962 and 1963. Lange thought the project of photographing in Africa would be "staggering" given her lack of knowledge of the region's history, economy, and society. And yet she became "absorbed" in taking photos there. Her photographs of date farmers near the Libyan border and Sudanese cotton farmers retain Lange's respect for labor. On this final trip, her clothes had to be safety pinned to keep them on her emaciated frame; she almost died from dysentery.

Despite her weakness, Lange returned to work once home. She continued to try to corral support for documentary photography. One plan that she had, called "Project One," sought to develop funding for a massive photographic project of American life, akin to the RA/FSA. She tirelessly promoted this idea to photographers, curators, magazine editors, foundations, and university presidents. She was concerned about the growth of the "megalopolis," how worldwide urbanization strained people, cities themselves, and the larger environment. She wrote to her friend Ansel Adams: "No nation that I know of has ever attempted this kind of close, hard scrutiny of themselves." Her concern was less with poverty, as she had explored it during the Depression, but a "poverty of the spirit." The U.S. permitted "privation within prosperity." Some Americans reveled in affluence, while others lacked basic medical care or went to bed hungry.[10]

In the last decade of her life, Lange entered into a more intimate exploration of everyday life, the life of women and families, of the reproductive labor that keeps humankind going, and the emotional labor that makes life sweet and bearable. As discussed in Chapter Ten, Lange focused much on rural women in her last years, those whose domestic labors were made more difficult on land with no electricity, refrigeration, and plumbing. Lange's country women were tenacious, mostly older women who were tied to the processes of life. But these women did not appear tethered to families alone. They were on their own, part of communities, homes, the land, insistent presences in a larger consumer culture that largely ignored such women. Lange's condensed study, *Dorothea Lange Looks at the American Woman*, was published after her death under the editorship of Beaumont Newhall.

Lange also explored domestic life through her own family, in a project she began in 1957 at "Steep Ravine" on the California coast where they took week-end refuge. Lange's observations on family snapshots were tart. "An emptier form of telling you about the family I don't know. Communication, zero." Family inti-macy makes investigation difficult, but she thought within domestic life, and spe-cifically in her family's unwinding at the cabin, some essential "circumstances... feel unlocked and free." Lange moved from the highly specific, to seeking to show American postwar prosperity and poverty, to exploring the universal, as it transpired on women's terrain, the home, stripped down to its essentials, eating, sleeping, conversing, walking, reading, playing. Author-photographer Margaretta K. Mitchell completed this project as *To A Cabin* (1973) with Taylor's support.

A MOMA retrospective of her work, slated for 1966, instead took Lange's attention. In late summer of 1964, Lange learned that she had esophageal can-cer, which has no cure. She hoarded her time, to put her stamp on the MOMA show. From the museum's founding in 1929, it took photography seriously as art. Nonetheless, well into the 1960s, photography, then more than a cen-tury old, was still fighting for respect. Lange was the first woman to have a MOMA career retrospective. She was adamant that her work be seen in social and political terms, at one point asking the curator, John Szarkowski, during a visit, "What's the background of the white owner sitting on the porch. Who's doing this work for him?" in regard to the Mississippi Plantation Owner, dis-cussed in Chapter Seven. She wanted to convey man's relationship to man. She also sought to shape how the exhibition would appear. She no longer believed in "bull's-eye photographs," or a photo that told the whole story. She sought "relationships, equivalents, progression, contradictions, positives and negatives." As with many exhibitions, the photos would be seen in groups. Unlike the curator, Szarkowski, who saw her photographs aesthetically, Lange thought his-torically and sociologically, and wanted to arrange the show based on specific locations and times. Her caption for a section devoted to her Depression-era work, describes her lifelong concern with "The Last Ditch."

> I am trying here to say something
> About the despised, the defeated,
> The alienated.
> About death and disaster,
> About the wounded, the crippled
> The helpless, the rootless
> The dislocated.
> About duress and trouble.
> About finality.
> About the last ditch.[11]

In the spring of 1965 Lange completed prints and wrote captions, but she was weakening. In June the author charged with writing the exhibition catalog's introduction was shocked at her condition; she weighed just over eighty pounds. But Lange worked relentlessly, from nine to four, with just a twenty-minute break for lunch. She received visits from photographers such as Robert Frank, and correspondence from Paul Strand and Margaret Bourke-White. Szarkowski visited her in August, to continue their discussions. That summer family also gathered around her. Into the fall she worked with her printer to communicate her desires for how exhibition prints should look. Her unique voice comes through in discussions about which photographs to feature. "Here's a photo of a lap that is a lap. They don't have laps any more today. Print it and let them see what a lap looks like." The lap, like "home," suggested intimacy, caring, support, relationships.

On October 8, 1965, Lange was hospitalized; she could no longer eat and she had a high fever. Some of her last words to her husband Paul were "Isn't it a miracle, that this comes at the right time." Lange died three days later, on October 11, 1965. She was seventy years old. Until the very end, she admitted, in a letter to Szarkowski: "I have not yet been able to break the habit of thinking that everything is ahead… That has been my lifelong attitude. I find that every day taken separately, with full weight given to every hour, has seen me through the last months."

Lange was no longer on this earth, but her vision, her probing eye continues to communicate with people around the globe. President Johnson, who believed in using the state to sustain American citizens through adversity, wrote of Lange's photographs: "Without retouching our blemishes, she showed the strength and gallantry of the American people under severe adversity," applauding "the magic of her camera." Johnson understood the power of Lange's work. MOMA curators spoke to fellow museum professionals of their regard for Lange, "We feel that both the philosophy and esthetics of modern documentary photography have been defined largely by the work of two great American artists," Walker Evans and Dorothea Lange. They defined Lange's "basic theme," as "the value and stamina, but also the destructibility of human beings." That ambiguity in her photos is often what gives them a charge.[12] Visitors to her exhibition wrote that Lange's photographs touched everyone, "from the janitors to the college president." A traveling exhibition sent to Germany, France, Italy, Brussels, and Yugoslavia received much press. Lange was the "grande dame of photography" who discovered in the Depression-era streets, "Dante in the first cycle of Hell." One writer asked, "Why does her style, with its lacerating sobriety, that makes all description banal and simplistic, move us so?"[13]

Lange's images endure, touching people a half-century after her death. Lange told a college student who interviewed her near her death that the camera gave "direct and powerful" communication. She amended her words;

photography instead was "a means of communion."[14] Lange's camera imbued her subjects, whether black Alabaman sharecroppers, white Oklahoman migrants on relief, Vietnamese peasants, or Mexican American Californians stooping in the fields, with dignity. Because of Lange we can seek and obtain communion with those alive nearly a century ago. Her photos asked people to enlarge their sense of shared citizenship and political possibility. And they pushed people to widen their vision. The questions her photographs provoke, about peoples' cares, about how people care for others and for the earth, and about how the nation responds to the needs of its citizenry are questions that U.S. citizens debate; the answers are politically unresolved. The exploitation of labor, particularly of migrant agricultural labor and of child labor, racism, extreme poverty amidst abundance, and environmental degradation; these injustices persist. The "work" of Lange's photographs continues. "The good photograph is not the object. The consequences of that photograph are the object. And I'm not speaking of social consequences. I mean the kind of thing where people will not say to you, how did you do it, or where did you get this, but that such things could be."[15]

Notes

1 Dayanna Taylor, director; *Grab a Hunk of Lightning,* available at: http://www.pbs.org/wnet/americanmasters/dorothea-lange-quotes-by-dorothea-lange/3159/.
2 Dorothea Lange and Daniel Dixon, "Photographing the Familiar," *Aperture* 2 (1952).
3 "Three Mormon Towns," *Life,* September 6, 1954, 91–100, available at: https://books.google.com/books?id=I1QEAAAAMBAJ&printsec=frontcover&dq=Life+Magazine+september+6,+1954&hl=en&sa=X&ved=0ahUKEwid-PbBjIHTAhUr4YMKHezMDNQQ6AEIHDAA#v=onepage&q&f=false.
4 "Irish Country People," *Life,* March 21, 1955: 135–143, available at: https://books.google.com/books?id=GVQEAAAAMBAJ&printsec=frontcover&dq=Life+Magazine+march+21+1955&hl=en&sa=X&ved=0ahUKEwjh9ajYqYvSAhWsy4MKHbmyDDEQ6AEIJTAA#v=twopage&q&f=false.
5 "Six Women Photographers," *NYT,* 22 March 1949; "Diogenes with a Camera," Press Release, May 21, 1952, available at: https://www.moma.org/d/c/press_releases/W1siZiIsIjMyNTg0NyJdXQ.pdf?sha=22d7cbd5132992ec.
6 "Camera Notes," *NYT,* 1 January 1956.
7 Jacob Deschin, "Family of Man: Panoramic Show Opens at Modern Museum," January 30, 1955; and "Families' Last Days," May 8, 1955, both *NYT.*
8 Press Release, October 18, 1962, available at: https://www.moma.org/momaorg/shared/pdfs/docs/press_archives/3063/releases/MOMA_1962_0122_119.pdf?2010.
9 "Stryker Exhibit: FSA photographers' pictures at Modern," October 21, 1962, *NYT,* available at: http://steichencollections-cna.lu/eng/collections/2_the-bitter-years; Nelson Lichtenstein, "From Corporatism to Collective Bargaining: Organized Labor and the Eclipse of Social Democracy in the Postwar Era," in Steve Fraser and Gary Gerstle, *The Rise and Fall of the New Deal Order* (Princeton, NJ: Princeton University Press, 1989), 122–152.
10 MOMA exhibits 711.21, August 7, 1962.
11 MOMA exhibitions, 789.27.

12 MOMA "Press Release for Dorothea Lange Retrospective," January 24, 1966, available at: http://www.moma.org/docs/press_archives/3581/releases/MOMA_1966_Jan-June_0015_8.pdf?2010, MOMA exhibition 789.27 Letter, November 8, 1965.
13 From *Femme D'aujourd'hui*, MOMA Exhibitions, 789.28 and 789.29.
14 Lange interview by Doud, and Suzanne Reiss's oral history included *Berkeley Review* interview.
15 Meltzer, *Dorothea Lange,* 305.

PRIMARY DOCUMENTS

Reading Photography in the Archives

Reading photographs seems seductively simple. The truth appears laid out in black and white. The nineteenth-century savant, Oliver Wendell Holmes, called photographs "the mirror with a memory," suggesting photography's direct transcription from nature. Other metaphors abound. Photographs provide witness; they are windows on the world, as if the cameraperson snatched a bit of reality. As discussed in the Introduction, documentary photography relies particularly on the power of the real.

Yet photographs obscure as much as they reveal, evident from the medium's inception. Holmes, for example, maintained that people could masquerade before the camera, altering their identity. Progressive-era Lewis Hine wrote: "Photographs don't lie, but liars may photograph." For Hine, the deception arose not in the photograph, but how it was taken. More recently, photography critic Martha Rosler quipped: 'Photography is dumb." As obvious as the information in photographs appears, it must be given meaning.[1] This essay explores ways to read images historically, and identifies digital collections that deepen insight into Dorothea Lange's photography, the New Deal, and the Depression.

Describing the photograph's contents is only the first step in understanding a photograph historically. What is the subject? Can we say with certainty what is it doing? Are there gestures or expressions to consider? In Lange's most famous photograph, "Migrant Mother," the mother supports her head with her hand; the two children turn their heads from the camera and curl toward their mother (Fig. 10.8). Chapter Six shows an early Lange documentary photograph, the unemployed migrant leans against his jalopy; he seems to lack enough energy to pull his foot forward (Fig. 6.2). Such gestures can relate the emotional traumas of the Depression. Take note of anything that stands out about the photograph. Artistic elements such as lighting, contrast, the space within the frame, the photographer's point of view, and the composition also shape what the photograph communicates. How did the photographer frame the subject, and what might lie outside that frame? "Migrant Mother" pushes the subject into the front of the picture plane, forcing us to look at her; there are no surroundings. This is also true for Lange's unemployed worker beside a wheelbarrow, pinioned against a wall (Fig. 4.1), and her eighty-year-old grandmother, on her knees against her tent (Fig. 6.1). And Lange rarely went inside the homes of her subjects. What do we not know about migrants' lives as a result? What kept her from entering their homes?

Other information often accompanies photographs, shaping or altering its meaning. Because Hine wanted his photographs to stand as truthful documents, not hucksterism or propaganda, he recorded basic facts about individual subjects as well as statistical information about social problems such as child labor. Similarly, Lange declared her distrust of "bullseye" photographs that ostensibly captured everything. She thought a careful, detailed exploration of a subject necessary. For Lange, multiple exposures of a subject, the transcription of subjects' stories, the logging of additional background information, and the agglomeration of tens of thousands of photographs addressing U.S. society in "the file" made it possible to employ individual photographs to establish truth claims. Because many Lange photographs were taken for the government's Resettlement Administration/Farm Security Administration (RA/FSA), researchers have an unusual opportunity to compare photographs such as "Migrant Mother" with other photographs taken from the same shoot, or against photographs of similar subjects from different times, different locales, or of different peoples.

Ironically, "Migrant Mother" has been embroiled in controversy over the nature of the documentary. Lange's obscuring of the subject, Florence Thompson's, thumb on the pole has led some to doubt the photograph's veracity. Can the photographer intervene in the scene or in printing, or does that detract from the image's truthfulness? Lange's multiple shots of the impoverished mother, which begin with distance shots showing the tent she lived in, its contents, and her larger brood of children, have led some to argue that Lange minimized confusing details that might limit sympathy. Those interested in such debates can begin with James Curtis's *Mind's Eye, Mind's Truth: FSA Photography Reconsidered* (Temple University Press, 1989), Martha Rosler's classic essay, "in, around, and afterthoughts (on documentary photography)," or the more recent *No Caption Needed: Iconic Photographs, Public Culture, and Liberal Democracy* by Robert Hariman and John Lucaites (University of Chicago Press, 2007).

Like Hine and Lange, historians treat photographic evidence with care, employing their conventional tools for primary sources. Historians attend to multiple contexts. Who is the artist? What propelled them to take their photos? What did they hope to communicate? But the artist's intent may not be the most significant factor explaining a work's meaning.

The photographer creates in a larger context. Their images appear on gallery and museum walls, in newspapers and magazines, and in reform campaigns, among other venues. Within those contexts, institutions strive to shape the image's interpretation. Cropping the photograph, captioning it, adding textual source material, changing its size, and sequencing it with other photographs, informs the image's meaning. Lange's government sponsor sought to place her photographs in top photojournals such as *Life,* in newspapers, before congressional hearings on migrant labor, at country fairs, university exhibitions, and other public spaces. The government did not always achieve its end. Chapter Eight details how *Life* printed Lange's photograph of three elderly Oklahomans on relief, taken to garner public support for California migrant camps, and cropped out two of the men to suggest one migrant's can-do spirit, tied to American westward pioneer narratives (Fig. 8.9). Chapter Ten suggests "Migrant Mother," published first in 1936, became the rationale for enhanced aid to a specific tent camp. Today, that photograph might grace an auction house catalog; the photo became a highly prized art object.

Lange's career matured concurrent to the increasing visualization of the news due to the picture press, the AP wire service, and faster films and cameras. Simultaneously, the news moved to become more national and standardized. Researchers should consider the available technologies the photographer used to take and to disseminate their photographs when addressing an image's significance.

Audience reception is also critical to understanding a photograph's meaning and influence. Some 1930s suburban train riders passing through an exhibit at Grand Central Station, New York's rail terminal, were offended by having to confront images of destitute Americans as part of their commute. But members of the radical New York Photo League applauded the social work of Lange's photographs when they saw them at their headquarters in the late 1940s.

Finally, photography historians Alan Trachtenberg and David Nye suggest reading for patterns of meaning across bodies of photographs—what particular themes emerge, or ways of viewing or approaching a subject, which might vary greatly by artist, disseminator, or assumed audience.

Two helpful guides for reading images historically are Kate Sampsell's "Student Centered Readings of Lewis Hine's Photographs," *The History Teacher,* 47 No. 3 (May 2014): 387–419, which offers recommendations for reading photographs, with superb background on Hine's documentary project, or James Curtis' online essay, "Making Sense of Documentary Photographs," for George Mason University's "History Matters" site at http://historymatters.gmu.edu/mse/photos/, which locates Depression-era documentary within a larger photographic history.

Digitization facilitates access to photographs and other archival materials, a boon to students of the past. Given Lange's repute and the traumas of the Great Depression, a wealth of digitally archived materials exists. The Library of Congress (LoC), Photogrammar, and the Calisphere best present Lange's works. At the LoC's Prints and Photographs Division, online catalog researchers can search for photographs taken by the dozens of RA/FSA photographers, including

Lange: http://www.loc.gov/pictures/collection/fsa/. The LoC explains how Paul Vanderbilt organized the 175,000 RA/FSA images in the 1940s: http://www.loc. gov/rr/print/coll/FSA-class-list-introduction.html. Searching by photographer's name, subject headings, or category headings, researchers can view in gallery or list formats, allowing comparison of photographs across time and space. Most helpful is the RA/FSA collection overview, which contextualizes the photographers within the Depression and the inner workings of one New Deal agency. Shooting scripts, correspondence, photographers' itineraries, captioning (including Lange's twenty-page hand-written listing of photographs, which identifies "Migrant Mother"), and exhibition descriptions are included: http://www.loc. gov/rr/print/coll/fsawr/fsawr.html.

Two other major digital repositories for Lange's RA/FSA photographs are the National Endowment for the Humanities and Yale-sponsored Photogrammar site, http://photogrammar.yale.edu/. In Photogrammar, researchers can use a map of the U.S. to screen for photographs by specific states, time frames, and photographers. Lange's photographs are also featured in the University of California's Calisphere, an online repository of university, archive, and museum collections: https://calisphere.org/. Paul Taylor donated her papers and negatives to the Oakland Museum, and the Calisphere presents Lange's photographs—from her early studio portraits of the 1910s and 1920s, photos indicating her budding interest in the documentary in the 1930s, to photographs from the war and postwar period.

Grounding Lange's work in the history of photography and the origins of photojournalism is possible with other LoC collections, the Bain collection, the Harris and Ewing Collection, and the National Photo Company Collection: http://www.loc.gov/pictures/collections/. The LoC holds a large collection of photographs by Arnold Genthe, who tutored Lange in portraiture: http://www. loc.gov/pictures/collection/agc/. And to follow the careers of early women professional photographers, Beverly Brannan, Curator of Photography's hyperlinked essay on women photojournalists is invaluable: http://loc.gov/rr/print/coll/596_womphotoj.html. It includes the Frances Benjamin Johnston Collection, http:// www.loc.gov/pictures/collection/fbj/, and an essay on Jessie Tarbox Beals, used for this biography, along with Lange's RA/FSA colleagues Marion Post Wolcott and Esther Bubley.

The RA/FSA's structure and impact within U.S. culture can be analyzed through the multiple online oral histories of photographers and agency staff, including the Archives of American Art, https://www.aaa.si.edu/, which have interviews with Lange, Rexford Tugwell who founded the RA/FSA, Roy Stryker, who directed the RA/FSA's Historical Section and supervised the photographers, Vanderbilt, the file's organizer, and nearly a dozen RA/FSA photographers.

Other Lange-related collections include the National Archives collection of photographs of the Japanese American internment (Record Group 210 of the War Relocation Authority): https://catalog.archives.gov/search?q=dorothea%20 lange&f.level=item&f.locationIds=31. Lange traveled with landscape photographer

Ansel Adams to the Manzanar camp; his photographs are available at the LoC: http://www.loc.gov/pictures/collection/manz/. The grassroots Densho Organization presents superb primary sources and analysis addressing the WWII internment of Japanese Americans: http://densho.org/.

A wealth of online material addresses the Great Depression. Excellent general background is available from the Living New Deal: https://livingnewdeal.org/oral-histories/. Eleanor Roosevelt's syndicated column, "My Day," is available through George Washington University: https://www2.gwu.edu/~erpapers/myday/. "My Day" chronicles nearly thirty years, beginning in 1935, and offers an elite reformer's view on a wide range of topics. The LoC's American Folklife Center provides online recordings from the 1930s; relevant collections include "Voices of the Dust Bowl," "Voices from the Days of Slavery," and "California Gold: Northern California Folk Music from the 1930s": http://www.loc.gov/rr/program/bib/newdeal/afc.html. Additionally, the LoC holds digitally archived manuscripts from the Federal Writers Project with its "American Life Histories: Manuscripts from the Federal Writers' Project, 1936 to 1940," https://www.loc.gov/collections/ federal-writers-project/about-this-collection/, and slave narratives conducted by the Works Progress Administration in the "Born in Slavery Collection": https://www.loc.gov/collections/slave-narratives-from-the-federal-writers-project-1936-to-1938/about-this-collection/.

A few relevant sites for other New Deal era cultural production include: Posters for the People: http://www.postersforthepeople.com/; The Wolfsonian Museum Digital Collections, which showcases art and design: https://digital.wolfsonian.org/; and the WPA Posters at LoC: http://www.loc.gov/pictures/search/?st=grid&co=wpapos. The New York Public Library's rich digital collections include two other photographers working in the documentary vein, Lewis Hine's "Photographic Documents of Social Conditions, 1905–1939," https://digitalcollections.nypl.org/collections/series-of-photographic-documents-of-social-conditions-1905-1939#/?tab=about, and Berenice Abbott's "Changing New York": https://digitalcollections.nypl.org/collections/changing-new-york#/?tab=about.

Note

1 A rich vein of literature explores the truth value and the political stakes of the documentary. An excellent recent discussion is found in Julian Stallabrass, ed. *Documentary: Documents of Contemporary Art* (London: Whitechapel Gallery, 2013).

STUDY QUESTIONS

1. Much of Dorothea Lange's childhood was spent in New York City and urban New Jersey. How did the city shape Lange's childhood and her ability to "see"?

2. What was the New Woman? How did shifting gender roles shape Lange's life options? How did Lange reject concepts of traditional womanhood, and how did she embrace them? What were the personal or professional costs of her choices?

3. Did Lange emphasize gender difference and female nurturance in her photographs? If so, how?

4. How did the Great Depression affect the nation's economy and citizens' lives? How did Franklin Delano Roosevelt's New Deal respond to the Depression? How did he reinvent government's role in citizens' lives?

5. How did the Great Depression create a decisive break in Lange's *oeuvre*? What is the documentary photograph, and why is it so hard to define? How was the documentary a response to the Great Depression?

6. Did the Agricultural Adjustment Act and the Resettlement Administration/ Farm Security Administration (RA/FSA) address agricultural laborers and farmers' distress, particularly sharecroppers, tenant farmers, and migrant laborers? What were the agency's limits?

7. Why did the federal government choose to use the camera to motivate support for the New Deal? How did Lange's singular efforts as a photographer get drawn into the collective governmental response of the RA/FSA and the New Deal generally? Was her work propaganda?

8. How did Lange portray the heterogeneity of America's rural workforce—its regional, racial, ethnic, and gender diversity? How did Lange convey agricultural workers' exploitation?

9. How did Lange's photographs comment on the civil liberties crisis occasioned by the mass internment of Japanese Americans?
10. How did World War II alter the U.S. economy and its political sphere? How did Lange, during World War II and after, continue to engage politically with her camera?

BIBLIOGRAPHY

This book synthesizes secondary scholarship and archival research. It relies heavily upon Milton Meltzer's *Dorothea Lange: A Photographer's Life* (New York: Farrar, Straus and Giroux, 1978) and Linda Gordon's *Dorothea Lange, A Life Beyond Limits* (New York: W.W. Norton, 2009). The latter situates Lange within the context of women's lives and the New Deal and is enriched by Gordon's deep knowledge of twentieth century politics and activist efforts to reshape the state. Lange gave a life history to the University of California, which provides much detail about her early life, her move to California, and her work with the New Deal through to her last years. *Dorothea Lange: The Making of a Documentary Photographer*, conducted by Suzanne Riess in 1960-1961, Regional Oral History Office, the Bancroft Library, University of California, Berkeley, 1968, available at http://digitalassets.lib.berkeley.edu/roho/ucb/text/lange_dorothea__w.pdf. Another interview by the Smithsonian offers slightly different perspectives. Reading them against one another is fertile. Dorothea Lange, 1964 May 22. Archives of American Art, Smithsonian Institution, available at https://www.aaa.si.edu/collections/interviews/oral-history-interview-dorothea-lange-11757. Quotations typically come from the two biographies, Lange's oral histories, her Field Notes at the Oakland Museum, and her *An American Exodus: A Record of Human Erosion* (New York: Reynal and Hitchcock, 1939), co-authored with Paul Taylor.

Archival research was done at the Oakland Museum (OMCA), where Lange's papers, negatives, and prints are housed, the Museum of Modern Art (MOMA), which has correspondence and records relating to the exhibition of her work, and the Bancroft Library at University of California at Berkeley (UCB), which holds Maynard Dixon and Paul Taylor's papers.

Because much of Lange's work was done for the federal government, her Depression-era work can be seen online, at the Library of Congress's American

Memory site. The National Endowment for the Humanities funded and Yale University sponsored Photogrammar site is one of the best ways to explore these photos by photographer, date, and location. It is an incredible resource. The National Archives has Lange's photographs of the Japanese American internment. The Oakland Museum has some 20,000 images online through the Calisphere.

Lange's granddaughter and filmmaker, Dyanna Taylor produced and directed an American Masters special, *Dorothea Lange: Grab A Hunk of Lightning*; Meg Partridge, produced *Dorothea Lange: A Visual Life*. Two public television programs of Lange in the last year of her life are available online, *Under the Trees,* https://diva.sfsu.edu/collections/sfbatv/bundles/191509 and *The Closer for Me,* https://diva.sfsu.edu/collections/sfbatv/bundles/191510.

There are many critical studies of Lange and her work; this biography relies upon the following: Anne Whiston Spirn, *Daring to Look: Dorothea Lange's Photographs and Reports from the Field* (Chicago: University of Chicago Press, 2009) offers a fresh perspective on a single year of Lange's photography for the FSA and is invaluable, as is Jan Goggans, *California on the Breadlines: Dorothea Lange, Paul Taylor, and the Making of a New Deal Narrative* (Berkeley, CA: University of California Press, 2010) which looks closely at Lange and Taylor's partnership using a gender lens. Elizabeth Partridge, daughter of Rondal Partridge, who traveled with Lange and who is Imogen Cunningham and Roi Partridge's son has written several books about Lange, and her collected set of essays that includes work by Sally Stein and Roger Daniel is insightful. Elizabeth Partridge, *Dorothea Lange: A Visual Life* (Washington D.C.: Smithsonian Institution Press, 1994).

Chapter Two's exploration of how women's lives shifted dramatically beginning in the late nineteenth century include Katherine Kish Sklar, *Florence Kelley and the Nation's Work: The Rise of Women's Political Culture, 1830–1900* (New Haven, CT: Yale University Press, 1995,) on nineteenth-century women's political culture, and Alice Kessler Harris's classic *Out to Work: A History of Wage-Earning Women in the United States* (New York: Oxford University Press, 1982). Jane Addams, *Twenty Years at Hull House* (Chicago: Macmillan Company, 1911) is an excellent primary source on women, reform, and cities. Annaliese Orleck's rousing *Common Sense and a Little Fire: Women and Working-Class Politics in the United States, 1900–1965* (Charlotte, NC: University of North Carolina Press, 1995) discusses New York labor activists; see also Kathy Peiss's *Cheap Amusements: Working Women and Leisure in Turn-of-the-Century New York* (Philadelphia: Temple University Press, 1986). Christine Stansell's *American Moderns: Bohemian New York and Creation of a New Century* (New York: Metropolitan Books, 2000) provides an excellent exploration of women, radicals, and challenges to gender roles. Also good on modernism and feminism is Nancy Cott's classic *The Grounding of Modern Feminism* (New Haven, CT: Yale University Press, 1987). Elizabeth Otto and Vanessa Rocco's (eds.) *The New Women International: Representations in Photography and Film from the 1870s through the 1960s* (Ann Arbor, MI: University of Michigan, 2011) offers a fascinating look at the New Woman in an international context; also interesting in

Martha Patterson, ed., *The American New Woman Revisited: A Reader, 1894–1930* (New Brunswick: Rutgers University Press, 2008). On this era's cultural production see Rebecca Zurier's *Art for the Masses: A Radical Magazine and its Graphics, 1911–1917* (Philadelphia: Temple University Press, 1988). Those interested in the Kodak Girl would enjoy John Jacob, ed., *The Kodak Girl: From the Martha Cooper Collection* (Gottingen: Steidl, 2011.)

California's thriving photography scene is discussed by Susan Ehrens, *Alma Lavenson: Photographs* (Albuquerque, NM: University of New Mexico Press, 1994); and Mary Street Alindor's *Group f.64: Edward Weston, Ansel Adams, Imogen Cunningham, and the Community of Artists Who Revolutionized American Photography* (New York: Bloomsbury, 2014). On the Southwest's avant-garde see Lois Palken Rudnick, *Mabel Dodge Luhan: New Woman, New Worlds* (Albuquerque, NM: University of New Mexico Press, 1984); Luhan's memoirs tell more about her ventures, *Intimate Memories: The Autobiography of Mabel Dodge Luhan,* also by University of New Mexico Press.

On the Depression and the New Deal for Chapters Four through Nine, see, David Kennedy's *The American People in the Great Depression: Freedom from Fear* (New York: Oxford University Press, 2003) and Robert McElvaine's, *The Great Depression, American 1929–1941* (New York: Times Books, 1984). It is impossible to discuss the rich body of scholarship on the RA/FSA photographers. Some classic works include William Stott, *Documentary Expression and Thirties America* (New York: Oxford University Press, 1973); Alan Trachtenberg, *Reading American Photographs: Images as History, Mathew Brady to Walker Evans* (New York: Hill and Wang, 1989); Roy Stryker and Nancy Wood, *In the Proud Land; America 1935–1943* (New York: Graphic Society, 1973); Carl Fleischauer and Beverly Brannan, eds., *New Deal Photography, 1935–1943* (Berkeley, CA: University of California Press, 1988). James Curtis, *Mind's Eye, Mind's Truth: FSA Photography Reconsidered* (Philadelphia: Temple University Press, 1991) has been extremely influential, as has been Cara Finnegan's *Picturing Poverty: Print Culture and FSA Photographs* (Washington, DC: Smithsonian Institution Press, 2003) and Maren Stange's *Symbols of Ideal Life: Social Documentary Photography in American Life, 1890-1950* (New York: Cambridge University Press, 1989).

Though our nation's mythology is tied closely to the land, agriculture and agricultural labor is not woven into the historical narrative. In addition to Lange and Taylor's *American Exodus,* two photo-books focusing on the South include Richard Wright, *Twelve Million Black Voices,* (New York: Basic Books, 2002 reprint), and Walker Evans and James Agee's *Let Us Now Praise Famous Men* (New York: Mariner Books, 2001). On the Dust Bowl and Chapter Eight, Timothy Egan, *The Worst Hard Time: The Untold Story of Those Who Survived the Great American Dust Bowl* (New York: Mariner Books, 2006), and Donald Worster, *Dust Bowl in the 1930s* (New York: Oxford, 2004). Chapter Nine addressing California's agricultural crisis relies on a rich body of scholarship about migratory labor and the 1930s. For background, the book relies upon David Vaught, *Cultivating California, Growers, Specialty Crops, and Labor, 1875–1920* (Baltimore, MD: Johns Hopkins Press, 1999), and Kevin Starr's multi-volume study of California, specifically *Endangered Dreams: California in the*

Great Depression both from Oxford University Press. James Gregory's work is critical: *American Exodus: The Dust Bowl Migration and Okie Culture in California* (New York: Oxford University Press, 1991). On Mexican American labor see Ernesto Galarza *Merchants of Labor: The Mexican Bracero Story* (New York: Mc Nally and Loftin, 1964) and Zaragosa Vargas's *Labor Rights Are Civil Rights: Mexican American Labor in Twentieth Century America* (Princeton, NJ: Princeton University Press, 2007) and *Crucible of Struggle A History of Mexican Americans from Colonial Times to the Present Era* (New York: Oxford University Press, 2016). Richard Steven Street's work on California agriculture is enlivened by his own photographic practice. He has multiple studies, the most relevant is *Everyone Had Cameras: Photography and Farmworkers in California:1850-2000* (Minneapolis, MN: University of Minnesota Press, 2008). On California's agricultural strikes, primary sources that were helpful include Taylor's *On the Ground in the 1930s* (Layton, UT: Gibbs Smith, 1984.)

Chapter Ten explores the pressures women faced as workers and draws heavily from the classic Jacqueline Jones, *Labor of Love, Labor of Sorrow: Black Women, Work, and the Family, from Slavery to the Present* (New York: Basic Books, 2009) and Kessler Harris' *Out to Work*. Pertinent scholarship on gender and the US welfare state are Linda Gordon's *Pitied Not Entitled: Single Mothers and the History of Welfare, 1890–1935* (Cambridge: Harvard University Press, 1998) and *Kessler Harris's In Pursuit of Equity: Women, Men, and the Quest for Economic Citizenship in 20th Century America* (New York: Oxford University Press, 2001). On women and reproductive issues see Nancy Cott, *No Small Courage: A History of Women in the U.S.* (New York: Oxford, 2000), and Sara Evans, *Born for Liberty: A History of Women in America* (New York: Free Press, 1997). The chapter also relies on Goggans' analysis in *California on the Breadlines*, along with Judith Fryer Davidov, *Women's Camera Work: Self/Body/Other in American Visual Culture* (Raleigh, NC: Duke University Press, 1998) and also Paula Rabinowitz, *They Must Be Represented: The Politics of Documentary* (New York: Verso, 1994).

On the internment, Linda Gordon and Gary Okihiro, *Impounded: Dorothea Lange and the Censored Images of Japanese American Internment* (New York: W.W. Norton, 2006); Evelyn Nakano Glenn, *Issei, Nisei, War Bride: Three Generations of Japanese American Women in Domestic Service* (Philadelphia: Temple University Press, 1986); Roger Daniels, *Guarding the Golden Door: American Immigration Policy and Immigrants since 1882* (New York: Hill and Wang, 2004); and Valerie Matsumoto, *Farming the Home Place: A Japanese American Community in California, 1919–1982* (Ithaca, NY: Cornell University Press, 1993). Some primary sources include: Masie and Richard Conrat, *Executive Order 9066: The Internment of 110,000 Japanese Americans* (Los Angeles: UCLA Asian American Studies Press, 1992)—Conrat was one of Lange's lab assistants, and Miné Okubo, *Citizen 13660* (New York: Columbia University Press, 1946, reprinted 1986, Seattle, WA: University of Washington Press). Lange's photographs of the defense industry's impact on California are available in Charles Wollenberg, *Photographing the Second Gold Rush: Dorothea Lange and the Bay Area at War, 1942–1945* (Berkeley, CA: Heyday Books, 1995).

INDEX